Orientation and Judgment
in Hermeneutics

Orientation and Judgment in Hermeneutics

Rudolf A. Makkreel

The University of Chicago Press   CHICAGO & LONDON

The University of Chicago Press, Chicago 60637
The University of Chicago Press, Ltd., London
© 2015 by The University of Chicago
All rights reserved. Published 2015.
Paperback edition 2017
Printed in the United States of America

23 22 21 20 19 18 17   2 3 4 5 6

ISBN-13: 978-0-226-24931-5 (cloth)
ISBN-13: 978-0-226-52776-5 (paper)
ISBN-13: 978-0-226-24945-2 (e-book)
DOI: 10.7208/chicago/9780226249452.001.0001

Library of Congress Cataloging-in-Publication Data

Makkreel, Rudolf A., 1939– author.
Orientation and judgment in hermeneutics / Rudolf A. Makkreel.
pages cm
Includes bibliographical references and index.
ISBN 978-0-226-24931-5 (cloth : alkaline paper) — ISBN 0-226-24931-X (cloth : alkaline paper) — ISBN 978-0-226-24945-2 (e-book) — ISBN 0-226-24945-X (e-book)
1. Hermeneutics.   2. Philosophy.   I. Title.
BD241.M2465 2015
121′.686—dc23
2014034906

For my daughter, Karen

CONTENTS

Preface xi

Introduction 1

PART 1 The Hermeneutic Situation

1 Philosophical Hermeneutics: Reassessing the Tradition in Relation to Dilthey and Heidegger 13
The Interrelations of Philosophy and Hermeneutics in the Tradition 14
The Extent to Which Dilthey's Hermeneutics Relates to the Cognitive Aims of the Human Sciences 18
Moving from Conceptual Cognition to Reflective Knowledge 21
Heidegger's Ontological Hermeneutics 23
Ontico-Ontological Understanding of Historical Time 27

2 Dialectics, Dialogue, and Communication 34
Feeling, Aesthetic Erlebnis, *and Artistic* Erfahrung 35
Hegel on Interpretation and Dialectics 43
Gadamer on Interpretation and Dialogue 48

PART 2 Interpretive Contexts, Judgment, and Critique

3 Reflective Orientation and the Bounds of Hermeneutics 55
Royce: Cognitive Exchange and Communal Conspectus 55
Reflective Judgment and Orientation 59
Kant's Transcendental Topic 61

	Reflective Topology and Judgmental Contexts	63
	Philosophy and the Reflective Specification of Bounds	69
	An Amphiboly of Reflective Orientation	74
	Worldly Orientation	78
4	The Hermeneutics of Attaining Knowledge: The Role of Judgmental Assent	81
	From Conceptual Classification to Judgmental Articulation	81
	Interpreting as Cognizing Meaning and Knowing Truth	84
	Kant on Opining, Believing, and Knowing	88
	Preliminary Judgments and the Provisionality of Reflective Judgments	93
5	Aesthetic Consensus and Evaluative Consent	100
	Levels of Aesthetic Consensus in Kant	101
	Reflective Schematization and Contextual Reconfiguration	105
	Exemplarity and Emulation	108
	Typification and the Intuitive Presentation of Meaning	111
6	Validity, Legitimacy, and Historical Attribution	116
	Knowledge and Legitimacy	116
	Hermeneutics and Adjudication	123
	Ascriptive and Attributive Modes of Imputation	127
	The Legitimacy of Interpretations	130
	Authentic Interpretation and Intersubjective Legitimacy	134
	Pragmatic Characterization	137
	Conscientiousness and Truthful Interpretation	141
7	A Reflective and Diagnostic Critique	146
	Critique as Constitutive and Categorial	146
	Critique as Regulative and Emancipatory	151
	Critique as Reflective and Judgment-Centered	161
	From Reflection to Reflexivity	164
	A Responsive Hermeneutics and a Transformative Critique	166
	Completeness in Critical Hermeneutics	169

PART 3 Applications and Adaptations

8	Genealogy, Narrative History, and Hermeneutic Transmission	175
	Nietzsche's Challenge to the Objectivity of Historical Interpretation	176
	Narrative Approaches to History	178
	Incommensurable Contexts and the Possibility of Universalist History	181
	Delimiting the Appeal to Causes in Historical Interpretation	184

Causes and Influences	186
Intentionalist Explanation and Hermeneutical Contextualization	188
Normative Judgment or Normalizing Genealogy	192
Hermeneutics and Historical Transmission	194
9 Contextualizing the Arts: From Originating to Medial Contexts	198
Meier on Representational Signs and Their Intentional Context	200
Kant and Expressing What Was Inexpressible	202
Dilthey on Manifestations of Life and Their Interpretive Contexts	205
The Earth-World Conflict in Heidegger's "The Origin of the Work of Art"	207
The Medial Contexts of Works of Art	211
The Medial Presentation of the Commonplace in Contemporary Art	216
Transitional Modes of Understanding	220

Bibliography 225

Index 233

PREFACE

This work is the product of a longstanding interest in the relation between philosophy and hermeneutics. It carries forward my explorations of Kant, Dilthey, and others to develop a reflective framework for interpretation. After reassessing the tradition of hermeneutics, I propose an orientational approach that enables hermeneutics to move forward and deal with the multicultural complexities of our contemporary global situation.

Hermeneutics will be reconceived as a critical inquiry into the appropriate contextual conditions of understanding. For this, reflective and diagnostic judgment are essential, not only to discern the differentiating features of whatever phenomena are to be understood, but also to orient us to the various contexts that frame their interpretation. It is one of the tasks of a hermeneutical critique to establish priorities among the relevant contexts that can be brought to bear on interpretation. Moreover, we need to consider how orientational contexts can be reconfigured to respond to the way the media of communication are being transformed by digital technology and other contemporary developments. A fuller characterization of the overall project will be given in the Introduction.

Several earlier essays of mine that anticipate some of the positions developed here are "Kant, Dilthey, and the Idea of a Critique of Historical Judgment," in the *Dilthey-Jahrbuch für Philosophie und Geschichte der Geisteswissenschaften* X (1996): 61–79; "Reflection, Reflective Judgment and Aesthetic Exemplarity," in *Aesthetics and Cognition in Kant's Critical Philosophy*, ed. Rebecca Kukla (Cambridge University Press, 2006), 223–44; "The Role of Judgment and Orientation in Hermeneutics," in *Philosophy & Social Criti-*

cism 34, no. 1–2 (2008): 29–50. One essay from which some parts have been substantially reproduced is "Life-Knowledge, Conceptual Cognition and the Understanding of History," in *Dilthey und die hermeneutische Wende in der Philosophie*, ed. Gudrun Kühne-Bertram and Frithjof Rodi (Vandenhoeck & Ruprecht, 2008), 97–107. My thanks to the editors and publisher of this volume for their permission to republish.

As always, I am grateful for the patience and perseverance of my wife Frances Tanikawa in editing my book manuscripts. With her insightful comments and probing questions, she has been my most helpful critic.

I would also like to thank colleagues, graduate students, and friends for their encouragement, stimulation, and interest in my work over the years. Among them are Karl Ameriks, David Carr, Alessandro Ferrara, Thomas Flynn, Manfred Frank, Kristin Gjesdal, Jean Grondin, Sebastian Luft, Jennifer Mensch, Eric Nelson, Lawrence Pasternack, Frithjof Rodi, Marco Sgarbi, Cindy Willett, and Eric Wilson. Finally, I am grateful for the support of David Brent of the University of Chicago Press and the helpfulness of Priya Nelson.

INTRODUCTION

Hermeneutics as reflection about interpretation has an extensive history going back to ancient and medieval efforts to make sacred texts accessible to the human understanding. The rise of modern philosophy generated more critical expectations, often morally based, about how scripture should be interpreted, and in the nineteenth century, the theologian Friedrich Schleiermacher initiated a transformation within religious hermeneutics itself by arguing that the study of holy books will remain a mere aggregate of observations until it is properly related to the understanding of secular books. In merging the results of scriptural exegesis and humanistic philology, nineteenth-century hermeneutics was expanded to interpret any manifestation or expression of human life as a meaningful text that can contribute to the understanding of historical and cultural phenomena. Wilhelm Dilthey is generally regarded as culminating this approach to hermeneutics by developing its methodology in relation to the goals of the human sciences.

Present wisdom has it that this methodological, human science approach to hermeneutics can now be replaced by a more broadly philosophical hermeneutics inaugurated by Martin Heidegger and Hans-Georg Gadamer. Whereas methodological hermeneutics is generally viewed as focused on the epistemological conditions of understanding, philosophical hermeneutics defines itself as ontological by prioritizing being-relations over the formal relations of cognition. By probing the ontological pre-understanding of being that is implicit in our everyday modes of existence, Heidegger relates hermeneutics to his project of retrieving our philosophical origins. Gadamer extends this ontological approach to locate the fore-structures of understanding in the still ongoing European humanist tradition. He believes that the prejudices we have inherited from this rich tradition must be given full play over against judgments arrived at on our own. Individual judgments are allowed to be productive only to the extent that they become part of the way a communal tradition fuses horizons.

One of the basic goals of the present work is to provide a more differentiated and multidisciplinary approach to hermeneutics that is attuned to the complexities of an ever-changing world. With that in mind, I shall propose an orientational and reflective approach to interpretation in which judgment will play an important role. When one communal tradition no longer provides the overarching framework that can direct interpretation, we must learn to reorient ourselves by surveying the field for other points of reference. The interpretation of a text becomes orientational when there is no self-evident context to determine its meaning. Then reflection and judgment must be applied to coordinate specific contexts with more general ones.

In working out a reflective orientational hermeneutics, I will explore some overlooked resources of transcendental thought that can be developed to contribute to contemporary theories of interpretation. Immanuel Kant's discussions of prejudices and preliminary judgments and his determinant-reflective judgment distinction will be useful in clarifying the nature of understanding and interpretation. In addition to focusing on the cognitive meaning-giving functions of human judgment, we will examine its evaluative role in relating what has been assimilated as experience to what we aim to appropriate through understanding. While prejudices and preliminary judgments may be important in locating the contexts that initially define what is to be understood, an informed judgment must also be applied to adequately consider other appropriate contexts. Hermeneutics will therefore be reconceived more broadly as a critical project capable of surveying a diverse range of contexts that converge on what is to be interpreted. Judgment can contribute a critical moment by properly differentiating the relevant contexts and setting priorities among them.

Even the mere exegesis of a text demands a decision about how broadly it should be contextualized. The intersection of orientation and judgment involved in interpreting human life can expand on a familiar procedure that occurs when expertise is used to diagnose a situation. Ordinarily, first-hand accounts of historical events by those immediately involved are compared with what contemporaries reported and then diagnosed in relation to what has since come to be known about the background conditions. The cognitive research of various disciplines can also contribute to recontextualizing what is to be understood. The challenge is to properly identify and coordinate these multilevel inputs.

Hermeneutically, the diagnostic task of judgment will be to sort out the various perspectives and discourses that stem from different contexts, whether topological or disciplinary in nature. Given the complexity of distinct intersecting approaches, it will be important to supplement the formal validating conditions that apply to theoretical *cognition* with an examination of the source-based legitimating procedures needed for the reflective *knowledge* of historical understanding. This way of defining what hermeneutics can contribute to critical inquiry includes more than the epistemology of the natural and human sciences. It also calls for knowledge resulting from normative assessments that are both theoretical and practical. Thus we will explore the relation between the cognitive considerations that characterize disciplinary inquiry and the evaluative reflective knowledge that completes the hermeneutic project.

Part One, "The Hermeneutic Situation," challenges the widespread assumption that philosophical hermeneutics begins with Heidegger's ontological approach by bringing out the philosophical premises of several earlier hermeneutical theories.

Chapter 1 highlights some often neglected aspects of the history of hermeneutics in order to indicate various ways in which hermeneutics and philosophy have been intertwined. The main focus of this chapter will be to characterize the distinctive ways in which Dilthey and Heidegger bring philosophical considerations to bear on hermeneutics. Points of convergence will also be acknowledged and some oft noted differences reevaluated. It has gone virtually unnoted that Dilthey considered epistemological inquiries into the human sciences as merely preparing the way for a more essential philosophical reflection about historical life. Similarly, it is generally overlooked that Heidegger did at times recognize the need to test our ontological understanding of being and time in terms of ontical interpretations of actual historical developments.

Chapter 2 examines Gadamer's hermeneutics in conjunction with Hegel's views on interpretation and dialectics. The approaches to history proposed by Hegel and Gadamer have played a constructive role in enriching the idea of universal hermeneutics. But their theories of *dialectical* conceptual reconciliation and a *dialogic* linguistic community do not fully address the multicultural diversity of contemporary life. Consideration needs to be given to more focused *diagnostic* modes of judgment that can address human diversity and the extant fragmentations based on distinct ethnic and national identities.

Part Two, "Interpretive Contexts, Judgment, and Critique," will pursue this diagnostic approach by exploring some of the conceptual tools needed for an orientational hermeneutics. This will lead us to relate reflective judgment to the different meaning contexts that intersect in the theory and practice of interpretation. A more general analysis of judgment in subsequent chapters will demonstrate how it contributes to the task of validating and legitimating interpretation. The normative aspects of interpretation will become an important theme as we develop the idea of a reflective hermeneutic critique.

Chapter 3 will show that a consideration of different contexts is needed not only to deal with the problem of mediating regional and linguistic differences, but also to help us understand the different forces and influences that intersect in all human life. It begins by examining Josiah Royce's insight that we cannot fully understand our own ideas until we can also express them in a "currency" of thought other than our own. The ability to convert one's linguistic medium into another and translate others into one's own has the pragmatic function of expanding the horizons of understanding. But there should be no illusion that clear equivalences will result or that Royce's projected ideal of convergence can be realized. Because each regional context has a distinctive currency or medium of ideational exchange, something will always be lost in the processes of translation and conversion. Moreover, the task of hermeneutics cannot be confined to bridging available languages and standard media of thought. Our orientational approach requires flexibility and imagination in dealing with a wider range of diverse contexts where only partial convergences may be possible.

We will gain our further bearings to the medial complexity of the world by developing four spheres of reference (field, domain, territory, and habitat) that are distinguished in terms of scope in Kant's Introduction to the *Critique of Judgment*. These will be delineated as judgmental contexts to provide reflective schemata for interpretation. *Field* and *domain* can be designated as primarily theoretical contexts. The cognitive judgments of outer experience as Kant defined them could be said to delimit the field of logically possible objects in order to establish within it the scientifically meaningful domain of objects that are determined by the laws of nature. But to reflect on the meaning of our own lived experience, the abstract theoretical contexts of field and domain need to be supplemented with the two other spheres of reference listed by Kant. I will treat these as more concrete contexts: the local *habitat* where we happen to reside and in which meaning is based on familiarity and the worldly *territory* within which things can be understood more broadly as humanly meaningful.

In Kant's case these additional contexts of habitat and territory are used to situate aesthetic judgments. The same phenomena, whose objective necessity was explained on the basis of universal laws of the domain of nature, may also be validly assessed in terms of a subjective, aesthetic response. Intersubjective agreement in matters of taste is possible if what is pleasing in our own habitat is judged in relation to the larger territory of the human species. Aesthetically, we can locate the territory of Kant's *sensus communis* somewhere between a universal horizon of the sciences and a local habitat with all its contingent limits. The task of aesthetic judgment—and reflective judgment more generally—is to recontextualize the limits of sense that are imposed from without by local, earthly circumstances and transform them into bounds of meaning that we supply from within to articulate the order of the human world. Broadly speaking, hermeneutics will need to adjudicate among these and other relevant contexts. The goal of interpretation is to assess how distinctive spheres intersect in what is to be understood, without allowing these contexts to fuse.

To develop a general theory of judgment more adequate to the task of interpretation, chapter 4 will reconsider the epistemic relation between meaning and truth in the *Critique of Pure Reason*. For Kant, knowing is a mode of holding something to be true (*Fürwahrhalten*). In knowing (*Wissen*), the subject goes beyond cognizing (*Erkennen*) by affirming that what is meant is also judged to be true. Hermeneutically, it is important to be able to distinguish what is objectively meaningful as cognition from what must also be subjectively assented to for it to count as knowledge. Cognitive judgments are anticipatory and project valid meaning claims whose truth must then be tested by referring back to its legitimating sources and by having individual judgmental assent confirmed by communal consent.

The nature of judgmental assent is also examined by Kant in his *Lectures on Logic*, where he deals at some length with the interplay between prejudice and judgment. In response to the claim by Heidegger and Gadamer that judgment as such has the pernicious effect of reductively fixing our understanding of things, we can look at the way Kant's differentiates between determinant, reflective, and his lesser-known preliminary judgments. Kant shows how a preliminary judgment can suspend a prejudice and transform it into a working hypothesis that is by nature open ended. Only the determinant type of judgment presents the danger of truncating the nature of things. And when reflective judgments do set bounds, as indicated in chapter 3, it is not to delimit things once and for all, but to locate the parameters within which they can be understood to function.

Chapter 5 explores the levels of consensus that are possible as we move from theoretical judgment (*Urteil*) to the kind of evaluative judgment (*Beurteilung*) involved in matters of taste. Kant allows that our cultural heritage has provided useful examples of good taste that appear worthy of imitation. However, as we advance in maturity, imitation must be replaced by emulation. Instead of relying on examples to imitate, we must look for exemplars to emulate. Emulation involves the use of precedents without a loss of autonomy and offers a way of making sense of historical influence hermeneutically. It allows us to distinguish between being determinantly conditioned by the past and being reflectively oriented and guided by it.

In turning our attention to the problem of interpreting historical change and influence more generally, I will further extend my previous explorations of how Dilthey's explanation-understanding distinction parallels Kant's determinant-reflective judgment distinction.[1] Determinant judgments are those in which the particulars of experience are explained by means of already accepted universals, whether these be concepts, rules, or laws. By contrast, reflective judgments are those where we proceed from a particular situation to seek a more universally accessible characterization to broaden our understanding. Often there are no ready spheres of discourse to rely on, so we proceed comparatively and may need to appeal to common sense to make our initial discriminations. Whatever horizons we orient ourselves toward in this search for new modes of characterization, they will tend to be indeterminate and produce a preliminary understanding. Yet it would be a mistake to conclude that reflective judgment is merely a step toward determinant concept formation. Its role is not so much to validate our cognitive determinations of experience as it is to contribute to a more overarching interpretation of it.

Chapter 6 addresses the problem of obtaining reflective legitimation for historical interpretations. Having distinguished between the disciplinary conditions of conceptual cognition and the more inclusive reflective knowledge aimed at by historical understanding, we go further in examining the role of evaluation in interpretation. Dilthey's drafts for a Critique of Historical Reason will be used to view the historical world as having a normative hold on us through the constraining bounds of sociocultural systems. This immanent way of locating sources of legitimacy for interpretation will be defended against Jürgen Habermas's appeal to absolute deontological norms. Since the norms of historical interpretation are about territorial power structures rather

---

1. See Rudolf Makkreel, *Dilthey, Philosopher of the Human Studies* (Princeton, NJ: Princeton University Press, 1975, 1992), 23–24, 218–62.

than strict legislative domains, it will be better to rethink Dilthey's project as a "Critique of Historical Judgment."

We have already pointed to an aesthetic model of reflective judgment that imputes agreement in matters of taste. However, such judgments project intersubjective agreement in a merely formal *ascriptive* mode. Historical judgments involve what I will call a stronger or *attributive* mode of imputation based on content that has been assimilated from the past. By developing a normative model of adjudication adapted from Kant's *Metaphysics of Morals*, we will explore a set of options for thinking about attributive imputations. They will include 1) the *dijudication* that makes a preliminary choice among the pre-given legal alternatives already made available by an institutional communal context and 2) the *adjudication* that renders a determinant courtroom verdict, but also 3) the more open-ended reflective *judication* required to deal with assessing situations that exceed the scope of the law. When making attributive imputations about historical agents, we must take into account not only the constraining normative conditions that regulate the performance of human tasks, but also the restraining contextual factors that present empirical obstacles to be overcome. Here it is important to consider the degree to which an action can be imputed, and this will be followed by an exploration of the different levels of legitimacy that can be expected of historical attributions. Kant established a hierarchy that proceeds from unilateral and bilateral legitimacy to a final omnilateral legitimacy when assessing legal claims. Because historical interpretations deal with actions that span multiple contexts, the ideal of a determinant omnilateral justification may not be possible and should leave room for a reflective multilateral legitimacy.

In chapter 7, I explore the theme of a critical hermeneutics by distinguishing three forms of critique: constitutive, regulative, and reflective. Starting with the primary model of a constitutive or foundational critique as exemplified by Kant and Dilthey, we move on to consider the emancipatory ideas of critique advanced by Habermas and Paul Ricoeur. Because they place hermeneutics in relation to the goal of nondistorted communication, I regard the Habermas-Ricoeur idea of critique as regulative in that concepts needed for ordinary understanding are extended beyond their normal scope and used to project ideal limits. Whereas regulative ideas are expansive by making hypothetical objective claims, reflection and reflective judgment also have the inverse function of specifying their subjective relevance. Accordingly, I will propose a reflective critique that relates general cognitive conditions and rational ends to what is specific to the situational contexts of the interpreter and the interpreted. Our hermeneutics calls for a judgment-centered critique that is reflectively oriented to regulative ideals without being determinantly directed by them. Instead of treating ideals as legislative for some abstract domain, we will regard them as self-prescriptive guidelines for interpreting the territory of human experience.

Part Three, "Applications and Adaptations," relates the orientational hermeneutics explicated in part two to contemporary cultural developments. Chapter 8 considers how our reflective hermeneutical approach to history compares with some of the narrative and genealogical conceptions of history that have played such an important role in the second half of the twentieth century. Using the distinct philosophies of life of Nietzsche and Dilthey as a starting point, I find there the basis for two types of narrative theory. The former stresses genealogical discontinuities and the latter generative continuities. A hermeneutic critique should be able to come to terms with both theories. It can acknowledge discontinuous contexts without assuming that they are inherently incommensurable and it can search for continuities that extend beyond local commonalities and are more than narrational.

What the genealogical, narrative, and hermeneutic approaches to history have in common is that they raise questions about the role of determinant causal explanations in making sense of historical change. But whereas the genealogical and narrative approaches are predominantly interested in finding alternative types of explanation, our reflective hermeneutical approach is also willing to consider to what extent causal explanations may still be possible with the proviso that any type of explanation must be framed by some kind of understanding.

Our initial bearings toward the historical world derive from the fact that we are ourselves participants in human life. We can understand history at least in part because we are already historical in our very being. But this ontologically oriented truth manifests itself to us most directly through the regional contexts in which we find ourselves. In a world of multiple and disparate contexts it is important to consider the contributions of cognitive disciplines so long as they are not given the last word. For Heidegger to trivialize these contributions as merely derivative is to court the danger of not gaining focus and clarity in what is to be understood. On the other hand, if cognitive clarifications and explanations of human affairs are to be furthered, then their contextual bounds will need to be recognized as well. Reflection will always be necessary to assess which mediating contexts are most relevant and which should have priority.

Chapter 9 explores various ways—traditional and contemporary—of contextualizing the interpretation of the arts. The understanding of a work of art involves a special appreciation of how its meaning content relates to the material content that provides the medium of its presentation. For this the general reflective contexts of historical understanding must be further specified in terms of what I will call "medial contexts." An artistic context is medial not only in being focused on a material medium, but also for exploring its communicative potential. This medial framing of understanding can be used as well to come to terms with how new technological and digital resources are changing the way information is transmitted and meaning communicated. Medial contexts often provide transitional modes of understanding that focus as much on informational content as on meaning analysis.

Throughout this work I have attempted to reframe the traditional distinction between different levels of understanding in a more context-focused way that is hermeneutically useful. The elementary understanding inherent in common sense life-knowledge is based on the limited context of a local heritage and earthly surroundings. Here understanding is primarily *assimilative* in nature. Secondly, the higher understanding produced by scientific inquiry appeals to a set of universal disciplinary contexts, each with its determinate bounds. This will be shown to involve the *acquisition* of conceptually mediated *cognition*. Finally, what Dilthey pointed to as a kind of individual reexperiencing will be replaced by a critical assessment that can responsibly *appropriate* what was previously assimilated and acquired in order to produce a more overarching *reflective knowledge*. The assimilative, acquisitive, and appropriative dimensions of hermeneutics are elaborated in various ways to show that hermeneutics is more than a methodological theory of interpretation. It must provide the basis for developing an overall worldly orientation without resorting to the speculative hypotheses of traditional systematic philosophy. A diagnostic use of reflective judgment will be crucial for hermeneutics as it assesses interpretations and probes whether their contributions to worldly intelligibility and human self-understanding adequately reinforce each other.

1

The Hermeneutic Situation

CHAPTER 1

Philosophical Hermeneutics: Reassessing the Tradition in Relation to Dilthey and Heidegger

According to a widely accepted view, there are two types of hermeneutics: 1) the "exegetical" theory of interpretation that was codified by Schleiermacher and Dilthey, and 2) "philosophical" hermeneutics as first articulated by Heidegger and Gadamer. Exegetical hermeneutics is characterized as primarily philological and concerned to methodologically reconstruct the meaning of texts. Philosophical hermeneutics, by contrast, is ontological and regards method as an obstacle to the disclosure of truth. Whereas the Schleiermacher-Dilthey school is said to be overly concerned with authorial intentions and the epistemological issues raised by trying to understand them, philosophical hermeneutics, the argument goes, conceives understanding in terms of its ontological presuppositions.

This chapter will show that Dilthey's contributions to hermeneutics are not confined to the reconstructive, methodological interests of philological theories of interpretation. While taking careful note of philological problems, he adopts a philosophical approach capable of being developed into a reflective hermeneutics that explores not only the epistemic, but also the normative conditions of historical understanding and interpretation. Indeed there is a distinction between cognition and knowledge at work in Dilthey that discloses the limits of the pure cognitive perspective of epistemology and will contribute to the fuller, multilevel analysis of the interpretive process provided in later chapters as well. This more encompassing view of Dilthey's hermeneutics will then be used to supplement Heidegger's ontological grounding of hermeneutics. Without denying important differences between Dilthey and Heidegger, I will explore some points of convergence in their philosophical approaches to hermeneutics and their bearing on issues that need to be addressed by a contemporary critical hermeneutics.

But before allowing Dilthey and Heidegger to encounter each other, let us consider a brief historical review of some earlier hermeneutical developments to give a preliminary indication that there are various ways in which hermeneutics and philosophy have been able to work together and can continue to do so.

THE INTERRELATIONS OF PHILOSOPHY AND HERMENEUTICS IN THE TRADITION

In his prize essay of 1860, "Schleiermacher's Hermeneutic System in Relation to Earlier Protestant Hermeneutics," Dilthey sketches a history of hermeneutics in which theological constraints are replaced by philosophical and historical considerations. This early *Preisschrift* demonstrates that even in the working out of technical problems in interpreting Biblical texts, philosophical ideas often proved to be operative and influential. One of the reasons Matthias Flacius was successful in developing a key to the interpretation of the Bible for Lutheran readers is that he could rely on certain changes that Philipp Melanchthon had introduced in the Aristotelian canon of rhetoric.[1] Similarly, Dilthey claims that "traces of the Wolffian School are visible . . . everywhere"[2] in the universal hermeneutics of Johann Martin Chladenius.

Considerable attention is given to Kant, who is said to deserve "an epoch-making place in the history of hermeneutics." According to Dilthey, Kant's *Religion within the Boundaries of Mere Reason* provides a coherent approach to interpreting the Bible as a whole that is "equal in importance to the philological approach to individual writings."[3] Just as "facts, dogmas, and articles of faith have significance only insofar as they manifest the moral-religious idea," so Scripture is explained as "the expression of a single, omnipresent spirit pervading the whole."[4] Thereby, Kant's work marks a "decisive turning point"[5] in the conception of Scripture.

---

1. Wilhelm Dilthey, "Schleiermacher's Hermeneutical System in Relation to Earlier Protestant Hermeneutics" (1860), in *Hermeneutics and the Study of History*, Selected Works (hereafter *SW*), vol. 4, ed. Rudolf A. Makkreel and Frithjof Rodi (Princeton, NJ: Princeton University Press, 1996), 37–39.
2. "Schleiermacher's Hermeneutical System," *SW* 4, 59.
3. "Schleiermacher's Hermeneutical System," *SW* 4, 91.
4. "Schleiermacher's Hermeneutical System," *SW* 4, 91.
5. "Schleiermacher's Hermeneutical System," *SW* 4, 91.

Dilthey acknowledges that Kant was not the first Enlightenment thinker to locate the value of Christianity primarily in its moral element. However, while others, like J. S. Semler, had explained away extramoral biblical claims as accretions of contemporary ways of thinking, Kant attempted to incorporate them into a cohesive account by interpreting beliefs about Christ, heaven and hell, etc., as forms of representing moral ideas inherent in spirit. "He explains the entire dogmatic content of Scripture," Dilthey writes, "partly as the representation of moral principles in the form of powers and persons external to man, and partly as a *schematism of analogy* deriving from the unity of the fundamental moral idea."[6]

We can add that Kant's views on biblical hermeneutics are formulated in light of his philosophical position that the basis for approaching the supersensible lies in practical reason and its moral postulates rather than in theoretical reason. Biblical representations of superhuman powers are endorsed as imaginative schemata to enliven our moral reflection, not to enable us to intuit some higher reality. The schematism of analogy produces a symbolical relation that can illustrate the significance of our moral ideas in aesthetic terms. Whereas Dilthey focused on this aesthetically enlivened moral symbolism for its relevance to the subsequent nineteenth-century "mythological approach to Scripture,"[7] I will give equal attention in chapters 3 and 4 to Kant's theoretical philosophy to also consider its import for hermeneutics more generally.

Turning to the romantic hermeneutics formulated by Friedrich Ast and Friedrich Schleiermacher, Dilthey makes much of the way they borrow from idealistic philosophy as they expand special (for example, biblical) hermeneutics into universal hermeneutics. Ast conceived the hermeneutical process in terms of a speculative model based on Schelling's philosophy. Thus interpretation proceeds through the three stages of 1) a unity of meaning that is merely anticipated, 2) a plurality that relates particulars to each other, and finally 3) a totality in which unity and plurality are fused. Ast's theoretical philosophical model with its use of the three Kantian categories of quantity is suggestive, but Dilthey criticizes it as still too formal and abstract.[8] By comparison, Schleiermacher's hermeneutics constitutes a considerable improvement in that its theoretical base is enriched by 1) relating all content of consciousness to language and 2) conceiving human creativity as much in terms of action and practice as of thought. Dilthey sees Schleiermacher's hermeneutical principle

---

6. "Schleiermacher's Hermeneutical System," *SW* 4, 93 (emphasis added).
7. "Schleiermacher's Hermeneutical System," *SW* 4, 93–94.
8. See "Schleiermacher's Hermeneutical System," *SW* 4, 97–99.

as interrelating the universality of language with the creativity of individual striving.

Schleiermacher distinguished two main modes of interpretation: the grammatical and the psychological. Grammatical interpretation is analytical and explicates those elements in a work that are "identical," or shared with other works. Psychological interpretation attempts to discern what is "distinctive," or individual, in a text and does so synthetically.[9] Dilthey goes to great lengths to show that Schleiermacher's attempt to synthetically reconstruct the individuality of the author of a work follows the dialectical method of Fichte's practical philosophy. But Schleiermacher also gives content to the originality of individual striving by relating it to the communal sphere of language. If the creative genius of a work is to be captured, it is necessary for the psychological and the grammatical modes of interpretation to cooperate.

Schleiermacher's move to locate hermeneutics in practical philosophy opened up a significant realm of philosophic discourse for articulating interpretive principles. Dilthey, for one, wrote approvingly of how the understanding of human speech and communication finds its more proper horizon in the world of ethical action and praxis. Looking back in light of subsequent developments, we can say that Schleiermacher's lasting achievement centered on his recognition that the individuality of human products is inseparable from the universality of the human project, whether understood in terms of a linguistic or ethical community. The words used by individuals to express what they think, feel, and strive for, can do so only because those words already explicate (*darstellen*) the human project in general. It is interesting to note that in his ethics Schleiermacher speaks of explicative action (*darstellendes Handeln*) as a kind of action which is suggestive of Habermas's communicative action.[10] Instead of expressing something distinctively personal, explicative action manifests the human spirit, which, like reason, is assumed to be the same in all of us.[11] Just as Kant can be seen to relate what is directly expressed in a symbol to what it indirectly explicates about our rational ideas of universal moral ends,[12] so we find in Schleiermacher's hermeneutics a concern to explicate the meaning of a specific ethical community in the most univer-

---

9. See "Schleiermacher's Hermeneutical System," *SW* 4, 146.

10. For more on Habermas and his relation to hermeneutics, see chapters 6 & 7.

11. See Friedrich Schleiermacher, *Die christliche Sitte nach den Grundsätzen der evangelischen Kirche im Zusammenhange dargestellt* (Berlin: G. Reimer, 1843), 510.

12. See Rudolf A. Makkreel, *Imagination and Interpretation in Kant: The Hermeneutical Import of the "Critique of Judgment"* (Chicago: University of Chicago Press, 1990), 125.

sal possible terms. Every human expression that needs to be interpreted has some larger meaning that constitutes a challenge.

Like Kant before him and Dilthey after him, Schleiermacher does not limit himself to understanding authors *just as* they understood themselves. His hermeneutical maxim is to understand authors *better than* they understood themselves. However, this maxim has a somewhat different significance in each of these three thinkers. For Kant it involves the conceptual clarification of the language used by an author. For Schleiermacher it is psychological clarification rooted in the romantic assumption that the work of an artist stems from an unconscious, seminal decision that must be made conscious. In his *Preisschrift*, Dilthey is concerned that Schleiermacher's idea of an underlying seminal decision imposes a closed explanative schema on interpretation. To leave open the possibility of external influences on a work of art, psychological interpretation must be contextualized. For Dilthey, interpreters have the opportunity to understand a work of art better than its creator if they can gain some distance, especially historical distance. By relating the work to its socio-historical context, it becomes possible to arrive at a better understanding of its complexity and overall meaning.

While he found much to admire in Schleiermacher's hermeneutics, Dilthey's concern for historical understanding marks a significant point of difference between them. Idealistic influences on Schleiermacher encouraged an ahistorical conceptualism that led him to explicate the reconstruction of the authorial creative act in terms of a dialectic of such concepts as the "identical" and the "distinctive." For Dilthey any attempt to account for historical outcomes by means of relations among such abstract concepts is bound to prove unsatisfactory. A more appropriate hermeneutics should be based on a philosophy primarily concerned with the functions of judgment. This will involve an approach in which concepts are related, not just to each other, but to the actual particulars of historical life. Only such a judgment-oriented philosophy can provide an understanding of historical change.[13] This is one of the first indications given by Dilthey that instead of being restricted to exegetical techniques, hermeneutics should be made integral to the project of historical understanding and the human sciences in general.

In a much later essay, "The Rise of Hermeneutics" (1900), Dilthey looks back to the exegetical and rhetorical theories of the Greeks with a view toward their suitability for a philosophical hermeneutics conducive to critical historical understanding. He shows how the conflicts between the Alexandrian and

---

13. See "Schleiermacher's Hermeneutical System," *SW* 4, 133.

Pergamene schools of philology set the stage for later interpretive controversies. In order to identify spurious works in their great library and exclude inauthentic passages, the Alexandrians developed an art of textual verification and criticism based on linguistic and historical research. By contrast, Pergamene philology resorted to speculative thought in adopting the Stoic principle of allegorical interpretation to resolve the contradictions between inherited religious texts and philosophical worldviews.[14]

Dilthey uses this contrast between philological criticism and speculative thought to distinguish two general hermeneutical approaches, one rooted in the linguistic considerations found in Aristotle's *Rhetoric* and *Poetics*, the other in the spiritual concerns of Platonic and Stoic philosophy. Aristotle's contributions to hermeneutics lie in his ability to organize our understanding of texts through the analysis of narrative structures and linguistic means. The Aristotelian approach to the metaphorical use of language is to see it as a modification of a literal use by means of a kind of transference. Although Dilthey himself adheres to Giambattista Vico's view that poetic meaning is more original than literal meaning, he finds Aristotle's approach to metaphor attractive in that it exhibits "similarity in dissimilars."[15] Whereas Aristotle allows us to see a continuity between literal and figurative meaning, the Platonic and Stoic approaches tend to separate them as the sensuous versus the spiritual. Their allegorical interpretations can be ingenious in overcoming anomalies and contradictions in a text by appealing to higher spiritual senses, but they do not resolve these problems in ways that promote historical understanding. For Dilthey, the Aristotelian linguistic-grammatical approach comes closer to the kind of critical understanding that is necessary for the philosophical interpretation of history.

THE EXTENT TO WHICH DILTHEY'S HERMENEUTICS RELATES TO THE COGNITIVE AIMS OF THE HUMAN SCIENCES

Dilthey characterizes his initial task as the articulation of a Critique of Historical Reason that examines the conditions that make the cognition of history possible while differentiating it from our cognition of nature. In the "Rise of Hermeneutics," he states that the main purpose of hermeneutics is

---

14. See Dilthey, "The Rise of Hermeneutics," in *Hermeneutics and the Study of History*, SW 4, 240.

15. Aristotle, *Poetics*, 1459a (Princeton, NJ: Princeton University Press, 1985), 235.

to preserve the universal validity of historical interpretation against the inroads of romantic caprice and skeptical subjectivity, and to give a theoretical justification for such validity, upon which the *reliability of historical cognition* is founded. Seen in relation to epistemology, logic and the methodology of the human sciences, the theory of interpretation becomes an important connecting link between philosophy and the historical sciences, an essential component in the foundation of the human sciences.[16]

Here hermeneutics turns to philosophy for the epistemological and methodological guidance it can give to the human sciences, but this link merely sets the stage for a more comprehensive relation between philosophical reflection and interpretation, as we will see in due course. The initial methodological task of the human sciences is to gain an understanding of the meaning of historical events and human activities in relation to their specific contexts. Only secondarily, if at all, are they to seek the kind of explanation characteristic of the natural sciences, where processes are subsumed under general causal laws. Although Dilthey makes a methodological distinction between understanding and explanation, he is opposed to any metaphysical divide whereby history is defended as the realm of freedom and singularity over against nature as the realm of universal determination. German historicists, who assumed such a sharp opposition between the historical and the natural, developed philological methods only for the interpretation of what is singular in history. A critical approach to history must go further, however, and balance the interpretation of historical singularity with an awareness of universality. This means that historical understanding must be related to the ways in which understanding functions in the other human sciences, some of which are systematic and seek to articulate universal structures in social, political, economic, or cultural life. The human sciences are not simply idiographic in Wilhelm Windelband's sense and must concern themselves with the problem of universal validity or objectivity.

The epistemological objectivity that Dilthey aims to preserve for the human sciences is not attainable by following the Rankean admonition that historians should efface themselves in their research. Instead of presenting a supposed neutral narrative, historians must examine the interests and needs that drive not only their human subjects, but also their own inquiry. Dilthey

---

16. "The Rise of Hermeneutics," *SW* 4, 250. The italicized words correct the print version of 1996.

writes that the historian's longing for objective reality cannot be satisfied "by mere contemplation or intuition, but only through analysis."[17] The analysis he has in mind is that of the various human sciences. Before looking for overall generalizations about history at large, we must focus on the special systems of relations that have been analyzed by the human sciences. Each such system, whether it be social, economic, or cultural, can delineate certain shared interests and context-specific patterns of human action. Some of the human sciences such as sociology and economics may arrive at uniformities of behavior and development in their spheres of interest. This means that the scientific ideal of historical objectivity will have to be refracted through the generalizations and structural relations specified by the different human sciences.

However, when we seek an overall truthful account of a historical event or movement, it is not a matter of simply synthesizing all the disciplinary results of the human sciences. No historical event will be exhausted by the various conceptual systems into which the historical world can be analyzed, nor should all of these systems be given equal weight when we assess how they intersect in real life. A full understanding of a historical event requires recognition of its factical singularity together with an evaluation of its more general significance.

Dilthey also rejects any claims to comprehensive historical truths based on a traditional metaphysical synthesis. Instead of a final, integrative metaphysical system à la Hegel's philosophy of history, we have various worldviews, which are overall interpretations of life encompassing the way a person perceives, evaluates, and responds to the world. These are expressed in great literature, in religions, and in philosophy. As conceptually formulated in philosophical systems, there are three recurrent types of worldview: naturalism, the idealism of freedom, and objective idealism. Each of these philosophical types of worldview exhibits reflection on reality and life at large—naturalism emphasizes those aspects of the world that are of special interest to our cognitive capacities (Epicurus, Hume); the idealism of freedom judges the world in light of our volitional ends and moral goods (Plato, Kant); and objective idealism searches for an overall sense of order that appeals to our aesthetic and evaluative capacities (Stoics, Schelling). According to Dilthey, these three types cannot be reconciled and will continue to challenge each other for supremacy.

With his theory of worldviews, Dilthey is generally thought to move toward a conceptual relativism. However, he is better seen as widening his perspective from an epistemological analysis of conceptual cognition to an integral

---

17. Dilthey, *Introduction to the Human Sciences*, *SW* 1, ed. Rudolf A. Makkreel and Frithjof Rodi (Princeton, NJ: Princeton University Press, 1989), 143.

kind of knowledge, one that assesses the world not merely intellectually, but on the basis of our whole being.

MOVING FROM CONCEPTUAL COGNITION TO REFLECTIVE KNOWLEDGE

A distinction between conceptual cognition and knowledge is often operative in Dilthey. This has been generally overlooked since Dilthey never adequately defined the meaning of the terms "cognition" and "knowledge." He does, however, briefly distinguish the terms in one early and one late work. Because Dilthey contrasts them somewhat differently in these two works, a more coherent and overarching account of the relation between cognition and knowledge will need to be developed.

Around 1880 in the Breslau draft for Book IV of the *Introduction to the Human Sciences*, Dilthey describes knowledge (*Wissen*) as the perceptual truth-intake (*wahr-nehmen*)[18] of things that comes with a factical sense of their being "present and certain (*Gegenwärtig-und-Gewißseins*)."[19] By contrast, conceptual cognition (*Erkenntnis*) is said to be "representational (*vorstellend*)"[20] and transforms the things we already know into objects that are "placed-before-me (*vor-mich-gestellt*)."[21] Cognition provides a distance on the world and seems to allow for a moment of re-cognition (*er-kennen*). This suggests a significant distinction between knowledge as directly presentational and cognition as indirectly representational. We can expand on this by calling such directly given knowledge "life-knowledge." Life-knowledge is what is taken as true (*wahr-genommen*) on the basis of the lived experience we grow up with, that is, through perceptual intake and common inheritance. Conceptual cognition differs from this by not merely taking in the world, but representing it discursively. Conceptual cognition projects the intelligibility of the world and classifies it in terms of theoretical forms.

In a later study of 1904 anticipating *The Formation of the Historical World in the Human Sciences*, Dilthey claims much more for knowledge (*Wissen*). Now knowledge actually encompasses the conceptual cognition *(Erkenntnis)* of reality and proceeds to evaluate it. While the role of conceptual cognition

---

18. See *Introduction to the Human Sciences*, SW 1, 280; *Gesammelte Schriften* (hereafter GS), (Göttingen: Vandenhoeck & Ruprecht, 26 vols., 1904–2006), XIX, 91.
19. *Introduction to the Human Sciences*, SW 1, 250; GS XIX, 62–63.
20. *Introduction to the Human Sciences*, SW 1, 281; GS XIX, 92.
21. *Introduction to the Human Sciences*, SW 1, 254; GS XIX, 67.

remains unchanged from the *Introduction to the Human Sciences*, knowledge becomes more comprehensive than conceptual cognition and involves the positing of values, the determination of purposes, and the establishment of rules.[22] Dilthey indicates that if the human sciences are going to be up to the task of understanding historical life, *epistemology* (*Erkenntnistheorie*) as the analysis of conceptual cognition must go over into "philosophical self-reflection."[23] Self-reflection, which involves an examination of self in relation to life, is subsequently broadened to include human nature and life in general and called "anthropological reflection." Whereas epistemology separates the theoretical from the practical, anthropological reflection attempts to understand how the theoretical and the practical intersect in life. For philosophy to illuminate all aspects of human existence it must supplement epistemology by applying anthropological reflection toward a more comprehensive *"theory of knowledge* (*Theorie des Wissens*)."[24]

The philosophical outcome of anthropological reflection I will call "reflective knowledge." Thereby, it becomes possible to again expand on Dilthey and distinguish between an initial *life-knowledge* that precedes conceptual cognition and a more considered and comprehensive *reflective knowledge* that follows it. The overall task of hermeneutics then will be to relate these two modes of knowledge to the intervening cognitive analyses made possible by the human sciences. What we have designated as life-knowledge is accumulated in lived experience, either as individually perceived or commonly inherited. The task of the human sciences is to gather this direct life-knowledge that already exists in ordinary life and to probe the extent to which it can be represented in terms of conceptual cognition.

However, all scientific efforts to make reality cognitively intelligible have the effect of dispersing our understanding into the general systems of different disciplines. The human sciences in particular raise doubts about our initial understanding of the sociohistorical world and attempt to replace the subjective certainty (*Gewißsein*) of life-knowledge with the objective reliability (*Sicherheit*)[25] of cognition. Yet the full understanding or interpretation of

---

22. Dilthey, "Studies Toward the Foundation of the Human Sciences," in *The Formation of the Historical World in the Human Sciences*, SW 3, ed. Rudolf A. Makkreel and Frithjof Rodi (Princeton, NJ: Princeton University Press, 2002), 25.

23. "Studies Toward the Foundation," *SW* 3, 27.

24. "Studies Toward the Foundation," *SW* 3, 24.

25. Dilthey, "The Delimitation of the Human Sciences," in *The Formation of the Historical World*, *SW* 3, 325.

the human historical world requires that we move on to reflective knowledge. Based on anthropological reflection, it is a more encompassing knowledge that can place conceptual cognition in context and evaluate it. In reflective knowledge there is often an "intuitive" moment that opens up an overall perspective on things. For Dilthey this is what worldviews provide and what historical interpretation should aim at.

A Dilthey-based approach to human understanding thus takes ordinary life-knowledge, analyzes it epistemically in terms of conceptual cognition, and then assesses it by means of reflective knowledge. Whereas epistemology functions primarily at the level of conceptual cognition, a broader theory of interpretation will need to be developed to do justice to the idea of reflective knowledge. This is where Dilthey can be said to have shown the way to a distinctive philosophical hermeneutics. We will explore this path further, beginning with chapter 4. For now we can conclude that hermeneutics as a general theory of understanding must give all three levels their proper due. Rooted in the immediacy of ordinary experience, life-knowledge provides an important background for hermeneutics as it proceeds to clarify the additional contributions made by conceptual cognition and reflective knowledge toward an understanding the human historical world. As part of this larger constellation, life-knowledge can be said to function like everyday pre-understanding in Heidegger.

HEIDEGGER'S ONTOLOGICAL HERMENEUTICS

In 1925 Heidegger delivered ten lectures in Kassel entitled "Wilhelm Dilthey's Research Program and the Present Struggle Concerning a Historical Worldview." Here Heidegger is not concerned with Dilthey's worldview typology nor with his reflections on the limits of our metaphysical interpretations. Instead, he follows up on Dilthey's recognition of the facticity of life and looks to him for the beginnings of a historical worldview that locates historicity as the source of our factical existence. Heidegger claims that Dilthey's ultimate interest lay in "historical Being (*geschichtlichen Sein*)"[26] rather than historical methodology. "Dilthey's authentic question was about the sense of history," he writes. "It went together with his tendency to understand life out of itself, not on the basis of some other reality. . . . Dilthey has shown and stressed that the basic character of life is its Being-historical (*Geschichtlich-Sein*)."[27]

---

26. Martin Heidegger, "Wilhelm Diltheys Forschungsarbeit und der gegenwärtige Kampf um eine historische Weltanschauung," ed. Frithjof Rodi, *Dilthey-Jahrbuch* 8 (1993): 157.

27. "Wilhelm Diltheys Forschungsarbeit," 173.

However, according to Heidegger, Dilthey failed to ask the deeper question of what Being-historical means, namely, its rootedness in time.

Since much of Dilthey's work was still unpublished in 1925, Heidegger was unaware that Dilthey had in fact explored the nature of time in relation to his reflections on life and history. But what is of greater interest here is that Heidegger introduces the historical worldview not as a reflective response to the riddles left unsolved by the sciences (Dilthey's sense of worldview), but as a fundamental ontological stance that grounds our very existence. In place of Dilthey's reflective life-horizon as the framework for our cognition of human life, Heidegger's understanding projects Dasein's future nonexistence. Human mortality is anticipated in terms of an ontological comportment rather than awaited or expected as an ontical event. Instead of being an extrapolation from present experience, the anticipated future is transcendent in the sense of being beyond our control. The arc that is projected in Heideggerian understanding is not outwards only; it also curves back towards Dasein itself. The existential future (*Zukunft*) harbors a "coming [*Kunft*] in which Dasein, in its own most potentiality-for-Being, comes towards itself (*auf sich zu-kommt*")."[28]

This power of temporality to bring Dasein back to itself, that is, to be self-referential or reflexive, is even more evident in its modality of having-been. Our past is never simply surpassed, but indicates a "situatedness in which Dasein is assailed by itself as the entity which it still is and already was."[29] The most derivative modality of temporality, the present, is paradoxically both the closest to Dasein and the one in which it most easily falls away from itself. The objects that are made present-at-hand by the theoretical sciences, whether they be the natural or the human sciences, can be assigned an ontical meaning. But we can understand why any of these epistemic results should matter to us only if we recall that the present is the future having-been-faced. The authentic facing of our future annihilation is the very existential response to Being-as-such that must frame our theoretical or ontical interests in objects. That is, if the ontical meaning of things is to become ontologically meaningful, it is necessary to relate the epistemic subject back to Dasein's existential questioning of the meaning of its Being and the possibility of its non-Being.

Two years later, in *Being and Time*, Heidegger characterizes his "existential-temporal analytic of Dasein" as an "appropriation" and "radicalization" of

---

28. Martin Heidegger, *Being and Time*, trans. J. Macquarrie and E. Robinson (New York: Harper & Row, 1962), 373; *Sein und Zeit* (Tübingen: Max Niemeyer Verlag, 1979), 325.

29. *Being and Time*, 376; *Sein und Zeit*, 328.

Dilthey's historical analysis of life.[30] Indeed, we can see Heidegger probing more deeply into the conditions of historical understanding that Dilthey sought to articulate. Thus Dilthey's hermeneutical circle becomes an ontological circle in Heidegger. For both, interpretation is necessarily circular in that it already presupposes some kind of understanding. In the case of Heidegger, it is an ontological pre-understanding that "discloses" the Being-in-the-world of Dasein. For Dilthey, the understanding presupposed is rooted in an overall sense of life and, as we will see, given historically in objective spirit.

It would seem that Dilthey's philosophical approach to hermeneutics, which aimed at both the cognition and knowledge of historical life, and Heidegger's philosophical hermeneutics in search of an ontological disclosure of temporality and human existence, could readily complement each other. Yet, Heidegger's attitude toward the ontical cognition sought by Dilthey's human sciences sometimes becomes so dismissive in *Being and Time* that any positive linkage may seem beside the point.[31] He contends that from the ontical perspective of ordinary experience, temporality loses its hermeneutical curvature and is leveled out into a mere linear sequence of nows. As a consequence, ontical understanding is reduced to the vulgar understanding of the "they." By stressing ever more insistently the importance of the difference between ontical beings and ontological Being, Heidegger stands in danger of forgetting his own claim that Being derives its meaning from its inherence in beings.

In *Being and Time*, the role of the intellect is minimized when authentic understanding of Being is identified with the attunement to the world that human beings possess through their moods (*Stimmungen*). Their existential attunement through moods provides an ontological pre-understanding that falls outside intellectual discourse. But in an earlier fragment on Aristotle from 1922, Heidegger defines authentic understanding as a mode of explicating *nous* or intellect. Instead of pitting existential understanding over against intellectual understanding, he works with a less deprecatory view of the intellect.

---

30. See *Being and Time*, 449, 455.

31. This dismissal of so-called ontical and epistemological approaches to hermeneutics is still echoed in Jean-Luc Nancy when he speaks of an opposition between a traditional hermeneutics that merely "anticipates meaning" and an "existential *hermēneuein*" that "creates the anticipatory or 'annunciative' structure of meaning itself." See his "Sharing Voices," in *Transforming the Hermeneutic Context: From Nietzsche to Nancy*, ed. Gayle Ormiston and Alan Schrift (Albany: SUNY Press, 1990), 223.

26   Chapter One

Just as Dilthey's hermeneutical heritage was related to the Aristotelian-Alexandrian tradition, so Heidegger attempted in 1922 to define his own hermeneutical situation through a phenomenological interpretation of Aristotle's *nous*. He begins the fragment "Phenomenological Interpretations in Connection with Aristotle (Indications of the Hermeneutical Situation)"[32] with a neutral sense of intellect or nous as a pure taking in (*reines Ver-nehmen*), which merely pre-gives the appearance of things.[33] It was already indicated that "taking (*nehmen*)" is also the root of Dilthey's perceptual knowledge (*wahrnehmendes Wissen*). Heidegger claims that Aristotle explicated nous by means of three modes of seeing[34]: 1) by means of *sophia*, which Heidegger renders as authentic or insightful understanding (*eigentlich-sehendes Verstehen*),[35] 2) by means of *phronesis*, which he equates with circumspection (*Umsicht*),[36] and 3) by means of *epistéme* or determinate observational understanding (*hinsehend-bestimmendes Verstehen*).[37] Concerning these three ways that nous is explicated, sophia and phronesis are considered superior to epistéme because they retain more of an affinity with the original process of taking in that is characteristic of nous. Sophia, which is often translated as wisdom, involves an ontological understanding of the *arché* of things for Heidegger, namely, insight into their where-from-ness (*das Von-wo-aus*).[38] Phronesis is ontically circumspective and recognizes that some things could have been otherwise. It keeps the nature of things open and considers their where-from-ness in relation to their where-to-ness (*das Worauf des Umgangs*).[39] Phronesis explicates nous as a circumspective mode of assessment that is prepared to move things toward some end. But when phronesis becomes too focused on specific ends it can lose sight of the fullness of life. Here sophia or authentic understanding can step in again to remind us that the preparedness to change things is part of the mobility of life itself. This mobility finds its resonance in the temporalizing nature of sophia. Gadamer has shown how impor-

32. Translated by John van Buren in Martin Heidegger, *Supplements*, Albany: SUNY Press, 2002, 111–45. All references below use my own translations of the original text.
33. See Heidegger, "Phänomenologische Interpretationen zur Aristoteles (Anzeige der hermeneutischen Situation)," ed. Hans-Ulrich Lessing, *Dilthey-Jahrbuch* 6 (1989): 250.
34. *Techne* is also related to nous, but not as a mode of seeing or insight.
35. See "Phänomenologische Interpretationen," 255.
36. See "Phänomenologische Interpretationen," 255.
37. See "Phänomenologische Interpretationen," 254.
38. See "Phänomenologische Interpretationen," 258.
39. See "Phänomenologische Interpretationen," 259.

tant phronesis was for Heidegger, but here at least, it is clear that sophia is more so.⁴⁰

Heidegger resists efforts to determine what life is, either in terms of its theoretical where-from-ness or in terms of its practical where-to-ness. Authentic understanding and interpretation must instead serve to keep the possibilities of things open. Heidegger is least satisfied with epistéme, the third mode of explicating nous. Here the aim is a determinate understanding of life in terms of observational judgments that serve to define and fix it propositionally. With this move, the interpretive "as," with all its broad suggestiveness, is reduced to a more narrow and fixed propositional "is." The understanding involved in epistéme is similar to the understanding associated with Kant's *Verstand*, the intellectual faculty that grounds the determinant cognitive judgments of science. Heidegger criticizes epistéme as concerned with truth (*Wahrheit*) in the merely derivative sense of cognitive correctness. Sophia, on the other hand, provides an indeterminate understanding that preserves and guards (*Verwahren*) the fullness and mobility of life. On this score, Heidegger's sophia seems very much akin to Dilthey's *Verstehen*. It is interesting to note that Dilthey too relates what is true (*wahr*) back to something more fundamental that has the power to preserve (*bewahren*).⁴¹

Despite the affinities between sophia as conceived by Heidegger and *Verstehen* as conceived by Dilthey, important differences remain. Heidegger focuses on the contrast between the authentic understanding of sophia and the cognitive understanding of epistéme because he views the content of the latter as a final outcome that loses contact with its sources in experience. Dilthey too discerns the limits of epistemology, but does not regard it as a dead end. He would locate its proper place within a developmental continuum. Full understanding or interpretation includes conceptual cognition as an intermediary between what we have distinguished as life-knowledge rooted in lived experience and a more mature reflective knowledge.

ONTICO-ONTOLOGICAL UNDERSTANDING OF HISTORICAL TIME

Although *Being and Time* provides a significant analysis of the ontological pre-understanding that is inherent in the moods of our existential condition,

---

40. See "Phänomenologische Interpretationen," 264.
41. See *Introduction to the Human Sciences*, *SW* 1, 269n.

it is not enough to analyze our everyday situatedness ontologically in terms of the Being-in-the-world of Dasein. The ontical results that exhibit themselves in our lives and what they disclose about human practices in general are more directly important for historical understanding. Here Dilthey's last essay on hermeneutics, "The Understanding of Other Persons and Their Manifestations of Life" of 1910, suggests a more fruitful approach.

By orienting historical understanding to objective spirit, Dilthey is able to capitalize on an ontical resource that Heidegger ignores. Dilthey borrows the expression "objective spirit" from Hegel but removes the speculative universality it assumed in Hegel's idealism. Rather, Dilthey reconceives the idea in terms of a more empirical and verifiable commonality.[42] Objective spirit designates the medium of inherited commonality on the basis of which we participate in our sociohistorical situation, find our place in it, communicate with each other, and interact. The idea of objective spirit is used to demonstrate that we are historical in our very being before we can even have historical cognition.[43]

As the medium of commonality in which each of us is nurtured, objective spirit endows what we experience with a whole range of public meanings. These meanings reflect attitudes, practices, and values that are held in common in the particular tradition and community in which I factically find myself. Even the way the trees have been planted in my village square, the way the furniture was arranged in my parental home, are understandable as part of a pattern of commonalities that was absorbed as I grew up.[44] Such meanings define an "us," not a Heideggerian "they."

We should not assume that Hegel's metaphysical idea of objective spirit is simply redefined epistemologically; to do so would be to lose sight of the cognition-knowledge distinction discussed earlier. Objective spirit does not provide conceptual cognition; it merely embodies that mode of life-knowledge that is passed down to us as a common inheritance. Epistemic or critical conditions of consciousness become relevant only when the knowledge of ordinary life is transformed by the human sciences into the concep-

---

42. See *The Formation of the Historical World*, SW 3, 172–73.

43. We can find further explications of objective spirit in what Husserl calls "sedimentation" and in what Sartre refers to as the "practico-inert." And when Derrida questions the primacy of what is present, he is invoking the traces and specters from the inherited past that always already affect us. Hermeneutically, "objective spirit" means history as lived inheritance.

44. See "The Understanding of Other Persons and their Manifestations of Life," *SW* 3, 229.

tual cognition of disciplinary discourse. In the language of Dilthey's essay, this involves a transition from "elementary understanding" rooted in objective spirit to "higher understanding." The transition makes possible the move from commonality to universality.

The common meanings of objective spirit are not strictly cognitive meanings, nor are they ever clearly formulated. Thus before understanding and interpretation can attain the universal cognitive intelligibility aimed at by the sciences, we are steeped in a more restricted knowledge of commonality. This elementary understanding, which informs our everyday existence, is a factical source of consensual meaning and could be said to provide an ontical background for hermeneutics. But as soon as we come upon events that deviate from the normalcy of the commonalities that are taken for granted, the being-certain associated with life-knowledge (*Gewißsein des Wissens*) and the self-evidentness (*Selbstverständlichkeit*) of elementary understanding break down. Then it becomes necessary to shift our mode of reference and study the particular situation more carefully by applying cognitive modes of higher understanding. This is where common sense is replaced with the universalistic demands of disciplinary consciousness. The indeterminate contexts of objective spirit can be analyzed into the more determinate contexts of the systematic human sciences that can help focus historical understanding. Those aspects of life that cannot be defined in this way can in turn be subjected to anthropological reflection.

As noted above, Dilthey's empirically reconsidered concept of objective spirit was developed in the service of his ontical approach to hermeneutics. But to argue for the relevance of the ontical does not, of course, entail the exclusion of any reference to the ontological and vice versa. On closer examination, the divisions between Dilthey and Heidegger have proven to be less clear-cut than is often assumed. Their dealings with the crucial question of temporality and history present another case in point.

In the well-known account of temporality of section 77 of *Being and Time*, Heidegger aligns his ontological analysis with that of Yorck von Wartenburg by claiming that the ontical cuts us off from the virtuality and force of the historical. The assumption that underlies this section is that the ontical fixes the vitality of history in terms of static ocular patterns. Thus he reiterates that our understanding of the temporality of the historical must be derived from an ontological rather than an ontical approach. Yet in the following section Heidegger acknowledges in effect that his ontological analysis of temporality must be related to the ontical concept of time. In section 78 of *Being and*

Time, he exposes the incompleteness of his own ontological analysis of temporality by adding an "ontico-temporal" analysis of "world-time"[45] necessary for understanding history. Whereas the ontological analysis of temporality yields the ecstatic structures of existential care about the meaning of Being, world-time manifests the structures of datability as significant for our circumspective concerns. Temporality and world-time, each in its own way, discloses a transcendent curvature which then gets leveled off in the ordinary or vulgar understanding of time as a linear sequence of "nows" that are merely "present-at-hand."

Heidegger's *ontico-temporal* analysis of world-time represents an effort to find a middle ground between the radical transcendence of his *ontological* temporality and the immanence of the *ontical* time-sequence of vulgar common sense. This world-time is really *ontico-ontological*. The datability of world-time is not referred to the present-at-hand, but to the ready-to-hand. Although this intermediate structure of a datable world-time moves us closer to history, it is still inadequate for understanding human history. To be sure, the ready-to-hand of circumspective concern (*Besorgen*) does add a practical element to world-time, but the equipmental structure (*Zeughaftigkeit*) that Heidegger attributes to the ready-to-hand is hardly sufficient to understand our involvement in history. It is too focused on the "in order to."[46]

What is really necessary to properly interpret the human practices involved in sociopolitico-cultural history is an *ontico-ontological analysis, not merely of time, but of life itself*. We need a philosophical hermeneutics that is not only oriented to our existential situation, but also provides an ontico-ontological awareness of our historical background. To despise what the commonality and consensus of objective spirit offer as an ontical starting point is unwise. If we situate ourselves in history too ontologically, we are left with the passivity of Heidegger's receptive modes of taking in (*Vernehmen*) things and of partaking (*Teilnahme*) in the disclosure of Being as a destiny (*Geschick*).[47] On the other hand, the equipmental contributions of circumspective concern are too limited and routine to do justice to our capacity for active participation (*Teilnehmung*) in the events of history.[48]

---

45. See *Being and Time*, 456–57.
46. See *Being and Time*, 97.
47. See *Sein und Zeit*, 168.
48. For more on the contrast between partaking (*Teilnahme*) and participation (*Teilnehmung*), see Rudolf Makkreel, "From Authentic Interpretation to Authentic Disclosure:

A case can be made that Dilthey's reflections on life also move toward an overlapping of the ontical and ontological. Anthropological reflection on lived experience leads Dilthey to describe time in ways that go beyond what Heidegger dismisses as the ontical time that represents a series of nows, each of which merely *is*. For Dilthey, time is experienced not just as given in the present, but as the continuum connecting it to the past and future. Instead of conceiving time as a Kantian linear *Ablauf* that runs down, he characterizes it as a "ceaseless advance (*Fortrücken*)"[49] that discloses itself in the "being-pulled-along (*Fortgezogenwerden*)"[50] of lived experience. About the relation of time to the past, Dilthey writes:

> Even the smallest part of the advance of time still involves the passing of time. The present never *is*; what we experience as present always contains the memory of what has just been present. Among other things, the continued efficacy of the past as a force in the present, namely, what the past means for it, imparts to what is remembered a distinct character of presence, whereby it becomes incorporated in the present.[51]

The reflective assessment of the ontical experience of time as a mediated "presence" suggests that it has an ontological import as well.

The primordial status of temporality (*Zeitlichkeit*) is evident in Dilthey's statement that "temporality is contained in life as its first categorical determination and . . . is fundamental to all the others."[52] Although he does not use the language of the ontical and the ontological, we can see that time is more than an inductively derived ontical concept. It is a category presupposed by the categories of meaning, value, and purpose, which are of special relevance to the human sciences. Each of the latter is then assigned a more specific temporal reference: meaning is linked primarily with the past, value with the present, and purpose with the future. Whereas Dilthey's category of meaning has

---

Bridging the Gap between Kant and Heidegger," in Heidegger, *German Idealism, & Neo-Kantianism*, ed. Tom Rockmore (New York: Humanity Books, 2000), 63–83.

49. Dilthey, "Fragments for a Poetics," in *Poetry and Experience,* SW 5, eds. Rudolf A. Makkreel and Frithjof Rodi (Princeton, NJ: Princeton University Press, 1985), 225.

50. *The Formation of the Historical World*, SW 3, 161.

51. Dilthey, "Plan for the Continuation of the Formation," in The Formation of the Historical Word, *SW* 3, 216.

52. "Plan for the Continuation of the Formation," *SW* 3, 214.

the function of retrospectively structuring the temporal relations of history to obtain a relatively stable mode of connectedness, another of his categories of life, that of productive force (*Kraft*), relates the present to the future in a more dynamic and open-ended way.

By revisiting some of the parallels we have seen between the analyses of Dilthey and Heidegger, we can indicate how they jointly contribute to historical understanding. Both chart an articulative movement from what is implicitly understood to a more explicit interpretation. In the case of Dilthey, this is a continuous and gradual process, but for Heidegger there is also a disruptive moment of unconcealing what has been concealed (*verborgen*).[53] However, from a larger perspective, both Dilthey and Heidegger start with a base of what is already taken for granted.

Both the life-knowledge that we have derived from Dilthey and Heidegger's ontico-temporal concerns of circumspection offer a kind of everyday understanding. We can also relate life-knowledge to another mode of circumspection that is less willful and more open, namely, phronesis. Together, life-knowledge and the circumspective assessment of phronesis provide a preliminary background for historical understanding by appealing to something shared. Life-knowledge embodies the inherited commonality of objective spirit; phronesis involves the use of common sense. Dilthey's conceptual cognition and Heidegger's epistéme are also alike in seeking to move from commonality to universality. But it is the combination of reflective knowledge and the authentic understanding associated with sophia that best discloses the full scope of human understanding. Any worldview achieved by philosophical reflection attains its overall coherence by being the work of self-reflection. Notwithstanding Dilthey's efforts to discern the recurrent types of worldview, every worldview is ultimately the expression of an individual's characteristic response to life. It draws on the "individuating ownness" often ascribed to authentic understanding.

We begin then with the elementary understanding of life-knowledge steeped in commonality, and proceed to universalize it cognitively through the higher understanding of the human sciences, but we can only achieve the overall interpretation needed for historical understanding by reflecting on our particular place in the world as individuals. The individuating insight of reflective knowing is not just a cognitive having but discloses one's mode of being.

When human understanding is conceived broadly enough to be both a *re-*

---

53. See *Sein und Zeit*, 33.

flexive or self-referential response to our ontological condition and a *reflection* of our ontical situation, it can provide the transition to a broadened philosophical hermeneutics that opens up a *reflective* critique of different possible modes of interpretation. The relation between the reflexive and reflective will be given further attention as we consider the theme of a critical hermeneutics. These considerations will also demonstrate that more than epistemological issues are involved in the knowledge that informs hermeneutics. The normative issues surrounding a critical hermeneutics will eventually lead us to deal with questions about the validity and legitimacy of interpretation.

CHAPTER 2

Dialectics, Dialogue, and Communication

Much of contemporary literature places the themes of communication and language at the heart of hermeneutics. We have seen that Schleiermacher is a forerunner of this trend, but the contributions of Schleiermacher and Dilthey are sometimes considered inadequate because they are thought to focus on individual expressions and authorial intentions. Such allegations have been given widest currency by Gadamer, who argues that language is hermeneutically disclosive only when it moves beyond monological expression and becomes dialogical. Language must be allowed to unfold itself in the art of conversation to open us up to more general truths.

In Gadamer's hermeneutics of tradition, the thematization of language and the search for general truths are broadly patterned after Heideggerian ontology and Hegelian dialectical mediation. Expanding the idea of linguistic understanding ontologically, Gadamer argues that our place in Being will disclose itself through a dialogue with the long-standing tradition of humanism going back to the Greeks and Romans. The attainment of truth involves a process of dialogical mediation that represents Gadamer's hermeneutical-historical adaptation of Hegel's dialectical theory of reason.

One of the most effective and influential ways in which Gadamer illustrates his hermeneutics of history is through his interpretations of the arts. Hence we will turn first to his discussions of the arts because they constitute an important element of *Truth and Method* and also serve as a vehicle for his criticism of modern aesthetics and hermeneutics as developed from Kant through Dilthey.

FEELING, AESTHETIC *ERLEBNIS*, AND ARTISTIC *ERFAHRUNG*

In his examination of the *Critique of Judgment*, Gadamer claims that Kant initiated the movement in epistemology and aesthetics toward a subjectivism that inhibits the attainment of communal truth. Here he follows Hegel in his attack on Kant for conceiving aesthetics primarily in terms of feeling, and ignoring the truth to be found in art. Kant's failure to do justice to the epistemic and ontological dimensions of aesthetic experience is said to be responsible for reducing its significance to a mere pleasurable state of mind. Treating Dilthey's *Das Erlebnis und die Dichtung (Lived Experience and Poetry)* as the culmination of Kantian subjectivization of aesthetics, Gadamer rejects the notion of aesthetic *Erlebnis* (lived experience) as limited to private consciousness. Such criticisms underscore many of the common assumptions about the aesthetics of Kant and Dilthey, assumptions that often ignore the complexities of their positions.

Hegel's earlier objection to the role of feeling in Kant's aesthetics reflects his concern that a feeling does not allow us to get beyond ourselves. "A feeling," according to Hegel, "is always at the same time the enjoyment of the self. Even when we are dealing with a matter outside us, feeling brings it back to ourselves and leads us to focus on how we are filled with it (*unsere Erfüllung von der Sache*). . . . He, who lives in a subject matter, whether scientific or practical, forgets himself in it, can have no feeling insofar as feeling is a reminder of himself."[1]

To be sure, feelings register how we are affected by things and thus remind us of ourselves, but they need not make us self-absorbed. Feelings (*Gefühle*) differ from emotions (*Rührungen*) in being able to transcend our bodily states. What Hegel describes as the subjective assimilation of content designates just one kind of feeling. There are many other kinds—including the feeling of something lacking that leads us beyond ourselves. In the most general terms, feelings indicate the way we relate to the world, and as such they can play a role in making judgments about things. Accordingly, feeling cannot be ignored in our efforts to develop a hermeneutics that is both reflective and critical.

For their part, Kant and Dilthey discuss not only subjective but also inter-

---

1. Georg Wilhelm Friedrich Hegel, *Vorlesungen über die Philosophie der Religion*, *Werke* (Frankfurt am Rhein: Suhrkamp Verlag, 1978) 15: 134.

subjective feelings such as aesthetic pleasure and moral respect. What differentiates aesthetic pleasure from other pleasures, according to Kant, is that it is disinterested. When we judge aesthetically, we are not interested in personal sensuous gratification. The aesthetic state of mind generates a peculiarly human pleasure involving a felt harmony of the faculties. Moreover, as I have argued elsewhere, aesthetic feeling can be considered an expansive life-feeling that pulls us outside of ourselves and orients us toward the human community.[2] The universality of the aesthetic judgment assumes a fundamental intersubjective feeling, that is, a *sensus communis*, defined "not as a private, but as a communal (*gemeinschaftliches*) feeling."[3]

Dilthey attempted to reinforce the relevance of aesthetic feelings by linking them more closely with the richness of our lived experience. The six spheres of feelings he analyzes in his *Poetics* of 1887 range from sensuous feelings to those deriving from cognitive connections and to others that project volitional and idealizing content.[4] Dilthey's reservations about Kant's aesthetics reflect a greater interest in his own more concrete, experiential approach. Unlike Kant, who looked on aesthetic feeling as purely formal, Dilthey insists that aesthetic feelings about form cannot be abstracted from content. Any formal aspects of art that are discerned aesthetically must be integral to the objective content of the works drawn from our lived experience of the world. In Dilthey's 1907–1908 notes for revising his *Poetics,* the reference to aesthetic feeling is replaced by considerations about meaning relations.[5] What remains a constant theme in both versions of the *Poetics* is the capacity of art to enhance our sense of life. All lived experience, aesthetic or otherwise, comes to be placed in the common sphere of objective spirit, and Dilthey reconceives Kant's idea of disinterestedness in light of this commonality.

Whereas Kant's disinterestedness applies to the impressions of aesthetic spectators, Dilthey goes further and extends the attitude of disinterestedness to the expression of the artist's lived experience. He writes: "Disinterestedness is . . . not only a property of the aesthetic impression, but also of the lived

---

2. See Makkreel, *Imagination and Interpretation in Kant*, 150–60. See also chapter 5 below.

3. Immanuel Kant, *Critique of the Power of Judgment*, trans. and ed. Paul Guyer and Eric Matthews (Cambridge: Cambridge University Press, 2000), 123 (translation revised). See also *Kant's gesammelte Schriften, herausgegeben von der Preussischen Akademie der Wissenschaften zu Berlin* (hereafter *Ak*), 29 vols. (Berlin: Walter de Gruyter, 1902–97), 5: 239.

4. See *Poetry and Experience*, *SW* 5, 77–86 for a detailed analysis of these spheres of feeling.

5. See *Poetry and Experience, SW* 5, 230–31.

experience of the creative artist. Thus Kant stands corrected."[6] The true creativity of poets and artists resides in their ability to transform our ordinary interested responses to the world into an overall attitude of disinterestedness through which light is shed on the interests of life itself.

The generic term Dilthey uses to classify various modes of expression is "life manifestation." Every expression is first of all a manifestation of a more general life-context; the expression of lived experience is not so much the externalization of inner psychic states as it is the articulation of shared patterns of meaning. What makes artists especially successful in moving beyond the personal is that they experience the world through the conventions of the medium in which they create. Because composers already experience the world tonally and poets linguistically, they do not merely translate some private psychic state into some public equivalent but articulate something truthful about life as such. This comes out most vividly in the late hermeneutical essay "The Understanding of Other Persons and Their Life-Manifestations," where Dilthey speaks of the enduring truthfulness of a great work of art that stands apart from its creator:

> There is something frightful in the realization that in the struggle of practical interests every expression can deceive and that its interpretation can alter with a change in our standpoint. But when in a great work a spiritual content is liberated from its creator, whether it be a poet, artist or writer, we enter a realm where deception ends. No truly great work of art can . . . want to put forward a spiritual content that misrepresents its author; indeed, it does not want to say anything about its author. Truthful in itself it stands—fixed, visible and abiding—and it is this which makes possible a methodically reliable understanding of such works. Thus there arises in the confines between knowing and doing a sphere in which life discloses itself at a depth inaccessible to observation, reflection and theory.[7]

Thus a great poem stands before us, not merely expressing truths about the author's lived experience but as truthful in itself.

In this late hermeneutical essay Dilthey most clearly distances himself from the subjectivization charged to Kantian aesthetics. However, his reference to a "sphere" between knowing and doing could lend some credence to Ga-

---

6. See *Poetry and Experience*, SW 5, 227.
7. *The Formation of the Historical World*, SW 3, 227–28.

damer's view that aesthetic *Erlebnis* involves a mode of aesthetic differentiation. To Gadamer, the danger of aesthetic differentiation is that it sets off a special region from the rest of reality. Instead of embedding the work of art in the institutional context that commissioned it, aesthetic differentiation posits the "free artist [who] creates without a commission."[8] The traditional work "measured by the standards of public morality" is replaced by a "creation out of free inspiration"[9] that is said to take place in an imaginary sphere of consciousness. Thus, Gadamer writes that "through 'aesthetic differentiation' the work loses its place [in] the world . . . [and] belongs instead to aesthetic consciousness."[10]

However, to read only a few of Dilthey's literary essays is to recognize how thoroughly he places his poets in their historical context. Referring to Goethe's governmental service and his scientific research on plant life and color theory, Dilthey writes, "These activities did not merely occupy him during the long periods in which he produced no poetry; they were indispensable to him for that engagement with life and with the world which he needed in order to fulfill his poetic mission."[11] Building on "the great achievements of the Enlightenment," Goethe's mission was to emancipate "the poetic imagination from the domination of abstract thought and 'good taste' which knew nothing of life."[12]

Even if it were true that Dilthey differentiates the aesthetic as a special sphere, this would not really isolate it from reality or from the world at large. While some of the ordinary interests of everyday life may be suspended in great art, the effect is not to escape them, but to more profoundly portray our lived situation. Thus we saw him speak of the aesthetic as "a sphere in which life discloses itself at a depth inaccessible to observation, reflection and theory." The disinterestedness of Dilthey's creative artist is simply a way of shedding light on the typical interests of life itself.

For Gadamer, however, Dilthey's focus on lived experience (*Erlebnis*) is in principle inadequate "to build a bridge to the historical realities."[13] He proposes his own theory of experience (*Erfahrung*) as an alternative that is

---

8. Hans-Georg Gadamer, *Truth and Method*, 2nd revised ed. (New York: Crossroad, 1992), 87; *Wahrheit und Methode*, 2nd ed. (Tübingen: J.C.B. Mohr, 1965), 83.

9. Gadamer, *Truth and Method*, 87; *Wahrheit und Methode*, 83.

10. *Truth and Method*, 87; *Wahrheit und Methode*, 83.

11. Dilthey, "Goethe and the Poetic Imagination," in *Poetry and Experience*, SW 5, 236.

12. "Goethe and the Poetic Imagination," SW 5, 236.

13. *Truth and Method*, 276; *Wahrheit und Methode*, 261.

attuned to "the pre-determinate influence"[14] of family, society and state. The paradigm of experiencing art is the participation by the actors and the audience in a public performance of a play. By following the transmission of a work from author to performers to audiences, Gadamer points to the ways in which the meaning of a work of art is public and plays itself out over time.

Just as Dilthey shifted the ground from aesthetic impression and feelings to the objective expression of aesthetic *Erlebnis*, Gadamer turns our attention to the way the work of art affects the artistic *Erfahrung* of its audience. Gadamer's theory of art is a theory of the effective or productive history (*Wirkungsgeschichte*) of works as they are performed, exhibited, or read subsequent to their creation. The task of understanding a work is not to reexperience the work as it was created by its author or even to reconstruct it as an ideal spectator of the time might have understood it. That would be to place the work in its own distinct horizon and set it apart from our present situation.

In addition to understanding the meaning of a work and interpreting how its original context can illuminate this meaning, Gadamer's hermeneutics involves a third task, namely, applying it to our present situation to discover its truth for us. Application gives historical interpretation a current relevance by relating the past to the present. The horizon of the past is not to be restored in its "authentic" originality as some special sphere subject to ever better understanding, but applied to the present for its relevance. Thus Gadamer dismisses what he believes to be the Schleiermacher and Dilthey ideal of better understanding with the rejoinder that we always understand differently. The claim for understanding differently through application makes sense in relation to our current situation, and it is in this specific context that the attempt to understand an author better than he understood himself could be thought of as "subordinating [that] other person to our own standards."[15] However, for Dilthey the project of better understanding is clearly directed at something like the higher universality that Gadamer himself invokes when speaking of his ideal of a fusion of horizons.

The fusion of horizons aimed at by Gadamer's hermeneutics forms "a single historical horizon"[16] that would have to include future generations as well as ours in the task of interpretation. It places human creations into a "reception history" in which no individual interpreter can become predominant. This reception history is an open horizon in which the work to be under-

14. *Truth and Method*, 276; *Wahrheit und Methode*, 261.
15. *Truth and Method*, 305; *Wahrheit und Methode*, 288.
16. *Truth and Method*, 304; *Wahrheit und Methode*, 288.

stood becomes a moving target. True understanding thus "involves rising to a higher universality that overcomes not only our own particularity but also that of the other."[17]

Although the practice of application allows a work to "be understood at every moment, in every concrete situation, in a new and different way,"[18] its placement within the theory of the fusion of horizons makes it difficult to define how any new understanding is effectively different. The goal of the "contemporaneity (*Gleichzeitigkeit*)"[19] that Gadamer expects from application is for the spectator to become involved in "an event"[20] that is part of the work's ongoing history. The link between understanding and application produces a contemporaneous *Erfahrung* of the work, but there seems to be little concern to generate the critical engagement made possible by relating understanding and interpretation.

Understanding becomes contemporaneous, according to Gadamer, when it allows a work to remain relevant over time and keep it alive as a "classic." By contrast, the quest by Schleiermacher and Dilthey for a more critical interpretation of a work is dismissed as being in the service of an antiquarian ideal of a "classical" work belonging to some past epoch. Their aesthetic *Erlebnis*, according to Gadamer, strives for a "simultaneity (*Simultaneität*)"[21] that artificially reconstructs the original.

The contemporaneity sought by Gadamer has the effect of placing the work of art in the real time of its tradition—a time that moves forward. The simultaneity that is attributed to the aesthetic differentiation of Schleiermacher and Dilthey is represented as referring us back in time with the aim of reliving the creative moment in which a work was conceived. But in fact, we saw Dilthey suggest that a great work stands before us, not as pointing to some truth about the author's past lived experience, but as truthful in itself and abiding through time.

It is misleading to characterize Dilthey's approach as holding "several objects of aesthetic experience . . . in consciousness at the same time with the indifference of equal validity (*Gleich-Gültigkeit*)"[22] Aesthetic disinterestedness is not a mode of neutral indifference, nor is it a prescription for an empty

---

17. *Truth and Method*, 305; *Wahrheit und Methode*, 288.
18. *Truth and Method*, 309; *Wahrheit und Methode*, 308.
19. *Truth and Method*, 127; *Wahrheit und Methode*, 121.
20. *Truth and Method*, 309; *Wahrheit und Methode*, 308.
21. *Truth and Method*, 127; *Wahrheit und Methode*, 121.
22. *Truth and Method*, 127; *Wahrheit und Methode*, 121.

formalism or an invidious relativism. The charge of "indifferent simultaneity" is really more applicable to the modern experience of the cosmopolitan museum and to what André Malraux called *la museé imaginaire*, the comprehensive art book. Here paintings are removed from their original context and are often placed side by side with others of a very different provenance. These cultural developments are the products of contemporary institutional and technological forces. Although Kant and Dilthey differentiated aesthetic experience from ordinary experience, they never proposed an ideology of art for art's sake. And what distinguishes Dilthey's more historically attuned aesthetics is that it allows a work of art to crystallize the world at large and lend it a heightened meaning.

Understanding need not aim at coincidence with the work—whether in terms of simultaneity or contemporaneity. The aim of understanding is to grasp what is distinctive about a work. Toward that end, interpretation brings more encompassing contexts and relevant variables to bear. Interpretation is a relational process that involves insight and judgment in restructuring what is to be understood—it is not a process of simple mediation where horizons become fused. There is a sense in which each of us can participate in a process whereby meaning develops through the tradition, but there are also critical limits that must be considered to avoid arbitrary and anachronistic readings. A potential danger of Gadamer's Hegelian model of mediation is that everything may dissolve into an overarching universal perspective. What makes a work of art significant, however, is that there is always a hard "factual core" that is stylistically distinctive as an intersection of the aesthetic and the historical.[23]

Hegel and Gadamer are correct to claim that a work of art is more than an expression of the particular experiences and attitudes of its author, for it also discloses communal truths that have a more general relevance. But they stand in danger of overlooking how particular *Erlebnisse* are expressed in art, and even more importantly, how the process of expression can contribute a distinctive perspective on the world. A work can thus express something contingently specific about the author's life and experience while at the same time articulating a universal truth. The contingent and the universal cannot be fully separated in the way Gadamer suggests when he describes the ideal of mediation as a process of liberating ourselves from contingency.[24] Not every

---

23. See the chapter "Style and the Conceptual Articulation of Historical Life," in Makkreel, *Dilthey, Philosopher of the Human Studies*, especially 398–413.

24. See Gadamer, *The Relevance of the Beautiful and Other Essays*, trans. Nicholas Walker, ed. Robert Bernasconi (Cambridge: Cambridge University Press, 1986), 44.

particular fact about a work can be subordinated to its universal potential and stripped of its contingency.[25]

Because of the indefinable convergence of particularity and universality in art, Kant and Dilthey refuse to consider aesthetic judgments as conceptual. By pointing to the enlivening effects of art, they may have placed too much stress on the feeling component of the aesthetic judgment. But as we have seen, they discern feelings that are intersubjective as well as those that are private. Although Kant's aesthetic judgments do not add cognitive content to our experience of the world, they are formally cognitive in that they have an import for the systematization of our experience. Kant's theory of symbolism allows him to go so far as to claim that through the expression of aesthetic ideas we can sometimes attain "symbolic cognition"[26] of things that exceed our ordinary experience. Through aesthetic symbolization our abstract rational ideas can receive a quasi-intuitive fulfillment in aesthetic ideas.

In the years following the publication of *Truth and Method*, Gadamer has indicated more appreciation of the contributions of the aesthetic tradition. In the essay "Auslegung und Anschaulichkeit," published twenty years after *Truth and Method*, Gadamer moves closer to recognizing Kant's insight when he finds in the *Critique of Judgment* the basis for understanding the special *Anschaulichkeit* or vividness that characterizes metaphor. Now Gadamer writes: "For the theory of metaphor, Kant's remark in Section 59 seems to me most profound: that metaphor at bottom makes no comparison of content, but rather undertakes the 'transference of reflection upon an object of intuition to a quite different concept to which perhaps an intuition can never directly correspond' (*CJ*, §59). Does not the poet do that with every word?"[27] Gadamer similarly softens his attacks on Dilthey in the essay "The Relevance of Beauty," when he allows that works of art "enhance our feeling for life."[28] Moreover, Gadamer seems to moderate his claims about directly grasping truth in art when he writes, "We learn that however unexpected our encounter with beauty may be, it gives us an assurance that the truth is not far off and inaccessible to us, but can be encountered in the disorder of reality with all its imperfections, evils, errors, extremes, and fateful confusions."[29] This view

---

25. In chapter 3 we will explore how Kant allows us to factor in contingency.
26. *Critique of the Power of Judgment*, 59, 198; *Ak* 5: 353.
27. *Relevance of the Beautiful*, 169–70.
28. *Relevance of the Beautiful*, 45.
29. *Relevance of the Beautiful*, 15 (translation revised).

of beauty as providing the promise of truth is not incompatible with Dilthey's aesthetics of truthfulness as shown above.

HEGEL ON INTERPRETATION AND DIALECTICS

Gadamer's new appreciation of Kant's views on aesthetic symbolism does not, however, take anything away from his greater affinity with Hegel. Whereas Kant's reflections on language and symbolism appear to be somewhat of an afterthought, Hegel's views on language are more deeply rooted in his philosophy. As Theodore Kisiel puts it in a suggestive essay on Hegel and hermeneutics, "It is language which is introduced from the start [of Hegel's *Phenomenology of Spirit*] to sustain the mediation of the immediate through the entire breadth of experience from sense-certainty to the self-transparency of thought thinking itself."[30] Hegel is indeed perceptive in recognizing the importance of language in shaping our experience and as the medium of communication. Deeply interested in the role of community in education, Hegel takes seriously all means of human mediation—language, work, and action.

With Kant, sociability is grounded transcendentally in a felt *sensus communis*, while with Hegel it is grounded in the communal spirit of a public state. Hegel distrusts feeling not only as a basis for artistic communication, but also as a source for religious communion. Feeling is again dismissed as a primitive mode of consciousness and in his critique of Schleiermacher's feeling-based theory of religion, Hegel condemns it as totally inadequate for knowing God. To commune with God humans need to turn to something more objective, namely, intuition as shaped by the arts. In his lectures on the philosophy of religion, Hegel claims that "art was produced because of the absolute spiritual need that the divine, the spiritual idea be available as an *object* . . . for immediate intuition."[31] Beautifully formed intuition presents itself both as immediate and as mediated by a divine idea of order. Beauty is thus the promise, not just of truth, but of divinely inspired truth.

Yet there is a limit to how much divine truth can be manifested in an intuitive image (*Bild*). The next stage of communing with God comes through representation (*Vorstellung*), which encompasses not only what can be directly imaged, but also what can be indirectly imaged. Hegel defines a rep-

---

30. Theodore Kisiel, "Hegel and Hermeneutics," in Frederick Weiss, ed., *Beyond Epistemology* (The Hague: Martinus Nijhoff, 1974), 201.

31. *Vorlesungen über die Philosophie der Religion*, *Werke*, 16: 135.

resentation as an image that has been raised to the form of universality or thought. But as internal and immediate, a representation possesses a mere abstract universality and needs language to express it: "representations are communicable through the word."[32] For Hegel, language is a necessary, albeit imperfect, means of communicating representations. No word is able to adequately merge what is sensuous (the letter) and what is universal (the meaning). The words used to embody religious representations are thus not to be taken literally (*in eigentlichem Verstande zu nehmen*). For example, a phrase such as "Son of God" or "God the Father" is merely an image derived from a natural relation, which we know is not meant in its immediacy; we know that its meaning involves a relation that is only approximate, and that this sensuous relation at most has something corresponding to the relation that is really meant by God.[33]

This kind of linguistic usage characterizes the level of hermeneutics traditionally identified with the interpretation of religious texts. The function of religious interpretation as defined by Hegel is to separate what is historical fact in the Bible from what points to a more universal meaning.

Throughout his work, Hegel acknowledges the natural and historical origins of our thought. He does not begin with a formal transcendental ego, as Kant does in the *Critique of Pure Reason*, and then move to the culturally situated subject of the *Critique of Judgment*. Hegel's subjects are historically situated from the start, which helps to account for his appeal to such hermeneutical thinkers as Gadamer and Ricoeur. It is not surprising then that it has been claimed that Hegel has an implicit hermeneutical principle that is based on the conviction that "we have no way to understand the universal except from within the particular situation in which we happen to find ourselves."[34] This conviction is, to be sure, hermeneutical in spirit, but when it comes to the way in which Hegel works out his philosophical system we see that this so-called hermeneutical principle is no more than a preliminary assumption. The *Phenomenology of Spirit* starts convincingly with the concrete situations in which sense-certainty and perception as well as desire place each of us, but very soon we are projected into the abstractions of force and understanding, skepticism, and the unhappy consciousness.

Paul Redding assigns a more explicit hermeneutics to Hegel and locates its

---

32. *Vorlesungen über die Philosophie der Religion*, 16: 145.
33. See *Vorlesungen über die Philosophie der Religion*, 16: 141ff.
34. Shaun Gallagher, "Hegel, Foucault, and Critical Hermeneutics," in *Hegel, History and Interpretation* (Albany, NY: SUNY Press, 1997), 161.

genesis in the role that is assigned to recognition (*Anerkennung*) in our "everyday understanding of life"[35] He points out that for Hegel, life was a system within which we can recognize opposed practical points of view. These are the everyday and practical aspects of Hegel's early thought that Dilthey was the first to appreciate in his groundbreaking publication *Die Jugendgeschichte Hegels* of 1905. It directed the attention of philosophers to newly discovered theological manuscripts of the young Hegel, which were then published two years later by Dilthey's student Herman Nohl. These previously unpublished writings disclosed a fuller understanding by Hegel of the affinities of life and spirit that Dilthey found sympathetic and led him to reassess the usefulness of the idea of objective spirit. Nevertheless, it remains the case that the dialectical logic that Hegel's philosophy imposes on our ways of understanding the history of spirit works against its hermeneutical starting point in life.

The root of this tension between hermeneutics and dialectics becomes evident when we consider Hegel's more detailed views about what is involved in interpretation. These views are further spelled out in Hegel's lectures on the philosophy of religion, and they manifest a considerable amount of ambivalence about the philosophical status of hermeneutics as a theory of interpretation. Language proves to be a merely natural mode of communication that must be superseded to do justice to the purely spiritual mediation required by philosophy. Thus, as we shall see, Hegel discusses two modes of interpretation: one applying to natural languages that express our subjective representations, the other to objective philosophical concepts. Religion may be content to approach God through the natural languages of subjective representations, but philosophy's task is to present God directly through objective concepts. This move from *representation* (*Vorstellung*) to *presentation* (*Darstellung*) is part of Hegel's effort to replace the narrowly focused understanding (*Verstand*) of early modern philosophy with his own more encompassing philosophy of reason (*Vernunft*).[36] As long as we understand the world representationally, we have abstract, piecemeal, and inferential knowledge—what we might call justified belief. Only through a reason that comprehends (*begreift*) everything from the perspective of the whole can we have true knowledge, including that of God. Accordingly, Hegel uses two different terms for interpretation: 1) *Interpretation* for modes of representational understanding and 2) *Auslegung* for presentational or rational comprehension.

1) *Interpretation* is defined by Hegel in his discussion of how positive or

---

35. Paul Redding, *Hegel's Hermeneutics* (Ithaca, NY: Cornell University Press, 1996), 107.
36. See *Vorlesungen über die Philosophie der Religion*, 16: 36, 66.

institutional religion seeks to make God intelligible to human understanding in terms of established modes of representation. This involves the use of written scriptures and church doctrines to determine our faith and beliefs as well as to formulate them in a creed. Hegel's conception of *Interpretation* thus focuses on the exegesis of biblical texts.[37] *Interpretation* can involve either a) *Worterklärung* (verbal explication), which clarifies an unfamiliar word by another more familiar word or b) *Sinnerklärung* (meaning explication), which clarifies the sense or import of the word.[38] Verbal explication is a mere mechanical process of substitution, achieving limited clarification. Meaning explication appeals to our representational understanding (*Verstand*) to attain enlightenment (*Aufklärung*).[39] As a critic of the Enlightenment's preference for understanding over reason, Hegel claims that meaning explication introduces abstract explanations to accommodate the content of the Bible to our fixed ways of representing the world. But the predicates of this world cannot fill in the conceptual infinity of the Idea of God and so leaves it an abstract infinity. This process of accommodation reduces reason to arbitrary but clever reasoning. What was to be the interpretive clarification of the meaning of God ends as an anachronistic explanation merely valid for the current situation.

2) *Auslegung* is a very different kind of interpretation, requiring a shift from the level of representational understanding and belief to the more important level of conceptual comprehension and knowledge. Hegel coordinates this with the move from positive religion to a philosophy of religion that can replace the "arbitrariness of reasoning" with "rational knowledge."[40] But this is not a simple move forward, for *Auslegung* also has its shortcomings and Hegel once again emphasizes the limitations of interpretation. In the *Wissenschaft der Logik*, *Auslegung* is the process by which the absolute interprets itself by laying itself out (*aus-legen*) in what actually exists.[41] In the English translation, this *Auslegung* of the absolute is usually called its "exposition."[42] Hegel considers Spinoza's system to be such an absolute exposition: everything is interpreted as either an attribute or mode of one all-encompassing or absolute substance, namely, God. Spinoza's impersonal divine substance assembles

---

37. See *Vorlesungen über die Philosophie der Religion*, 16: 35.
38. See *Vorlesungen über die Philosophie der Religion*, 16: 36.
39. See *Vorlesungen über die Philosophie der Religion*, 16: 37.
40. See *Vorlesungen über die Philosophie der Religion*, 16:39.
41. See Hegel, *Wissenschaft der Logik*, *Werke* (Frankfurt am Rhein: Suhrkamp Verlag, 1976), 6: 194–5.
42. See Hegel, *Science of Logic*, trans. W.H. Johnston and L.G. Struthers (London: Allen and Unwin, 1961), 161.

everything that is, but neither understands it in terms of the unity of a subject nor comprehends it in terms of spirit according to Hegel. Spinoza's world is the mathematically extended world of nature that is modally limited in merely reflecting what is given in actuality. It fails to do justice to the possibilities of the subject and the unfolding necessity of spirit.

The laying out or exposition of the Idea of God is thus merely preliminary in nature and does not yet provide the reinteriorizing memory (*Er-innerung*) of the history of spirit. What has been externalized must be reappropriated in thought to produce rational insight (*Einsicht*).[43] Interpretation cannot comprehend necessity, but is either about positive factual givens or about those possibilities of reason that have already been actualized. Pure possibility and pure necessity are beyond the scope of interpretation. Thus as far as Hegel is concerned, hermeneutics, whether it be a theory of *Interpretation* or of *Auslegung*, or even a combination of them, must fall short of a proper dialectic. It would seem then that the discipline of hermeneutics can at best illuminate things externally, whether ex-egetically or ex-positionally. Dialectics alone can provide the inner differentiations necessary for the adequate comprehension of reality.

One of the contributions of Hegel's dialectics is its attempt to conceive the movements of historical spirit through a logic of negation. But this raises the question whether actual historical changes can be adequately defined in terms of contradictions that arise and are then overcome. From Dilthey's perspective, reducing the many tensions that occur in history to a dialectical progression of negations creates the illusion of a panlogism. This is certainly the overall impression that Hegel's project of dialectical reconciliation tends to produce. Considered more closely, however, his works can also reveal suggestive ways of applying negations. Hegel invariably dismisses immediate negations as abstract and inadequate. They must give way to more mediated and concrete modes of negation. The modes of negation that are historically valuable do not simply cancel their opposites; they transmute and refine them. In the dialectical histories of Hegel and Marx, the importance of human work lies precisely in its capacity to take crude matter that would normally disintegrate or decay and transmute it into something that can be integrated and preserved.

For us, Hegel's importance for understanding the human world is to have turned the abstract recognition that history develops by negating previous

---

43. Hegel, *Enzyklopädie der philosophischen Wissenschaften im Grundrisse* (1827), in *Gesammelte Werke*, vol. 19, 1989 (Hamburg: Felix Meiner Verlag), §§465, 467: 342–44.

stages into the more complex capacity to discern whether historical change involves an undifferentiated or differentiated negation. Dialectics can be comprehensive not merely by positively exposing the extension of the world but by imposing internal conceptual differentiations that probe spiritual depth. Dialectical theories can be heuristic, even if they lack the greater sensitivity characteristic of hermeneutics.

GADAMER ON INTERPRETATION AND DIALOGUE

Gadamer seeks to preserve the comprehensive scope of Hegel's dialectic by thematizing the role of language rather than of logic in hermeneutics. Kisiel, in discussing some parallels between Hegel's dialectic and Gadamer's hermeneutical dialogue, writes that, for Gadamer, "every word is not simply a fixed and given being but rather mirrors the whole of language as its suggestive unsaid."[44] He compares this to Hegel's speculative sentence that "overflows into a whole system of sentences in order to express the comprehensive unity of the concept."[45] Clearly, Gadamer agrees with Hegel that the philosophical significance of language does not lie in fixed assertions or judgments. Thus Gadamer writes that the very effort to determine the sense of a word "forces us to think its opposite."[46]

Yet, the conclusions drawn from these considerations about language and thought differ. Hegel's dialectic is a "serious" telic logic that attempts to demonstrate that these shifts in meaning reflect a developmental process in which each conceptual stage both cancels and preserves the results of earlier stages. At the end of the process, everything will have been systematically comprehended. Gadamer's hermeneutic dialogue, by contrast, involves the more "playful" movement of a linguistic conversation that is not guided by an implicit answer but by questions that leave the outcome open. Under the influence of Dilthey and Heidegger, Gadamer can no longer share the Hegelian optimism that at some point everything will have been conceived and said. Every disclosure of thought must close off something else, every saying leaves something unsaid. This radical sense of finitude that marks hermeneutics as it was developed in the twentieth century requires Gadamer to transform Hegel's dialectical theory of truth projecting a telos of absolute knowledge

---

44. "Hegel and Hermeneutics," 207.
45. "Hegel and Hermeneutics," 207.
46. Gadamer, *Hegel's Dialectic: Five Hermeneutical Studies*, trans. D.C. Smith (New Haven, CT: Yale University Press, 1976), 23.

into a dialogical theory that finds its basic access to truth through the prejudices that we inherit from our traditions.

Gadamer's hermeneutics focuses on prejudices as the source of the kind of pre-understanding typically relied upon by interpretation. Charging Enlightenment philosophers with blindness to the value of prejudices, Gadamer relates Kant to the beginning of an overly methodological approach to hermeneutics that is hostile to prejudices and culminates in Dilthey's attempt to make hermeneutics the method of the human sciences. But in *The Blomberg Logic* of the early 1770s, Kant states that we should not reject each and every prejudice. Instead, we should "test them first and investigate well whether there may not yet be something good to be found in them."[47] Then, anticipating Gadamer's well-known claim that an outright discreditation of prejudice is itself a prejudice,[48] Kant asserts: "One can actually find a kind of prejudice against prejudice, namely, when one rejects everything that has arisen through prejudices."[49] Although by no means a champion of prejudices, Kant is realistic enough to know that we are shaped by them in important ways. Admitting that it is almost impossible to overcome all prejudice, he defines enlightenment as the more limited project of a "deliverance from superstition." Superstition is not just prejudice, but gross prejudice.[50] Some prejudices may be repositories of truth, but until we transform their blind acceptance into a seeing acceptance, we are not justified in acting on them. As we shall see later, Kant examines how prejudices may be converted into proper judgments.

Gadamer, who regards prejudices as historical modes of fore-having in the Heideggerian sense, distinguishes between legitimate prejudices and illegitimate prejudices of overhastiness. A legitimate prejudice is rooted in the authority of tradition and has withstood the test of time. While we might agree that there should be room for such prejudices, to linger with them and refuse to transform them into more explicit judgments could betoken a prejudice against judgment itself. It may be true, as Gadamer writes, that "the prejudices of the individual, far more than his judgments, constitute the historical reality of his being."[51] However, we would not be willing to also say that the

---

47. Kant, *Lectures on Logic*, ed. J. Michael Young (Cambridge: Cambridge University Press, 1992), 133; Ak: 24: 169.
48. *Truth and Method*, 276.
49. *Lectures on Logic*, 133; Ak 24: 169.
50. Superstition is called "the greatest prejudice of all." See *Critique of the Power of Judgment*, 174; Ak 5: 294.
51. *Truth and Method*, 276–77; *Wahrheit und Methode*, 261.

prejudices of historians, far more than their judgments, constitute historical knowledge. To be sure, historical research must exploit the prejudices of tradition as a resource for understanding beliefs, but it is going too far to think that prejudices themselves can be "productive of cognition (*Erkenntnis*)."[52] This way of thinking produces a monolithic continuum of history in which "a living tradition and the effect of historical study must constitute a unity of effect (*Wirkungseinheit*)."[53]

As with Heidegger, there appears to be a reluctance to move beyond prejudgment to judgment and a preference for the suggestiveness of fore-understanding to explicit understanding. Methodologies that can be judged by the human sciences and put at everyone's disposal are rejected and understanding is conceived as a *subtilitas* or talent that draws on finesse or innate tact. As far as Gadamer is concerned, method vulgarizes the profundity of truth. Method is presumed to impose some technique or calculus as a substitute for insight into the nuances of historical life. But Dilthey's concern with the methods of human sciences was to indicate not only the limits but also the legitimate role of the explanative models of the natural sciences and to consider distinctive procedures more receptive to the complexities of human affairs. Questions about method in the human sciences were really aimed at a broader question about the kind of knowledge we can expect from these modes of inquiry. When Dilthey does discuss particular methods like description and comparison, he argues that they need to be applied reflectively.

What is needed is a hermeneutics that proceeds reflectively and is willing to give both prejudgment and judgment their due. To insist on a fusion of horizons is to court confusion. There must be a place for the discernment of judgment as well as for the received wisdom of prejudgment. The differentiated alternatives that Hegel expects from dialectics require the very reflection that Gadamer rejects. When he writes that "a person who reflects himself out of a living relationship to tradition destroys the true meaning of this tradition,"[54] it is assumed that reflection can come only from without. Here Gadamer seems to associate reflection with the optical image of reflected light that barely catches the superficial surface of things.[55] But there are other kinds of reflection that are more probing and thoughtful. Indeed, reflection

---

52. *Truth and Method*, 279; *Wahrheit und Methode*, 263.
53. *Truth and Method*, 282; *Wahrheit und Methode*, 267.
54. *Truth and Method*, 360; *Wahrheit und Methode*, 343.
55. *Truth and Method*, 483; *Wahrheit und Methode*, 457.

should be able to both engage with the tradition and be open to alternative possibilities.

*

Gadamer has contributed importantly to hermeneutics with his ideas about the way the effective history of human achievements unfolds and about the importance of a dialogue with tradition. But his approach leaves little room for the initiative of individual judging subjects. We see this first in the way Gadamer contrasts the Kant-Schiller conception of aesthetic play with his own theory of artistic play. Kant and Schiller stress the freedom of human subjects as their imagination actively plays with the aesthetic possibilities suggested by a work of art. Gadamer, however, argues for the "primacy of play over the consciousness of the player."[56] He writes in *Truth and Method* that the structure of play established by a work of art "absorbs the player into itself, and this frees him from the burden of taking the initiative (*die Aufgabe der Initiative*)."[57] As one recent commentator puts it, for Gadamer "the experience of art resembles religious experience in that it offers . . . a movement in which the subject participates only by losing itself."[58]

At first glance, Gadamer's account of the experience of dialogue or conversation seems to allow for a more active engagement that encourages reciprocity. This is because he claims that in a true conversation no one party should dominate. But in exploring the nature of language, he writes: "There is no reflection (*keine Reflexion*) when the word is formed, for the word is not expressing the mind but the thing intended."[59] It is not surprising then that Gadamer concludes his discussion of language and dialogue by also applying his concept of artistic play to it. The conversation draws the players into itself and plays itself out on its own terms. We are said to "fall into conversation"[60] and expected to concur with its outcome. When we understand linguistically, we are again largely passive as in the experience of art.

Gadamer's hermeneutics leaves us with the question whether the model of

---

56. *Truth and Method*, 104; *Wahrheit und Methode*, 100.
57. *Truth and Method*, 105; *Wahrheit und Methode*, 100.
58. Kristin Gjesdal, "Between Enlightenment & Romanticism," *Journal of the History of Philosophy* 46, no. 2 (April 2008): 304.
59. *Truth and Method*, 426; *Wahrheit und Methode*, 403.
60. *Truth and Method*, 383; *Wahrheit und Methode*, 385.

dialogic communication is adequate for hermeneutics in general. A dialogue or conversation is an idealized mode of communication that may make sense within one continuous tradition, but unfortunately our world today is more complex than that. The world involves the intersection of various traditions for which the ideas of fusion and concurrence appear remote and inapplicable. Today, more than ever, we are confronted with a global situation in which different heritages stand in such conflict that no dialogue seems possible.

An adequate hermeneutics must be also able to cope with the way we are marked by our regionality and historical background. It should point to those regions where communication is possible while also taking note of those gaps that make it problematic. Hermeneutics must take account of both the media that make commonality possible and those obstacles, real or imagined, that divide us. It is possible that even when we listen to each other, we speak past each other and fail to understand. When a common language produces this crisis, we confront what Jean-François Lyotard calls "the differend." He writes that "in the differend, something 'asks' to be put into phrases that do not yet exist."[61] It is a state of language that points to its own insufficiency—a state that is signaled by "the feeling of pain which encompasses silence."[62] Analogously, we come upon a legal differend when disputing claimants in a court of law cannot have their differences resolved by the existing rules of judgment. This is the point at which Lyotard is willing to call on Kant's reflective judgment.

In what follows we will explore reflective judgment, not just for its juridical use, but for its hermeneutical import. We will also examine Kant's theory of judgment more generally as a framework for a critical hermeneutics that can address questions of both the possibility and impossibility of communication and practical exchange.

---

61. Jean-François Lyotard, *The Differend: Phrases in Dispute*, trans. Georges Van Den Abbeele, *Theory and History of Literature*, vol. 46 (Minneapolis: University of Minnesota Press, 1988), 13.

62. *The Differend*, 13.

* 2 *

Interpretive Contexts, Judgment, and Critique

Part 2 consists of the central five chapters and is an attempt to rethink hermeneutics in orientational and reflective terms. In chapter 3, interpretation will be oriented to some of the distinctive spheres of reference suggested by Royce's theory of cognitive exchange and Kant's theory of reflective judgment. These spheres are then developed as meaning contexts and reflective schemata for interpretation. Chapter 4 offers an analysis of how cognition and knowledge can be differentiated in the *Critique of Pure Reason*. This is then used to clarify the meaning-truth relation and show what is at stake in validating understanding and legitimating interpretation. A more general treatment of how judgments function in Kant will also examine their relation to prejudices and how the latter can be made useful as preliminary interpretive judgments.

Knowledge involves judgmental assessment and after showing how this is borne out in arriving at scientific consent, we will examine the evaluative striving for aesthetic consensus in chapter 5. The next chapter addresses some of the normative considerations that must be brought to bear on historical interpretation according to Habermas. This requires a move from the ascriptive imputation that defines aesthetic judgment to a new model of attributive imputation. To develop such a model, I will expand on what Kant has to say about juridical legitimacy and authentic interpretation. Finally, the idea of a reflective hermeneutic critique will be developed in chapter 7 and contrasted with the more traditional models of constitutive and regulative critique.

CHAPTER 3

Reflective Orientation and the Bounds of Hermeneutics

We are now ready to move beyond the models of *dialectical* reconciliation and *dialogical* communication to pursue a *diagnostic* approach to hermeneutics. It became clear that both the dialectical and dialogical approaches to human understanding tend to regard history as a homogeneous sphere, conceived either as universal human spirit or as a continuous tradition. Instead, we will consider two more differentiated ways of thinking about interpretation: a triadic cognitive exchange approach, as elaborated by Josiah Royce, and a reflective orientational approach, as suggested by Immanuel Kant. They will help provide more realistic accounts of interpretation that acknowledge the mundane and contingent origins of our perspective on the world. Each in its own way can disclose how both ideal and pragmatic considerations apply to hermeneutics. Our task will be to show how these considerations intersect, as we bring out the role of judgment and diagnosis in interpretation.

ROYCE: COGNITIVE EXCHANGE AND COMMUNAL CONSPECTUS

Royce's views on interpretation are of interest because he sought to develop some insights from German idealism and make them relevant to pragmatism as it was being developed in America. In 1913 he published a set of lectures, three of which focus on interpretation. The first of these is entitled "Perception, Conception, and Interpretation," in which he introduces a cognitive exchange model. According to this model, interpretation is essentially a mode of theoretical problem-solving that tests ideas for their ability to be exchanged.

He points out that traditionally the cognitive process has been defined in terms of our powers to conceive and perceive. In considering the transactions that occur between these two powers, pragmatism regards conceptions as promissory notes that must find their "cash-value" in perceptions.[1] But even this more mundane, monetary way of characterizing cognition assumes that conceptions and perceptions trade in a private currency, namely, the mental representations of the Cartesian ego.

Genuine cognitive exchange cannot get started, according to Royce, until one considers the currency of thought as a public currency. The credit-values of concepts must be convertible into the cash-values of a generally accepted currency. Cognitive exchange needs to become interpretive when one enters another nation where a different currency is in use. Interpretation requires a self to go beyond his or her native currency to transact an exchange with others who use a foreign currency.[2] Interpretation can thus be said to extend cognition into the world as a transnational sphere.

Cognition becomes an art of social exchange whereby the self attempts to understand things that transcend its own sphere of familiarity. Royce adds a Fichtean dimension to this when he suggests that you must "postulate your fellow-man as the interpreter of the ideas which he awakens in your mind, and which are not your own ideas."[3] The other is not just another object to be interpreted by me, but addresses me as a subject also capable of interpreting. Under the further influence of Hegel, Royce sees interpretation as instituting reciprocal social relations, whereby an interpreter addresses a problem to another interpreter, who is expected to answer in turn. But neither the self nor the other, the first or second interpreter, can provide an answer to the problem without some "third," or intermediary. What can serve as such an intermediary?

In searching for an answer to this question in the lecture "The Will to Interpret," Royce adapts Charles Pierce's views about "thirdness" and its mediating function. If each of the two interpreting subjects has a distinct idea of a situation, they need to be compared by means of a "third idea" that will explicate how the original two both resemble and differ from each other.[4] The comparison involved here "is neither merely conceptual, nor merely per-

---

1. Josiah Royce, "Perception, Conception, and Interpretation," in *The Problem of Christianity* (Chicago: University of Chicago Press, 1968), 280.
2. See "Perception, Conception and Interpretation," 277–95.
3. Royce, "The Doctrine of Signs," in *The Problem of Christianity*, 361.
4. See Royce, "The Will to Interpret," in *The Problem of Christianity*, 299.

ceptual," according to Royce, nor does it produce a Hegelian synthesis. It involves an interpretation that goes beyond the conceptual and perceptual to seek a unifying visionary insight.[5] Interpretive insight involves "a third type of knowledge [that] . . . surveys from above. It is an attainment of a larger unity of consciousness. It is a conspectus."[6] What would constitute this larger conspectus of interpretation is not clear, but it leads Royce to posit a third independent subject. He relates the mind of the interpreter not only to "the mind which he undertakes to interpret" but also to a third "mind to which he addresses his interpretation."[7] This third, addressed as another neighbor who listens, also makes it possible for "a Community of Interpretation"[8] to arise. But in explicating this community, Royce begins to leave pragmatism behind and returns to his sources in speculative idealism. He acknowledges that he does not expect to perceive the unity of a conspectus "as any occurrence" in his own life. "I have to define the truth of my interpretation of you in terms of what the ideal observer of all of us would view as the unity which he observed. This truth cannot be defined in merely pragmatic terms."[9]

In the final analysis, Royce's community of interpretation is not merely a secular community of inquiry, but a religious one. His move beyond the pragmatic is also a move beyond the norms of scientific inquiry and brings hermeneutics back to the idea of disclosure from on high. However, instead of appealing to an original revelation, it projects a future illumination.[10] Although Royce's will to interpret was rooted in the will to know of the scientific community, where every hypothesis about the world is intersubjectively tested, the lecture on "The World of Interpretation" goes further by also making the community of interpreters constitutive for what is to be known. The world of sense is redefined idealistically as a more inclusive spiritual world that is the complex of interpreters and interpretations.

Despite the vagueness of their results, Royce's lectures remain useful in that he recognized many of the complexities associated with interpretation and replaced dialogic translation with a more worldly triadic conversion process. He saw the need for thought to be convertible into public currencies and for a communal solution to the interpretive problems generated by cognitive

---

5. See "The Will to Interpret," 307.
6. "The Will to Interpret," 306.
7. "The Will to Interpret," 314.
8. "The Will to Interpret," 315.
9. "The Will to Interpret," 317.
10. "The Will to Interpret, 319.

exchange.[11] While acknowledging the territorial borders that must be crossed in arriving at a proper interpretation, Royce assumed that the different media for expressing thought can be converted into each other and produce a consensus whose truth will be validated by an ideal interpreter. This is an assumption that cannot be usefully made for interpretation in the global world of the twenty-first century. Our task will be to think of interpretive insight not just in terms of conspectual convergence, but also in terms of perspectival divergence. Each of the various contexts that hermeneutics must take into account needs to be analyzed for its specific scope as well as its distinctive medium. Media of communication and information are not all like currencies that can be converted into each other. This becomes especially evident in our concluding chapter, where the medial contexts of the arts will be surveyed.

Royce's concern to transcend finite national currencies of thought and make the international community the standard for interpretation was motivated by the concern for legitimating truth. However, any particular interpretation can only approximate a final outcome, and absent an overarching unity provided by a divine observer, we must find an alternate way of addressing the problem of truth. We can no longer rely on the model of continual and incremental progress toward a final system of knowledge and truth. Hermeneutics must be ready to acknowledge the possibility that different perspectives may never be reconciled. In discerning the limits of national, ethnic, religious, or any other particular cultural perspectives, we should not assume that our understanding of historical phenomena necessarily improves by continually widening our scope of reference.

Understanding is always contextual and requires reflection to discern and specify the kinds of contexts that can be appealed to. Some of these contexts will be regional like those just mentioned. They are the product of history. Other contexts will arise through disciplinary efforts to make the world intelligible. The regional contexts from which we start in interpretation are a function of what we have called life-knowledge as accumulated through experience. Here we find local commonalities that cannot necessarily be widened. Even though each discipline will tap only certain aspects of the complex whole of reality, it is through disciplinary approaches to conceptual cognition that we can best hope to approach universal results.

The task of reflection will be to coordinate the various contexts of cognition and knowledge. Royce's idea that interpretation involves a triadic public process of ever-expanding scope will be modified into the proposal to treat

---

11. "The Will to Interpret," 339.

interpretation as a reflective triangulation of perspectives, whether they be regional or disciplinary. Instead of assuming that there will be a converging final consensus, we project the coordination and intersection of distinct perspectives.

The understanding of the historical world requires both an appreciation of commonalities and an awareness of irreducible differences. The interpretation required for such understanding cannot appeal to a Roycean conspectus that illuminates us from above. Instead it must proceed reflectively and by means of orientation from within this world. As a first step toward articulating a hermeneutics based on reflective orientation, I will consider some resources that can be found in Kant's examination of reflective judgments.

REFLECTIVE JUDGMENT AND ORIENTATION

If interpretation is to be applied to a world that is more fluid and diverse than has been traditionally assumed, then Kant's conception of reflective judgment will be more useful than the standard determinant judgment that defines intellectual inquiry. In the *Critique of Pure Reason*, Kant was primarily concerned with the determinant or explanative judgments that the mathematical natural sciences can make about phenomenal objects. Such judgments involve the thesis that the behavior of all experienced objects can be subordinated to laws of nature. In the *Critique of Judgment*, Kant finds room for the reflective judgments made when experience is approached either aesthetically or teleologically. In aesthetic judgment, we consider sense not just for its informational content about objects but for its feltness—how it affects the subject. Here we look for a felt harmony among the elements of our experience. Moreover, reflection about teleology and the overall order of nature leads to the realization that the constitutive claim of the first *Critique* that all natural events have an *efficient* cause does not commit us to the stronger claim that they are the exclusive product of *mechanical* moving forces. In the third *Critique*, Kant considers it possible to conceive of some objects as not merely subject to mechanical forces from without but as exhibiting immanent purposiveness or formative forces from within. For this he introduces a teleological judgment that can specify its own purposive context. Reflective judgments about aesthetic harmony and teleological order thus distinguish themselves by appealing not only to the intellect, but also to feeling and purposive interests of will. Reflective judgment moves beyond the faculty of understanding (*Verstand*) in Kant's sense to the process of understanding (*Verstehen*) in the broader Diltheyan sense that draws on all our capacities.

Reflective judgment is contrasted with determinant judgment as follows: "If the universal (the rule, the principle, the law) is given, then the power of judgment, which subsumes the particular under it . . . is determinant. If, however, only the particular is given, for which the universal is to be found, then the power of judgment is merely reflective (*reflectirend*)."[12] Determinant judgments employ available concepts to subsume particulars under them. Thus we can use ready concepts such as "chair" and "table" to classify the objects in a room. But in aesthetic appreciation we consider aspects of objects or their relation to us for which we have no adequate concepts. Then we judge phenomena reflectively. We may look for similar phenomena and thereby approximate a new concept through comparison. In aiming at such a universal, our reflective judgment has no clear-cut class of things or sphere of discourse to rely on. Hence, while determinant judgment is directed by the rules of the available spheres of discourse, reflective judgment seeks its own rules to orient itself. Only the reflective power of judgment can "give itself . . . a transcendental principle,"[13] says Kant. Rather than being directed or necessitated from without, reflective judging can be considered self-orienting. The principle by which it proceeds is to discern a purposive arrangement among particulars, even when they initially appear to be merely externally juxtaposed. Kant shows that we may reflectively regard a natural body as purposive if we are able to describe its parts as adjusting to each other to better serve the whole. Considered mechanistically, each part of a body is subordinate to the laws that govern that body, but considered teleologically, the parts are coordinated among themselves in the service of the whole.

Reflective judgment moves beyond the standard reading of the world and is interpretive in seeking new universals that can coordinate more content than available concepts are capable of. For hermeneutical ends, we are not only interested in the purposive aspects of nature. Thus the principle of reflective judgment will also be employed to orient us to the organizational structures of the sociohistorical world. Here individuals interact within shared social and cultural wholes that can be judged to be more or less purposive. Many of these spheres of human practice and culture have their own rules or conventions, but there are no ready rules to interrelate them. To understand history is to be able to articulate the way these holistic systems relate and intersect as well as to coordinate the various modes of discourse associated with them.

---

12. *Critique of the Power of Judgment*, 66–67; *Kant's gesammelte Schriften (Ak)* 5: 179.
13. *Critique of the Power of Judgment*, 67; *Ak* 5: 180.

KANT'S TRANSCENDENTAL TOPIC

In the *Critique of Pure Reason*, Kant does not yet discuss reflective judgment and its power to specify various worldly contexts for understanding. But he does speak of reflection as the consciousness of our representations relative to their subjective sources. Reflection is the capacity to compare representations and locate them in the faculty that gave rise to them. It distinguishes whether a representation belongs to sensibility or to understanding. Once this subjective differentiation has been made, we can relate representations by means of four paired concepts of reflection: identity and difference, agreement and opposition, inner and outer, as well as matter and form.[14] Kant uses these concepts of reflection, not to give determinant knowledge of objects as categories and empirical concepts do, but only to sort out what kind of object a representation can be about. Reflection can thus be said to be orientational, for as it compares representations, it also assigns them their place in relation to possible objects of sense or understanding. Concepts of reflection establish what Kant calls a "transcendental topic,"[15] which can be used to decide whether a representation should be referred to a phenomenal or a noumenal world.

Although reflective concepts such as matter and form are comparative in being reciprocally related, they are also contrastive and demand a weighing of alternatives. Thus, according to whether representations are located in sense or in the understanding, the priority of form or matter will differ. For phenomenal objects of sense, form is claimed to precede matter, but for intellectual objects of the understanding, matter precedes form. Since representations of sense come from without and are externally related, we cannot according to Kant make inner determinations about the matter of their objects except through the formal means whereby we apprehend them. By contrast, representations referred to the pure understanding must give precedence to what is inner as that which "has no relation . . . to anything that is different from it."[16] For such intelligible objects of the understanding, matter is the determinable that is then determined by form. Kant's assumption that inner content is best defined in the intellectual terms of the pure understanding may be open to

---

14. See Immanuel Kant, *Critique of Pure Reason*, trans. and ed. Paul Guyer and Allen W. Wood (Cambridge: Cambridge University Press, 1998), A263/B319–A266/B322.

15. *Critique of Pure Reason*, A268/B324

16. *Critique of Pure Reason*, A265/B321.

question, but his discussion serves to illustrate the considerations involved in applying reflective concepts as part of a transcendental topic.

Transcendental reflection provides procedures for orienting ourselves to possible objects before arriving at cognitive claims about actual objects.[17] Properly locating our representations through transcendental reflection is important if we are to avoid what Kant calls an "amphiboly of concepts of reflection."[18] He gives two examples of this confusion, namely, the amphibolies of "sensitivizing" concepts and of "intellectualizing"[19] appearances. Locke is mentioned as being guilty of the former, while the latter is discussed at some length as the confusion created by Leibniz's rational philosophy in which the principle of the identity of indiscernibles is extended from the intelligible world of metaphysics to the intuitable phenomena of science. Kant renounces metaphysics as the direct foundational base for the scientific understanding of the phenomenal world, but retains it as what I would call a reflective, orientational framework.

Having left dogmatic metaphysics behind, Kant considers the remaining alternatives of charting the phenomenal world of the sciences either skeptically or critically. Hume's skepticism dwells on the limits of experience and dismisses any role for reason beyond its empirical use. Kant speaks of Hume as one of those "geographers of human reason"[20] who chart the earth solely in terms of sensible appearances and leave its horizon indeterminable. Critical philosophy, while also basing knowledge claims on the empirical understanding, must, however, remain open to what might lie beyond the horizon of sense. A critique of reason must, according to Kant, supplement "the *limits* of my actual knowledge of the earth at any time" with "the *boundaries* of all possible description of the earth."[21]

This distinction between limits and boundaries is further explicated in Kant's *Prolegomena*. Limits (*Schranken*) are merely negative. They are empirical markers that cannot take into account what lies beyond them. Boundaries (*Grenzen*), however, are positive in that they "presuppose a space existing outside a certain definite place and enclosing it."[22] The earthly limits that confine

---

17. We will develop an analogous approach for hermeneutical reflection by considering the meaning and validity of interpretations before broaching the question of their truth.
18. *Critique of Pure Reason*, A260/B316.
19. *Critique of Pure Reason*, A271/B327.
20. *Critique of Pure Reason*, A760/B788.
21. *Critique of Pure Reason*, A759/B787, emphasis mine.
22. Kant, *Prolegomena to Any Future Metaphysics*, trans. Paul Carus, ed. Beryl Logan (London and New York: Routledge, 1996), 111; *Ak* 4: 352.

the empirical understanding are re-conceptualized as worldly boundaries that leave room for reason to have a more extensive role, even if it is mainly for orientational purposes. *Grenze* is to be taken positively and conceptualized as a boundary that points to possibilities beyond itself.

However, the term *Grenze* can also be translated as "bound," which carries the implication of a binding constraint. The idea of a boundary leaves room for the possible use of reason, but that very use may in turn entail necessary constraints on cognitive claims. When Kant indicates that a critique of reason must be able to determine "the ignorance that is unavoidable for us,"[23] we can say that he is not merely drawing a boundary, but pointing to the necessary bounds of what we can and cannot know. Bounds signify what is rationally binding and have "*a priori* grounds,"[24] and *Grenze*, as a critical concept, must be related to what is necessary as well as to what is possible. In exploring the idea of a reflective hermeneutics, we will consider to what extent these distinctions between the actual limits of experience, the boundaries of possible inquiry, and the necessary bounds of rational intelligibility can be adapted and applied to the relevant contexts of interpretation.

REFLECTIVE TOPOLOGY AND JUDGMENTAL CONTEXTS

The ancient image of Hermes as the messenger god shows him navigating between heaven and earth. A more modern image of Hermes as the figure of hermeneutic transport would require that he be able to negotiate the various locations and terrains of the natural and human sciences. The world of discourse is not a continuous plane or homogeneous sphere. Each science has its own mode of discourse that is at least partly discontinuous from others. And where there is some overlap of terrain or terminology, the scope of application will be quite different. Ultimately, the articulation of a theory of interpretation (*Auslegung*) will involve the laying out (*aus-legen*) or exposition of the various disciplines that lay claim to cognize reality.

Whereas the transcendental topic of the *Critique of Pure Reason* was largely geared to the universal framework of the natural sciences, in the *Critique of Judgment* Kant suggests a reflective topology that can be elaborated to be equally useful for the human sciences, with their more differentiated contexts. In the transcendental topic, Kant referred to his concepts of reflec-

---

23. *Critique of Pure Reason*, A767/B785.
24. *Critique of Pure Reason*, A758/B786.

tion as "titles for all comparison"[25] to properly locate representations. This dual reference of "topic" to both a title and a place (*topos*) will prove especially useful for the human sciences in referring interpretations to their relevant disciplinary and regional contexts. This new reflective topology of judgment allows us to relate concepts to objects while at the same time contextualizing them. In the Introduction to the third *Critique*, Kant states that when a concept is referred to an object, this object can be located in the world as part of either 1) a field (*Feld*), 2) a territory (*Boden, territorium*), 3) a domain (*Gebiet, ditio*), or 4) a habitat (*Aufenthalt, domicilium*).[26] This is the only place where this kind of contextualizing imagery often found in Kant's writings is brought together to allow us to delineate the regional scope of each term. The way Kant differentiates these four referential contexts can be used to specify the relative scope of judgments. But our hermeneutic concern will be to also fill them in as meaning contexts.

Kant begins by giving the following characterization of a *field*:

> Insofar as we refer concepts to objects without considering whether or not cognition of these objects is possible, they have their field, and this field is determined merely by the relation that the objects of these concepts have to our cognitive powers in general.[27]

To merely think of objects without determining whether their cognition is possible, that is, whether they can be actualized in experience, is to judge them as part of a field. To be part of a field is to be conceived as merely logically possible for thought, but not yet as transcendentally possible or actualizable for experience.[28] A field is the most neutral way of framing objects and allows us to judge unicorns and centaurs as belonging to the context of what can be conceived, even though they are presumed to be illusory beings. Kant also speaks of the field of the supersensible.

The second context is called a *territory* and denotes that part of a field "in which cognition is possible for us."[29] A concept locates an object in a terri-

---

25. *Critique of Pure Reason*, A269/B325.
26. See *Critique of the Power of Judgment*, 61–62; *Ak* 5: 174.
27. *Critique of the Power of Judgment*, 61 (translation revised); *Ak* 5: 174.
28. In the *Critique of Pure Reason*, possibility, actuality, and necessity are inseparable because they are taken as transcendental conditions of experience. In the *Critique of the Power of Judgment*, they are merely reflective modalities of thought and separable.
29. *Critique of the Power of Judgment*, 61; *Ak* 5: 174.

tory when it refers to or means (*bedeutet*) an actual sensible object. A territory (*territorium*) provides the base (*Boden*) of what can be experienced by human beings.

The third context represents a *domain* and is constituted by the legislative function of concepts. A domain is that part of either a logical field or the territory of experience in which concepts can provide laws that govern it. Since there are two sources of legislation—theoretical reason and practical reason—we can approach the world as the domain of either natural law or moral law.

The fourth context, a *habitat*, designates a locality in our territory of experience where we have only been able to arrive at empirical concepts. By contrast, categorial concepts such as causality apply to all possible objects of experience and lead us to expect that the whole territory of experience is in principle lawful. But not until universal mathematical laws like those of physics have been determined can conceptual legislation delineate a domain of nature within the territory of experience. With habitats, however, we have attained no more than inductive generalizations based on empirical concepts. As such they are marked by a somewhat contingent order. As Kant puts it, "empirical concepts . . . are, to be sure, lawfully generated, but are not legislative, rather the rules grounded on them are . . . contingent."[30] The contingent and transient order of this fourth context make it more difficult to define and name. The usual translation of *Aufenthalt* as "residence" misses the sense of contingency associated with this context. Instead the term "habitat" will be used to refer to the locality where we happen to be and which most directly affects us.[31] Here the particular situatedness of a judging subject is most obvious and can be contrasted with how the initial worldly context of a logical field was related to the cognitive powers of any potential thinking being.

Although these contexts of field, territory, domain, and habitat are presented in spatial or regional terms, we will develop them as judgmental contexts that can provide reflective schemata for interpretation. They project a reflective topology that orients us to the world at large by providing inter-

---

30. *Critique of the Power of Judgment*, 62; *Ak* 5: 174.

31. The term "residence" should be reserved for the legal term *Sitz*, for this is how it is used in the *Metaphysics of Morals*. "Residence (*Sitz*)" is a legal term indicating a chosen location where one has the right to stay permanently. A "habitat (*Aufenthalt*)" as I will use the term in what follows, represents a sphere where neither the laws of nature nor the laws of nation states have been considered or applied. See also chapter 6 about legal and interpretive ownership (*Besitz*).

mediate organizing contexts. A field can be projected purely by thought. A territory has the more limited scope of what we human beings can actually experience. A domain is a part of a territory that we can legislate to with a priori concepts. Finally, a habitat as the context of empirical concepts is a part of nature for which a human subject can find order only a posteriori.

Further elaborating the scope of these four kinds of judgmental context, we can roughly correlate field with the logically possible, territory with what is humanly actualizable, domain with objective and necessary order, and habitat with subjective and contingent order. This enables us to speak of the field of the possible, the territory of the actual, the domain of the necessary, and the habitat of the contingent[32] as four modal contexts for judging objects. When we locate an object in a territory or a domain, we are in a position to make either descriptive or predictive determinant judgments about it. By contrast, the field of the possible is merely the correlate of logical reflection, and the habitat of the contingent the correlate of reflective judgment.

Reflective judgment would not have the hermeneutical import that I ascribe to it if it could not relate the contingency of a local habitat to other contexts. Therefore habitats are merely the starting points for reflective judgment. Kant seems to acknowledge this possibility of relating contexts when he indicates that reflective judgment has the capacity to discern a domain-like "lawfulness" in what is ordinarily thought to be contingent. In section 76 of the *Critique of Judgment*, he reflects on contingency and shows that what we humans call the "purposiveness of nature" is the "lawfulness of the contingent."[33] The habitat of the contingent involves a collocation of facts that demonstrate no objectively necessary connection. What reflective judgment looks for, then, is a more limited orderliness that restricts lawfulness to a specific system like an organism. Indeed, the problem of contingency also raises its head when the topic of the overall systemization of the laws of nature is addressed. From the standpoint of Kant's faculty of the understanding and the capacity for determinant judgment, every event is subsumable under some law, but the explanative laws of nature could be so numerous and diverse that not all of them will be discovered. Consequently, nature as a whole would never be grasped as anything more than a contingent aggregate. Because the

---

32. Contingency can of course also display itself in nature understood as the domain of scientific order. But then contingency manifests gaps in an overall objective order. By contrast, the contingency of a habitat represents a local and subjective sense of order. Later we will speak of it as order based on familiarity.

33. *Critique of the Power of Judgment*, 274; *Ak* 5: 404.

overall coherence demanded by reason cannot be legislated to nature, reflective judgment "presumes [it] of nature . . . only for its own advantage" as a formal purposiveness.³⁴ Kant makes it evident that his concept of a purposiveness of nature is a subjective mode of representing nature, and, to that extent, interpretive.

When these four orientational contexts are related to our previous discussions of the concepts of limit, boundary, and bound, we can say that while the territory of experience is limited by what is actualizable, the field of possibilities is relatively unlimited. To the extent that rules are constitutive for our experience of nature, they are binding laws that positively bound a domain; to the extent that rules are regulative and transcend experience, they transform the actual limits of experience into boundaries beyond which they project an ideal or hypothetical limit. Whereas the territorial limits of experience are negative, the limits of regulative reason are abstract in that they transcend experience. Finally, a habitat can be said to be an empirically discovered location marked by transient or provisional limits. Reflective judgment can relate such a contingent context to others that converge on it and thereby attempt to transform negative limits into positive boundaries. We find the beginnings of such a transition from a contingent to a more appropriate context in Kant's efforts to relocate psychology as a discipline.

Traditionally, psychology had been seen as part of metaphysics and subject to rational analysis. Psychology as the theory of mind was defined as having its own spiritual substance or soul. Rational analysis had been used to argue for the simplicity of the soul and therefore its immortality. In his *Critique of Pure Reason*, Kant exposed the transcendental illusions involved in such inferences. Thus the claim that we can theoretically *know* ourselves to have an immortal soul must be transformed into the practical claim that it is rational to *believe* it.

With the traditional rational psychology of the soul disposed of, any remaining psychological claims would have to be restricted to an empirical psychology. Empirical psychology appeals to inner experience to attempt to determine the nature of our states of mind. But Kant regards inner experience as far less reliable than outer experience and holds out little hope that empirical psychology can make good on its cognitive claims. Yet, because the questions raised by psychology remain important, Kant allows psychology to retain its place in metaphysics, but only as a temporary habitat (*Aufenthalt*) until it can find its more permanent dwelling (*Wohnplatz*) elsewhere. Its habi-

---

34. *Critique of the Power of Judgment*, First Introduction, 10; *Ak* 20: 204.

tat in metaphysics is contingent and must be replaced with a more adequate domicile that will transform its empirical and earthly limits—as evidenced by the unreliability of inner experience—into the reflectively justified boundaries of a new discipline that also considers outer experience, but reorients it to the world of human interaction.

Kant contends that psychology must renounce its aspirations to be part of academic philosophy and transform itself into an empirical worldly discipline called anthropology. But in making this turn, psychology must resist being reduced to a physiological anthropology. Adequate anthropological self-cognition will come less from investigating what nature has made of the human being than from examining what "*he* as a free-acting being makes, or can and should make of himself."[35] Anthropology as the proper framework for psychological questions should be conceived pragmatically, which in this context means viewing human beings as active participants in the historical world. Merely cognizing the world must be replaced by "participating (*mitspielen*)" in the world so that we can be said "to *have* the world."[36] Kant speaks of a pragmatic disposition that civilizes humans by developing their social qualities. It falls short of the moral disposition by allowing individuals to use others as means rather than as ends in themselves.[37] But by cultivating civil concord, the pragmatic disposition moves humans to regard themselves as more than citizens of their own limited state and become citizens of the world. In pragmatic anthropology, the geography of theoretical reason becomes a cosmopolitan mode of reflective orientation with practical import. When Kant spoke of the geography of human reason, he attempted to transform the empirical limits of the earth into the boundaries of the domain of nature. The cosmopolitan scope of anthropology defines the human world as a territory whose limits must be specified as bounds by reflective judgment in light of human activities and interests.

If psychology had been relocated in physiological anthropology, it would have been considered a natural science. But Kant's call for psychology to become part of a pragmatic anthropology is in effect a proposal to steer it away from the explanative natural sciences with their universal laws and locate it in what we now call the human sciences. Once the limited self-awareness gained through psychological introspection is related to the observation of what hu-

---

35. Immanuel Kant, *Anthropology from a Pragmatic Point of View*, trans. Robert B. Louden (Cambridge: Cambridge University Press, 2006), 3; *Ak* 7: 119.

36. See *Anthropology*, 4; *Ak* 7: 120.

37. See *Anthropology*, 226; *Ak* 7: 322.

man beings are able to make of themselves in the world and toward cultivating civil concord, we can establish the boundaries of pragmatic anthropology in relation to contiguous disciplines concerning cultural and political life, economics, and history.[38] Through the systematic context that anthropology can establish in conjunction with these disciplines, psychology can be given a new lease on life.

PHILOSOPHY AND THE REFLECTIVE SPECIFICATION OF BOUNDS

In *The Conflict of the Faculties*, Kant complains that the philosophical faculty at universities had not been placed with the higher faculties such as Theology, Medicine, and Law. Although he never indicates the precise location of philosophy among the disciplines, he is quite insistent that philosophy should not be too closely tied to mathematics. In the *Critique of Pure Reason*, the differences between the two are illustrated by contrasting the demonstrative or constructive use of reason in mathematics with the "discursive use of reason"[39] in philosophy. In this section, I will argue that there is also a reflective use of reason that can make philosophy less abstractly discursive and render it hermeneutically relevant for specifying the disciplinary contexts of the various sciences.

Both mathematics and philosophy are rational disciplines that start with a priori concepts. However, mathematics alone can provide the demonstration or intuitive proof of its a priori concepts. Its knowledge comes from the construction of such concepts, "that is, from intuition, which can be given a priori in accordance with the concepts."[40] Philosophy differs in gaining knowledge through the discursive use of a priori concepts whose meaning can be fulfilled only in relation to empirical intuition, which is a posteriori. Philosophy must discipline itself and not expect a direct presentation of either its transcendental concepts of the understanding or its ideas of reason.[41]

With its discursive use of concepts, philosophy cannot match mathematics in meeting the requirement for the demonstration of a priori concepts, that is, their direct presentation in particulars. According to Kant, mathematical

---

38. For a more extended discussion of the relation of psychology and anthropology, see chapter 5.
39. *Critique of Pure Reason*, A719/B747.
40. *Critique of Pure Reason*, A734/B762.
41. *Critique of Pure Reason*, A737/B765.

claims about magnitude can be intuitively demonstrated either through the constructive delineation of individual geometric figures or through the "symbolic construction"[42] of algebraic notation. Because philosophical concepts like causality cannot be directly presented or intuited in particular objects that undergo change, an intermediary mode of schematic presentation is necessary. Schemata are produced by the imagination to relate the understanding to sensible intuitions. The imaginative schema for causality explicates what it would mean for one intuitable state A to always be followed by another state B. Logical dependence is translated into a temporal irreversibility that is in principle intuitable. We can thus distinguish between the mathematical use of demonstrative presentation, which is direct, and the philosophical use of schematic presentation, which is formal and indirect.

In the *Critique of Judgment*, Kant speaks of symbolic presentation as a third way of presenting a priori concepts—in this case, ideas of reason. Symbolic presentation attempts to exhibit the meaning of rational ideas by way of intuitive analogies. It can be said to fall between the schematic presentation of discursive concepts and the demonstrative presentation of mathematical concepts. On the one hand, symbols are like schemata in being produced by the imagination, and on the other hand they approximate mathematical constructs by being quasi-intuitive.

Unfortunately, when he compares symbolic presentation with schematic presentation, Kant does so by stating that the symbolic is indirect while the schematic is direct and demonstrative.[43] This goes against his earlier position that only mathematical constructions can be direct and demonstrative. Schemata and symbols are really both indirect as media for presenting concepts. For us, the significant contrast is that demonstrative and schematic presentation as used in the *Critique of Pure Reason* are about objective relations, while symbolic presentation in the *Critique of Judgment* is about contextual relations. If demonstrative and schematic presentations are, so to speak, more "direct," it is because they exhibit relations among possible contents of experience; if symbolic presentation can be called more "indirect," it is because it exhibits relations among the orientational contexts that are needed to interpret experience.

Symbolic presentation is introduced in the *Critique of Judgment* as a way of overcoming the abstract discursive use of concepts. It uses reflective judgment to apply a rule that makes sense of how things are related in a familiar

---

42. *Critique of Pure Reason*, A717/B745.
43. *Critique of the Power of Judgment*, 226–27; Ak 5: 352.

and intuitable context in order to illuminate how things are related in another less familiar context. Thus Kant suggests that the rather abstract contrast between despotic governments ruled by a "single absolute will" and constitutional governments ruled by "laws internal to the people"[44] can be made more intuitively concrete by considering the former as a machine and the latter as an "animate body." There is no congruence of content here because we are comparing how things function in a natural context to how they function in a political context. Nevertheless, there is an analogy that can serve a heuristic function. We can apply "the form of reflection"[45] suggested by the more tangible natural context to the less tangible political one. To make a machine the symbol for a despotic state is to bring out that its governance is artificially controlled and imposed from without; to think of a constitutional state as an organism is to see it as being self-regulating and organized from within. The poles of machine and living organism establish the bounds for a whole range of possible political states.

Although Kant had disciplined discursive philosophy not to expect rational ideas to be intuitively presented, symbolic presentation provides a way for them to obtain intuitive analogues. To be sure, philosophers should not expect the rational idea of God to be intuitively demonstrable and to provide determinate knowledge. But through reflective judgment we can draw on intuitive analogies from the territory of human experience to illuminate the field of the transcendent. When it is asserted in the *Critique of Judgment* that we can have "cognition of God" that is "symbolic,"[46] this will not be knowledge determining the nature of God, but merely a reflective interpretation of our possible relation to God. Kant's main hope for this work was to locate certain affinities between the otherwise conflicting domains of nature and freedom by using sensuous beauty to exemplify the moral attributes of human freedom.

Of the three uses of reason that we have distinguished, the constructive use will be the least relevant for the delineation of hermeneutic contexts. Whereas constructive demonstration is direct, interpretation is, by nature, indirect. Since mathematical demonstration intuits the coincidence of the particular and the universal, its claims do not require contextualization and interpretation. For both the discursive and reflective uses of reason, there will be a disparity between particulars and universals. The discursive use attempts their

---

44. *Critique of the Power of Judgment*, 226, *Ak* 5: 352.
45. *Critique of the Power of Judgment*, 225; *Ak* 5: 351.
46. *Critique of the Power of Judgment*, 227; *Ak* 5: 353.

mediation by legislative means that will subordinate particulars to universals. The reflective use will coordinate them within interpretive contexts.

According to Kant, the constructive and discursive uses of reason "admit of limits, but not of bounds."[47] That is, neither the infinite series generated in mathematics nor the indefinite series confronted by the discursive understanding can "find completion in its internal progress."[48] This lack of completion is not a problem for mathematical constructions dealing with fields or series of ideal objects. But it is a problem for the discursive use of reason in natural philosophy, where the understanding is limited to explaining the events of nature by conditions that are themselves conditioned. To account for all that happens in nature, the discursive understanding is forced into endless regressions and progressions. These indefinite series in the domain of natural science can be completed only by the rational idea of an unconditioned condition, which gives the understanding its limits from without. But as we will see, the reflective use of reason can provide the territory of human experience a measure of completion from within, so that the appropriate contexts for relating particulars and universals can be established. Here reflective judgment can set the contextual bounds of interpretation immanently.

The most general way in which reason sets the boundaries for the understanding is through the idea of "the purposive unity of things"[49] in the *Critique of Pure Reason*. Kant uses the idea of a unifying purpose regulatively to project an inner connectedness for what appears phenomenally as merely externally connected. Purposive unity posits the abstract ideal of an overall system of nature. In the *Critique of Judgment*, however, the idea of purpose is used both regulatively and reflectively. The latter use serves to specify the idea of systematic order into more locally organized systems. In this process of reflective specification, the abstract idea of purpose is employed more restrictively to delineate concrete terrains of the lifeworld manifesting an immanent purposiveness within the territory of experience.

To describe a particular organism as exhibiting an immanent purposiveness is to specify the context and scope of the regulatively used rational idea of purpose. Whereas a regulative system transcends the limits of experience by projecting a more encompassing context as a hypothetical boundary, reflective judgments are more restrictive and can establish bounded contexts within experience, which can then be coordinated. A particular can exemplify a uni-

---

47. *Prolegomena to Any Future Metaphysics*, 111; *Ak* 4: 352.
48. *Prolegomena*, 111; *Ak* 4: 352.
49. *Critique of Pure Reason*, A686/B714.

versal for reflective judgment only if the universal has been made "more specific by adducing or taking into account (*anführen*) the manifold under it."[50] The reflective explication of the particular must be matched by the reflective specification of the universal concept. The universal is no longer purely rational but adapted to the empirical world. For particular beings to be considered organisms, it must be possible to structurally specify them as organized systems with their local coordinates within the territory of our experience. An organism may at first appear as a limited habitat but can be reflectively rethought as a special system that establishes its own immanent bounds as it actively responds to its surroundings. The idea of a self-bounding reflective system will prove to be an important addition to the other means of contextualization provided by Kant's topology. Such systems will figure prominently in the rest of this work as a fifth kind of hermeneutical context.

Kant's idea that purposiveness is the "lawfulness of the contingent" is ultimately elucidated by regarding organic systems as habitats displaying domain-like behavior. However, the lawfulness of an organism is not strictly legislative but that of a well-organized, functioning whole. Here we can specify systematic bounds that are organizational rather than legislative. Legislative bounds unify things by subordinating them to some universal rule; organizational bounds do so by coordinating them within some functional context or system.

The hermeneutic relevance of reflectively specified systems will become more evident when we extend the preceding reflections on the nature of organic life to the complex problem of understanding historical life. Thus when we turn to the less determinate discourses or disciplines that delineate order within the sphere of historical life, we refer them to localizable contexts, which are bounded by constraints deriving from common human interests. Here bounds are not simply imposed from without like the causal laws that govern Kant's domain of nature. Instead, formal bounds establish themselves within the organized practices and purposive systems that arise in human history. This will become apparent when we consider the productive systems of history that are delineated by the human sciences. From the perspective of Kant's anthropology, such historical systems should specify the pragmatic purposiveness of human activity. But not all historical order can be delineated in terms of organized purposive systems. In chapter 1 we spoke of objective spirit as the medium of inherited commonality. This medium can be extended

---

50. *Critique of the Power of Judgment*, First Introduction, 18 (translation revised); *Ak* 20: 215.

beyond the contingent local habitat of our birth to encompass other common patterns of human interaction that have accrued over time without necessarily manifesting clear purposes. It is with the help of the human sciences eager to replace commonality with universality that we can begin to delineate the more broadly organized purposive systems that develop territorial contours.

Although the four referential contexts adapted from Kant and the idea of systematic order were originally oriented to nature, they can and will be applied to the historical world as well. The medium of inherited commonality, however, is clearly historical from the start. It constitutes the meaning context that nurtures each of us and provides us with a native language and a cultural background for communication and action. This inherited context is the most difficult to define, and some more forward-looking analogues will be proposed in my final chapter. There, the contextual medium of commonality, as conceived by Dilthey, and the media of exchange, as explored by Royce, will be further specified as medial contexts for making sense of artistic communication in the contemporary world of global information transmission.

We can thus add systematic and medial contexts to the original four orientational contexts for interpretation. Each defines the scope of judgment in a distinctive way. In the case of Kant's general fields and lawful domains, judgment conceives the natural world in purely intellectual terms and is capable of establishing objective and universal order. However, in the case of the territory of human experience and more local habitats, judgment also takes into account our sensible nature and is forced to acknowledge subjective limits and find ways of overcoming them. The contexts defined by either a communicative medium or a more organized historical system will become especially useful for understanding how human beings can both compete with each other in striving to attain their ends and have a basis for setting bounds for themselves to make cooperation possible.

AN AMPHIBOLY OF REFLECTIVE ORIENTATION

So far we have begun the differentiation of referential contexts and have also considered the possibility of discerning boundaries and internally bounded systems. It has become increasingly clear that limits and boundaries are primarily descriptive, while bounds are prescriptive or normative. Whereas legislative bounds were conceived by Kant as rational and formally binding, organizational bounds are more concretely structural and help to articulate the functional values of systems from within.

Hermeneutics, however, cannot content itself with merely locating and specifying the appropriate contextual frames for inquiry; it must also consider the different relations among them. The full orientational task of hermeneutics echoes reason's quest for an overall coherence of things, but in light of the failure to establish the subordination of everything to one overarching system, hermeneutics seeks instead the coordination of varied frames of reference. Coordination is often thought of as a simple process of juxtaposing things and relating them externally, but the coordinative task of hermeneutics includes a consideration of the ways different meaning systems may converge, intersect, and at times partially coalesce. For example, by correlating systems with disciplines, we can generate functional contexts capable of interacting to some extent. Several contexts can frame the same object—we saw Kant define objects by their territorial location as well as by the laws of a domain. And as we will see, various social and cultural systems can converge on the same historical subject. As part of its orientational task, reflective judgment must consider questions of priority and decide which referential context takes precedence. Otherwise, mistakes about meaning and illusions about the truth can arise.

The confusion resulting from not properly adjusting to different contexts is a form of what was referred to earlier as Kant's amphiboly of concepts of reflection. For our hermeneutical approach, this amphiboly points to the need to treat distinctively each of our six ways of contextualizing a subject matter. Thus while it may make sense to prioritize formal considerations within a legislative domain, it is inappropriate when exploring the territories we come upon in experience. Many actual territories on this planet have borders that extend from land to water, requiring us to be amphibious. To chart a territory—whether it refers to some physical landscape or a disciplinary terrain—requires a capacity to adapt to a changing baseline. To explore a legislative domain requires a cognizance of levels of dependence, but in a field, possibilities can be explored independently of each other. Most of all we must cultivate a structural awareness of how fields, domains, territories, habitats, and system-based and medium-focused contexts may or may not intersect.

In the *Metaphysics of Morals*, Kant adds a practical counterpart to his theoretical amphiboly in a section entitled "On an Amphiboly in Moral Concepts of Reflection." This practical amphiboly comes about when we misconstrue the proper scope or context of our moral duties as rational human beings. Kant begins this section as follows:

> As far as reason alone can judge, a human being has duties only to human beings (himself and others), since his duty to any subject is moral constraint by that subject's will. Hence the constraining (binding) sub-

ject must, *first*, be a person; and this person must, *second*, be given as an object of experience, since man is to strive for the end of this person's will and this can happen only in a relation to each other of two beings that exist.[51]

Normative confusions occur when our way of thinking about duties to ourselves and fellow human beings is improperly extended to other kinds of beings. The amphiboly here is to mistake a "duty *regarding (in Ansehung)*" these other kinds of beings for a "duty *to (gegen)*" them."[52] A duty regarding non-human beings is, in Kant's words, a "supposed duty"[53] and is not the same as a direct duty owed to each other as moral persons. Although the moral law requires us to treat all human beings as equals, for Kant this duty does not strictly extend to animals. Nevertheless, he indicates that they should be treated with decency and not be allowed to suffer, for their proper treatment is an indirect duty owed to our humanity. This also applies to our relations with inanimate nature. When using its resources for our sustenance, we must avoid the "wanton destruction of what is beautiful"[54] in nature. Natural beauty deserves our appreciation much as sacred beings deserve our reverence.

Kant's moral amphiboly allows us to distinguish between direct duties that determine us as a rational self (*autos*) in the moral domain and indirect duties that relate us to larger territories of beings. What Kant says about the wide duty to perfect oneself and to promote the happiness of other human beings also applies to an indirect duty, that is, it "determines nothing about the kind and extent of actions themselves but allows a latitude of free choice."[55] A direct duty involves legislative determination, whereas an indirect duty leaves it for us to decide what is appropriate, by means of reflective interpretation. Through a reflective-orientational sense of a more individuated human self (*heauton*) as one among other kinds of being, the abstract idea of a duty regarding all other beings can be specified into that of a duty to have regard for them as distinctive.

The amphiboly of moral reflection can also arise for Kant when we consult our conscience and misinterpret duties owed to ourselves as duties owed to God. Although conscience "is a business of a human being with himself," rea-

---

51. Kant, *The Metaphysics of Morals*, trans. Mary Gregor (Cambridge: Cambridge University Press, 1996), 192; *Ak* 6: 442.
52. *Metaphysics of Morals*, 192; *Ak* 6: 442.
53. *Metaphysics of Morals*, 192; *Ak* 6: 442.
54. *Metaphysics of Morals*, 192; *Ak* 6: 443.
55. *Metaphysics of Morals*, 195; *Ak* 6: 446.

son constrains a person to "carry it on as at the bidding *of another person*."[56] In being conscientious, we interpret ourselves not merely by how other humans bind us, but by how a superhuman "scrutinizer of hearts"[57] would regard us. From the perspective of human reason, this ideal interpreter is a regulative idea, and the amphiboly of moral reflection stands as a warning not to conflate the need to refer to this ideal other with the belief that we have a duty to that being. Although Kant's idea of God as an ideal other provides a regulative limit that we should take into account, we are not positively bound to that being. If we consider ourselves as having duties to a higher being, we lose our autonomy as rational human beings. Conscience must not be heteronomously directed by a superhuman being, but it still makes sense to be reflectively oriented by the limiting idea of an ideal interpreter. God is referred to not in order to give us an absolute Roycean conspectus, but to help us define our own perspective and accordingly bind ourselves. Whatever one thinks about Kant's value-hierarchy concerning animals, humans, and purely rational beings, his normative amphiboly makes it necessary to differentiate between what is directly binding and what is indirectly limiting on the basis of a regulative appeal to a wider or ideal context.

When we turn to the interpretation of the changing terrains of historical life, it becomes even more important to avoid disorientation by keeping in mind the basic referential frameworks that have been previously distinguished. To chart a territory in terms of contexts that range from the physical and organic to those resulting from human activity requires a capacity to discern changing baselines. The possibilities of reflective amphibolies increase when we indiscriminately extend our understanding of a familiar region to others that are less familiar. For our hermeneutical approach, the amphiboly of reflection also shows the need to consider interrelations among meaning contexts and to judge what point of reference should take precedence in a given case.

Each discipline must be probed for how it frames its objects and proceeds in accordance with the perspective it provides. Whereas the natural sciences tend to subordinate their objects to universally binding laws, disciplines like anthropology, while limited by such laws, set their bounds differently, namely, by means of commonalities. One of the tasks that Kant assigns his pragmatic anthropology is to judge behavioral patterns by the norms of the *sensus communis*.[58] Moreover, practices that may make limited sense in terms of their

---

56. *Metaphysics of Morals*, 189; *Ak* 6: 438.
57. *Metaphysics of Morals*, 190; *Ak* 6: 439.
58. See chapter 4.

originating localities need to be legitimated in relation to our cosmopolitan destination. By so doing, we can relate limited terrains or contingent habitats to a broader territory in which we can nevertheless feel at home as citizens of the world.

Although the historical world is not the homogeneous sphere that determinant judgment tends to project for nature, reflective judgment can aim for the historical world's structural articulation by coordinating specific disciplines, modes of discourse, and other relevant frames of reference. The challenge is to find the key factors or crucial conditions within this complex of relevant contexts so that the different kinds of discourse they provide will be properly interwoven in the fabric of interpretation.

WORLDLY ORIENTATION

In considering the various meaning contexts for human understanding and historical attribution, we should not forget that these modes of reflective orientation have their experiential basis in our geographical orientation to the earth. The original sense of orientation refers to the capacity of the subject to locate itself spatially and to navigate through its territory. Spatial orientation involves more than a visual relation to my earthly surroundings; it is rooted in the way I feel my locatedness in the world. Here the intuitive can encompass both what is perceived and what is felt. Kant writes that "even with all the objective data of the sky, I orient myself *geographically* only through a *subjective* ground of differentiation."[59] This subjective ground is "the feeling of a difference between my two sides, the right and left."[60] Whether or not this capacity to distinguish the right and left sides of my body is a priori as Kant claims, it reveals the importance of feeling in making certain essential orientational discriminations. The role of feelings has been increasingly recognized in contemporary neuropsychological research, resulting for example in the proposal that feelings like joy serve to map our bodily as well as mental states.[61] In reflective interpretation, feelings of sympathy and solidarity can correlate our own inner states with those of other subjects. The feeling of ori-

---

59. Kant, "What Does It Mean to Orient Oneself in Thinking?," in *Religion within the Boundaries of Mere Reason and Other Writings*, trans. and ed. Allen Wood and George Di Giovanni (Cambridge: Cambridge University Press, 1998), 5; *Ak* 8: 135.

60. "What Does It Mean to Orient Oneself in Thinking?," 5; *Ak* 8: 135.

61. See Antonio Damasio, *Looking for Spinoza: Joy, Sorrow, and the Feeling Brain* (San Diego: Harcourt Inc., 2003), 85–86.

entation goes beyond our own states and those of others in eventually relating us to the world at large.

We noted earlier that when it comes to reflective contrasts, such as inner and outer, which takes precedence will depend on the context. When considering representations of sense, the outer is primordial and the interiority of what is felt is a mere vanishing limit. Cognitively, the senses point us in the direction of the external world. But when we focus on the felt aspect of what is sensed, we are recalled to ourselves and our specific place in the lived world—here the inner is at least equiprimordial with the outer.

The orientational distinction between left and right only makes sense for a world observed from a lived body. For a pure intellect, the right and left sides of the body would be conceptually indiscernible. The indexical capacity to differentiate them accompanies our "taking a stand" so that when we step forward to assert ourselves, we may favor either the left or the right. This felt preference will not be relevant to a world conceived in terms of fields of logical possibility or domains of legislative determination, but it is operative when the world is articulated in terms of actual territories and contingent habitats. Functional and pragmatic systems established by humans still make use of this lived distinction, as when we speak of political associations being left or right of center.

The task of reflective orientation is to elicit those conditions that allow us to relate our basic feeling of orientation to some more encompassing frame of reference. In *The Jäsche Logic*, Kant states that one should *"orient oneself in thought* or in the speculative use of reason by means of the common understanding."[62] It must be noted, however, that the orientational framework provided by Kant's "common understanding," or by any other encompassing frame of reference such as the *sensus communis* and the inherited medium of commonality, will not give us determinate directions. They only provide markers to help chart our bearings and keep us from straying beyond the bounds of what is communally or historically reasonable as we pursue our own goals or make sense of those of others. The further task of interpretation is to diagnose the most appropriate points of reference and specify such indeterminate horizons into the more worldly reflective contexts that we have differentiated.

By advocating a reflective orientational approach, we are extending philosophy in the academic sense into what Kant calls "philosophy in the worldly sense (*Philosophie nach dem Weltbegriffe*)."[63] Academic philosophy involves

---

62. Kant, *The Jäsche Logic*, in *Lectures on Logic*, 563; *Ak* 9: 57.
63. *Jäsche Logic*, 537 (translation revised); *Ak* 9: 24.

the theoretical skill of classifying all available cognitions and giving them an ideal systematic coherence. Worldly philosophy also brings into focus our practical and pragmatic concerns in evaluating all cognition and uses of reason in the service of future human ends. It is of interest not just to those skilled in scientific cognition, but to all human beings concerned with the kind of knowledge that enables them to live wisely.

In the first *Critique*, Kant lists the three basic questions we must consider: What can I know? What should I do? and What may I hope for?[64] In *The Jäsche Logic* he claims that for philosophy in the "cosmopolitan sense (*weltbürgerlichen Bedeutung*)"[65] these three questions relate to a fourth question: What is man?[66] The latter question suggests that the ultimate concerns of philosophy have anthropological import. Michel Foucault viewed Kant's discipline of pragmatic anthropology as marking the transition from a philosophical conception of the human subject as both sovereign and controlling to a subject who will be disciplined and controlled by the human sciences. However, our hermeneutic appropriation of Kant locates a human subject who cannot be defined as either entirely controlled or controlling. We see instead a finite subject who is both responsible in accepting rational bounds and responsive in ways that allow for overcoming some limits. Critique should be able to provide an interdisciplinary framework for hermeneutics that will not just discipline by imposing external limits, but develop self-discipline by setting bounds from within.

Hermeneutics can orient us to the territory of the human world as we evaluate how cognition is of use to us in the practice of living. For such an orientational hermeneutics, the general cognitive subject who represents reality contemplatively and, in Thomas Nagel's words, "from nowhere,"[67] is reconceived as a particular living subject with its distinctive habitat who is able to assert his or her place in the world. Interpreting this world involves relating pragmatic situational conditions to ideal orientational meaning contexts.

64. *Critique of Pure Reason*, A805/B833.
65. *Jäsche Logic*, 538; *Ak* 9: 25.
66. *Jäsche Logic*, 538; *Ak* 9: 25.
67. See Thomas Nagel, *The View from Nowhere* (Oxford: Oxford University Press, 1986).

CHAPTER 4

The Hermeneutics of Attaining Knowledge: The Role of Judgmental Assent

Our hermeneutical approach has stressed the importance of disciplinary differentiation and coordination as well as the discernment of judgment in orienting ourselves to multiple contexts. Just as interpretation involves indirect modes of understanding, so orientation as a way of providing preliminary contexts for interpretation is an indirect process that arrives at its destination only by way of some already familiar markers. Although we have discussed some of these meaning frameworks in quasi-spatial terms, there are also temporal considerations in how we come to know the world. Now we turn to the temporal aspects of reflective orientation and consider the important role played by both prejudgment and judgment in the process of attaining knowledge.

FROM CONCEPTUAL CLASSIFICATION TO JUDGMENTAL ARTICULATION

As an early proponent of incorporating the temporal and historical dimensions of reality into philosophical analysis, Dilthey criticized Schleiermacher's hermeneutics for classifying reality in terms of timeless concepts. For Schleiermacher, he wrote, "the whole task of philosophy is to impose a philosophical form—the form of inner necessity and unity—on a world of appearances that is already present in a complex of concepts."[1] Such a classificatory approach amounts to a theory of concept formation that assumes a preexisting

---

1. Dilthey, "Schleiermacher's Hermeneutical System," in *Hermeneutics and the Study of History*, SW 4, 133.

convergence of form and content, of concept and reality. To overcome such a timeless system, Dilthey points to the need for a philosophy of history in which judgment-formation takes precedence over concept-formation. We will develop this suggestion by showing that judgment is essential for articulating an ever-changing world in which conceptual convergences must be validated rather than assumed.

A hermeneutics oriented to the formation of judgments allows us to relate concepts, not only to each other as in Schleiermacher's classificatory system, but also to the particulars of historical reality. In the ideal world of mathematics, there is no need to mediate between particulars and universals, for with mathematical intuition it is possible to exhibit particulars that coincide with universals by means of continuous delimitation. But in the real world, judgment is needed to bridge the discontinuities that may be found in nature and historical life. If continuity is to be attained in the way things are experienced over time, it will not be intuitable like a mathematical continuum. What is partially present in the perception of nature must be supplemented by what is represented in general terms. Connectedness in nature may be cognized conceptually by appealing to universal causal laws to which particular events are judgmentally subsumed. While we largely accept the idea of laws governing nature, we must question their adequacy for apprehending historical continuities. The historical world is not a domain as we have defined it, but a territory that presents itself through partial continua or systems that must be explicated by different kinds of judgment.

In history, continuity is perhaps more felt than perceived. Much of the past is lost forever, yet the present incorporates aspects of the past. The present, after all, is not a vanishing limit between the immediate past and the future, but their mobile boundary. We are able to preserve parts of the past through efforts of memory. Beyond that, ancient parts of the past are unexpectedly thrust into the present as sedimentary traces or remnants of historical life. But this captures history only in a passive way. Even when we are not focused on our social or cultural past as such, its influence is embedded in our customs and at work in our institutions. All these effects that have been accumulated over time must be differentiated and aligned through judgment with their proper contexts.

Although Dilthey stressed the importance of judgment-formation for historical understanding, his own accounts of judgment were brief and rather conventional. Nor did he explicate how a judgment-based approach relates to the distinction between knowledge (*Wissen*) and cognition (*Erkenntnis*) that we found to be operative in his writings on historical understanding.

We elaborated on this knowledge-cognition distinction by delineating three phases leading up to historical understanding: 1) life-knowledge, 2) conceptual cognition, and 3) reflective knowledge. Life-knowledge was conceived in terms of an experiential intake where the subjective certainties of everyday life coalesce with what we inherit from the past and take for granted in our local community. The resulting elementary understanding is rooted in this inherited commonality. We can say that this everyday life-knowledge is based on *assimilation.*

Conceptual cognition attempts to expand this commonality and adopts the universal aims of the natural and human sciences. Cognition gives up the immediate certainty (*Gewissheit*) of life-knowledge for a mediated reliability (*Sicherheit*) that is acquired on the basis of disciplinary method. Here we can say that the reliability of conceptual cognition is gained through a process of *acquisition.*

The final product, reflective knowledge, involves evaluation and aims at an encompassing perspective on reality. Although a perspective is always individuated, it requires historical consciousness to be comprehensive. Rooted in self-reflection, reflective knowledge articulates the worldview by which an individual assesses reality. Here what is judged to be of value is the product of reflective *appropriation.* In sum, reflective knowledge relates what we have assimilated as life-knowledge and acquired as cognition to what can be appropriated as worth knowing.

We can relate these three phases to what was said about hermeneutical contextualization. Assimilation situates us relative to the familiarity of a local habitat and the commonality of heritage, which acquisition then reorganizes in terms of various theoretical and practical domains that appeal to universal rules. Finally, appropriation relates these conceptual systems to the broader territory of human experience that provides the framework for reflection. In each instance, we see a process of recontextualization that leads to reflective knowledge.[2]

Reflective knowledge is explicitly judgmental, but we must also consider what forms of judgment may or may not be involved in life-knowledge and conceptual cognition. For a more fully developed theory of judgment relevant to our hermeneutical aims, it will prove worthwhile to further explore Kant's

---

2. Experientially, assimilation, acquisition, and appropriation define three phases or levels. But when we interpret how others have already made sense of their experience, those phases may disclose themselves in a different sequence. Then they become aspects that need to be triangulated.

many groundbreaking views on judgment. We have already employed Kant's distinction between the determinant judgments that delimit the domains of scientific cognition and the reflective judgments that orient us in the territory of aesthetic experience. By also examining Kant's *Lectures on Logic*, it becomes possible to consider other types of judgment as well as the prejudgments that can be linked to life-knowledge.

But first we will consider how judgment as such contributes to the tasks of cognition and knowledge in the *Critique of Pure Reason*. Although Kant never adequately distinguishes between cognition and knowledge, it will be argued in the next section that he does treat them differently.

INTERPRETING AS COGNIZING MEANING AND KNOWING TRUTH

It is often assumed that cognition and knowledge differ simply as process and product, but it can be shown that for Kant the difference goes deeper. The *Critique of Pure Reason* will be analyzed to establish how cognizing serves to assign meaning to experience and how knowing involves confirming the truth of meaning claims through judgmental assent. On that basis, we will differentiate cognizing and knowing as two phases in the process of interpreting the world.

All of Kant's initial epistemic claims in the Aesthetic and Analytic of the *Critique of Pure Reason* are about cognizing and cognition (*Erkenntnis*) and pertain to judgmental thought. It is only near the end of the work in "The Canon of Pure Reason," which is part of "The Transcendental Doctrine of Method," that Kant discusses the nature of knowing (*Wissen*). In the Kemp Smith translation, both *Erkenntnis* and *Wissen* were translated as knowledge. The Guyer/Wood translation has made it clear to English readers of Kant that he uses two different terms, but up to now the distinction has not drawn much attention.[3]

In the "Transcendental Analytic," our cognition of objects of experience is made possible by the categories of the understanding together with the forms of intuition. They are the a priori conditions that we bring to experience on the basis of our cognitive faculties of sensibility and understanding. The categories provide universal rules of thought, but they are more than logical con-

---

3. I first explored it in "The cognition-knowledge distinction in Kant and Dilthey and the implications for psychology and self-understanding," *Studies in History and Philosophy of Science* 34 (2003): 149–64.

cepts that relate mental representations merely to each other. Categories are transcendental concepts because they relate representations in the subject to the objects that appear to it in the world.

If the categories were mere general logical concepts, then they would allow us to *think* of objects without intuitively *cognizing* them.[4] Simply thinking of objects is governed by the truth conditions of general logic, but in cognizing objects our thought is governed by the truth conditions of transcendental logic as well. By introducing a transcendental logic, Kant complicates the usual way in which truth conditions are conceived to constrain meaning. Since the truth conditions provided by general logic are formal and empty of meaning content, he considers them as negative.[5] What distinguishes the truth conditions of transcendental logic at the level of cognition is that they are positive in providing what I will call the "meaning parameters" for the eventual determination of truth in knowledge. A transcendental logic entails that in addition to there being certain logical truth standards for what can be meaningful, there are also certain cognitive meaning standards for what can be known to be true.

Kant's transcendental logic supplies cognitive categories (e.g., causality), which differ from other pure universal concepts (e.g., identity) in not abstracting from all intuitive content. It is this reference to possible intuitive content that provided Kant's categories "with sense and meaning (*Sinn und Bedeutung*)"[6] and gives them an inherent judgmental grip on the world. This judgmental function of categories is not to differentiate the most generic classifications of things but to locate the most general marks that relate the meaning of things. Because the categories refer (*deuten*) to all possible objects of experience, they are able to produce cognition that is meaningful (*bedeutend*). They predelineate a world in ways that allow us to structure our experience objectively. Such a conception of categories can be applied to the historical world as well as to Kant's Newtonian nature.

Kant elaborates on the positive meaning-endowing potential of the categories of cognition in section 24 of the B Deduction, where the imagination is assigned the function of projecting the "objective reality" of the categories.[7] He writes: "The transcendental synthesis of the imagination . . . is an effect of the understanding on sensibility and its first application (and at the same time

---

4. *Critique of Pure Reason*, B146.
5. *Critique of Pure Reason*, A59/B84.
6. *Critique of Pure Reason*, B149.
7. *Critique of Pure Reason*, B150.

the ground of all others) to objects of the intuition that is possible for us."[8] With this first formal application of the categories, the imagination anticipates the meaning that can be given to the objects of our sensible and empirical intuition. This is reiterated in his chapter on the Schematism, where the imaginative schemata of the concepts of pure understanding are said to be "the true and sole conditions for providing them with a relation to objects, thus with *meaning (Bedeutung).*"[9] Schemata predelineate the judgmental structure of these a priori concepts by indicating how universal rules can apply to objects of sense. Each of the categories is said to have a schema as "a transcendental product of the imagination"[10] that translates conceptual content into a temporal set of instructions for ordering the manifold of sense. The schema of substance allows us to imaginatively anticipate "the persistence of the real in time," and the schema of causality "consists in the succession of the manifold insofar as it is subject to a rule."[11] Without such schemata, the categories would have a mere abstract logical meaning and lack the real objective meaning that applies to the sensible manifold of experience. Having characterized schemata as the "true" conditions for the empirical use of the categories, Kant concludes that "transcendental truth . . . precedes empirical truth and makes it possible."[12]

Hermeneutically, transcendental truth conditions provide the general cognitive meaning parameters on the basis of which actual empirical truth claims can then be established as knowledge. We can confirm a shift from cognizing to knowing by turning to Kant's discussion of the correct method of applying our cognitive faculties in "The Canon of Pure Reason." Whereas pure logic sets the formal truth conditions for thought in general, and transcendental logic establishes the cognitive meaning-structures that are particular to how thought relates to human sensibility, what Kant calls "method" in the Canon locates the criteria that any individual subject must apply to test what is understood about nature in relation to a systematic interpretation of the world. In determining what it is to know, individual subjects must take rational responsibility for their cognitive claims. Knowing involves reason, but unlike the dialectical speculations of pure reason, it restricts itself to ascertaining what can be understood.

8. *Critique of Pure Reason*, B152.
9. *Critique of Pure Reason*, A142/B185.
10. *Critique of Pure Reason*, A142/B181.
11. *Critique of Pure Reason*, A144/B183.
12. *Critique of Pure Reason*, A146/B185.

While *cognizing* was described in terms of general rules of anticipating objective meaning relations within the temporal manifold of sense, *knowing* involves assessing such cognitive meaning claims for their truth. In claiming to know, the subject goes beyond cognition by affirming that what was meant is also taken to be true. Knowing, as the final stage of interpretation, is in Kantian terms a mode of taking or holding to be true (*Fürwahrhalten*).[13] No matter how much objective meaning a cognitive claim may provide, it will not count as an actual truth claim until it is also supported by "subjective causes in the mind of him who judges."[14] The cognitive function of judgment is to refer concepts to objects, but knowing also requires something more from the judging subject. I will call this the judging subject's "assent." Judgmental assent may stem either from our particular psychological constitution or from our universal rational constitution. In the particular psychological instance, a subject is moved by persuasion to accept a claim as true; in the universal rational case, the subject affirms its truth through conviction. The final test for a truth claim will require the subject to reflect and consider the "possibility of communicating it and finding it to be valid for every human being."[15] It is through scientific communal agreement that we can attain the certainty that Kant assigns to knowledge.

Kant himself at times compares coming to know nature as a process of interpretation, as when he writes in one of the *Reflections on Metaphysics* that "nature is the text of our interpretations."[16] We can use this to expand on his claim that our reason leads "our power of cognition to feel a far higher need than that of merely spelling out appearances according to a synthetic unity in order to be able to read them as experience."[17] This higher need can be explicated to mean that what has been spelled out as the manifold of sense in time and read as experience by means of concepts of the understanding must be supplemented with ideas of reason if nature is to be properly interpreted.[18] Without positing anything that transcends nature, ideas of reason can be used regulatively as rules of interpreting experience as part of a complete system of nature. What "The Canon of Pure Reason" does is to provide an analogue

---

13. *Critique of Pure Reason*, A822/B850.
14. *Critique of Pure Reason*, A820/B848.
15. *Critique of Pure Reason*, A820/B848.
16. Kant, *Reflexionen zur Metaphysik*, in *Kant's gesammelte Schriften*, Ak 18: 274.
17. *Critique of Pure Reason*, A314/B370-71.
18. For a more detailed treatment of how Kant applies the spelling-reading-interpreting metaphor, see Makkreel, *Imagination and Interpretation in Kant*, ch. 2.

for this systematic rational completion by insisting that individual knowers must test their cognitive results through communication with the whole community of inquirers. Only thus can the move from persuasion to conviction be completed by the certainty that Kant demands of knowledge.

KANT ON OPINING, BELIEVING, AND KNOWING

By also considering what it means to have opinions and to form beliefs, Kant comes to distinguish three stages in the rational process of moving beyond psychological persuasion to the certainty of knowing. In the following passage, opining, believing, and knowing are assessed in terms of the strength with which a subject takes something to be true:

> *Having an opinion* is taking something to be true with the consciousness that it is subjectively *as well as* objectively insufficient. If taking something to be true is only subjectively sufficient and is . . . held to be objectively insufficient, then it is called *believing*. Finally, when taking something to be true is both subjectively and objectively sufficient, it is called *knowing*.[19]

Although persuasion and having an opinion are often treated as synonymous, Kant underscores an important point of difference between them. Thus, when he claims that having an opinion brings with it an awareness of its insufficiencies, he is placing opinion on a reflective level, while persuasion remains unreflective. In *The Jäsche Logic* he makes this very clear. Persuasion is "uncertain cognition [that] appears . . . to be certain," whereas "opinion . . . is an uncertain cognition, *insofar as it is held to be uncertain*."[20] Both persuasion and opinion are uncertain, but only opinion involves awareness of its uncertainty. Whereas Kant asserts that persuasion is illusory in taking subjective grounds as objective,[21] no such charge is made against holding an opinion.

Persuasion is unreflective in being based, not only on subjective needs and private interests, but also on historical and cultural influences that are internalized and taken for granted. We will come back to this when prejudices are discussed in relation to what can be known. Using the distinction we have made between types of knowledge, we can say that persuasion pertains to

---

19. *Critique of Pure Reason*, A822/B850.
20. *Lectures on Logic*, 577; *Ak* 9: 73.
21. *Critique of Pure Reason*, A820/B848.

what is accepted at the level of life-knowledge, and opinion represents a first step toward reflective knowledge. Opining begins the process of reflection by recognizing that many things of which we are persuaded lack justification. With this self-awareness, opinion is held in a tentative way and suspends the presumption of persuasion.

We indicated earlier that persuasion must be replaced with conviction if we are to approach the certainty that Kant attributes to knowledge. Conviction exceeds the private presumption of persuasion in that it is rooted in the subject's rational capacities that strive for universal validity. Whereas persuasion is a "mere semblance"[22] rooted in a provincial habitat and is unconcerned with universal communicability, conviction provides the confidence that other terrestrial rational beings will agree. Thus conviction goes beyond the suspended judgment of an opinion by assenting to the truth of a cognitive proposition. This raises the question whether conviction amounts to belief. Believing was given an intermediary place in the sequence cited above that starts with opining and ends with knowing. Nevertheless, Kant's claim that belief is "held to be objectively insufficient,"[23] or to lack objective validity, seems to devalue it as a step toward knowledge. Andrew Chignell is correct in having such reservations about belief, but I disagree with the way he separates it from conviction. Chignell claims that the conviction needed for knowledge amounts to "objective sufficiency" and has nothing to do with belief, which is subjective and based on "non-epistemic considerations."[24] But Kant explicitly equates the conviction needed to move toward knowledge with "subjective sufficiency" and reserves "objective sufficiency" for the certainty of having knowledge.[25] Moreover, the fact that belief is subjective does not stop Kant from speaking of belief as a kind of conviction.[26] Thus belief cannot be so easily dismissed.

22. *Critique of Pure Reason*, A820/B848.
23. *Critique of Pure Reason*, A822/B852.
24. Andrew Chignell, "Belief in Kant," *Philosophical Review* 116: 3 (2007): 323–60.
25. See *Critique of Pure Reason*, A822/B850. There is, however, one passage that could suggest that conviction can be objectively sufficient. But it is conditional on our being purely rational beings, which we are not. Thus Kant writes that *if* taking something to be true "is valid for everyone merely as long as he has reason, *then* its ground is objectively sufficient, and in that case taking something to be true is called conviction" (A820/B848). Since we are both sensible and rational creatures, the subjective causes that lead us to accept the truth of something may also include factors that are peculiar to our sensible constitution and therefore cannot be objectively sufficient.
26. See the passage "subjective conviction, i.e., firm belief" in the *Critique of Pure Reason*, A824/B852.

Lawrence Pasternack also thinks that belief has no epistemic import for Kant and pertains only to the moral reasons that support religious faith.[27] Kant does, to be sure, stress the practical-moral considerations that prompt us to form religious beliefs, but this need not rule out the relevance of all beliefs to cognitive inquiry. Indeed, Kant writes that "there is in merely theoretical judgments an *analogue* of practical judgments, where taking them to be true is aptly described by the word belief."[28] For instance, the empirical belief that there are "inhabitants of other worlds" is considered to be "theoretical" and "doctrinal"[29] because if we could travel to a planet like Mars, we would be able to accumulate the needed cognitive experience to test the belief.

My position is that empirical beliefs that are not religious may be relevant to the question whether something is cognizable, but even they cannot contribute to the rational appropriation of cognition as knowledge. This is because "belief provides a conviction that is not communicable."[30] Belief does not suffice to create knowledge, for according to Kant, "knowledge must be communicable and demands concurrence (*Beystimmung*)."[31] One can rationally endorse a cognitive claim as knowledge only through a mode of conviction whose subjective sufficiency exceeds belief. What is needed to attain knowledge is the rational confidence that others will agree with what one assents to. It is thus possible to distinguish between the incommunicable conviction$_1$ of belief and the communicable conviction$_2$ of active confidence.

To know something to be true requires that the "subjective sufficiency . . . called conviction$_2$ (for myself)" be matched by "objective sufficiency, certainty (for everyone)."[32] Thus the final step in appropriating universally valid cognition as legitimate intersubjective knowledge demands that the judgmen-

---

27. See Lawrence Pasternack, "The Development and Scope of Kantian Belief," *Kant-Studien* 102 (2011): 290–315.

28. *Critique of Pure Reason*, A825/B853. Pasternack acknowledges this analogue I point to in the *Critique of Pure Reason* but considers it an "odd exception" that was later abandoned. He points to Kant's claim in the third *Critique* that only ideas pertaining to the highest good, immortality, and God can be *Glaubenssachen*. See Pasternack, "The Development," 300–303. But even in the third *Critique,* Kant distinguishes between "matters of faith" or "belief as *habitus*" and the more general "act of belief (*Glaube als actus*)" that can still be applied to cognitive issues about factual matters. This will be referred to in the next section as "historical belief." See *Critique of the Power of Judgment*, 333–35; Ak 5: 469–71.

29. *Critique of Pure Reason*, A825/B853.

30. *Reflexionen zur Logik*, 2489; Ak 16: 391.

31. *Reflexionen zur Logik*, 2489; Ak 16: 391.

32. *Critique of Pure Reason*, A822/B850.

tal assent of my conviction$_2$ be confirmed by the consent of others. In order for objectively meaningful cognition to also be objectively sufficient to justify a truth claim, it needs to be agreed to by the community of all investigators. Not only must the formal objective structures of cognition be intuitively filled in, but they should also be inductively confirmed to produce the intersubjective agreement that constitutes certainty for Kant. What distinguishes knowing as the final mode of holding something to be true is that the subjective conviction$_2$ attached to an objective cognitive claim also be recognized as intersubjectively certain through communication.

In effect, the individual *assent* of conviction$_2$ needs to be expanded into a communal *consent*. What the subject takes to be true in knowing is something about which it must be certain that the community of investigators agrees. We can thus sum up Kant's account of truth-assessment (*Fürwahrhalten*) with the conclusion that knowing (*Wissen*) involves cognition that has attained the certainty (*Gewissheit*) of being confirmed by the community of science (*Wissenschaft*).[33] Opinion involves problematic judging, belief or conviction$_1$ amounts to assertoric judging, and the knowing in which conviction$_2$ and certainty merge makes possible apodictic or necessary judging.[34] Whereas for Dilthey's hermeneutics of history, certainty is a mere subjective starting point, in Kant's rational interpretation of nature, certainty represents an intersubjective end point. It projects the transformation of universally valid cognition into legitimate knowledge.

Kant's initial distinction between persuasion (*Überredung*) and conviction (*Überzeugung*) remains relevant for the interpretation of texts because they can either "talk us into" (*über-reden*) things or "bear convincing witness" (*über-zeugen*). For Kant, reason is that convincing witness that can lead us from the false confidence of persuasion and the uncertainty of opining toward the final goal of certain knowing. Hermeneutically, however, there can be no such closure. Interpretation will always be on the way and approximative. The hesitancy and uncertainty of opining will remain part of the equation.

In response to Kant's view that cognitive claims can be convincing if they are rationally warranted, one could say that opinions have another kind of warrant—they may be based on some experience that is, however, insufficient to come to a conclusion, or they may rely on hearsay, which appeals to the experience of others in a nonsystematic way. This makes it clear that knowing demands that cognition be systematized. Of the three subjective modes of

33. See *Lectures on Logic*, 575; *Ak* 9: 72.
34. See *Lectures on Logic*, 571; *Ak* 9: 66.

assenting to or taking something as true, only knowing adds systematic order to cognition. Put more generally, knowing is cognition that meets both the discursive *meaning* standards of the understanding and the systematic *truth* standards of reason.

To reinforce our thesis that the power of judgment also plays a role here, we can reformulate Kant's cognizing-knowing distinction one more time to say that cognition schematizes or *realizes* meaning claims that knowing legitimates or *actualizes* as truth claims.[35] Both schematization and legitimation are inherently judgment-producing functions. The schematism that allows concepts to be realized relative to possible objects constitutes the subject matter of the first chapter of "The Transcendental Doctrine of the Power of Judgment." Here the categories are cognitively validated as the a priori concepts necessary for objective experience. However, we cannot know if a truth claim about a particular object is legitimate without also considering its actual "agreement with the object, with regard to which, consequently, the judgments of every understanding must agree."[36] Unlike the cognitive validity of the "Transcendental Analytic," the legitimacy of knowledge in "The Canon of Pure Reason" cannot be arrived at a priori, for it requires evidence and communal consent. Being inferential, legitimating judgments actualize universal cognitive claims by reflectively linking them with each other and testing them through communication. They relate what we think we know to what we can justify as knowing.[37]

The way we take things to be true is important in expanding hermeneutics from a mere analysis of meaning into a search for truth. Kant's linear progression—from 1) unwarranted persuasion to 2) opinion as a neutral assessment to 3) conviction$_2$ as rationally warranted confidence to 4) a final certainty of knowing—will need to be developed further to do justice to the perspective of a post-Enlightenment hermeneutics and its more circuitous paths. So far we have spoken about the role of judgment in recognizing what we cognize and in communicating it to others. But in response to hermeneutical objections that have been raised against judgment, more needs to be said about its role in assessing truth claims and arriving at legitimate knowledge.

---

35. For Kant, realization is intensional, and actualization extensional. *Realität* refers to the qualitative intensity of our experience and *Wirklichkeit* to the modality of the object of our experience. See *Critique of Pure Reason*, A80/B106 and A225/B272.

36. *Critique of Pure Reason*, A820/B848.

37. We will return to the validity-legitimacy distinction in chapter 6.

PRELIMINARY JUDGMENTS AND THE PROVISIONALITY OF REFLECTIVE JUDGMENTS

We have seen both Heidegger and Gadamer devalue the role of judgment in hermeneutics in favor of pre-understanding and prejudices. According to Heidegger, judgment fixes the fluidity of life and flattens out the fullness of authentic understanding. To be "judgmental" in this pejorative sense is to lack openness and sensitivity so that in the proverbial rush to judgment we too hastily categorize things and congeal our mode of thinking. The same may be charged against the prejudices of tradition focused on by Gadamer. But as he defends them, they have a capacity to adapt to new circumstances and thereby display a productive history. It is thus important for a reflective orientational hermeneutics to examine the way judgments and prejudices interact with each other in our overall experience. In this context, we will focus on judgment as an ongoing process of assessing things, rather than simply a final outcome, and will consider prejudices in relation to a larger field of prejudgments opened up by Kant. By making all this part of an attempt to rehabilitate the role of judgment in hermeneutics, we should also obtain a better sense of how, in addition to the judging involved in his transcendental theory of cognition and rational knowing, Kant deals with the everyday judgments and prejudgments of historical experience and empirical inquiry.

There are two kinds of prejudgment for Kant, *Vorurtheile*, or prejudices, and *vorläufige Urtheile*, standardly translated as "provisional judgments." Prejudices are prejudgments that resemble the private persuasions we discussed earlier. Like persuasion, a prejudice is unreflective, but it is even more problematic in that it functions as a commonplace that generates further unreflective claims. By contrast, the other type of prejudgment requires reflection. To better highlight the transitional role of *vorläufige Urtheile* in empirical inquiry, they will be called "preliminary" rather than "provisional" judgments. Provisionality is really a hallmark of reflective judgments, for in being interpretive they are still subject to revision.

It is interesting to note that in the lectures on logic, Kant distinguishes between *rational* certainty, which is apodictic, and *empirical* certainty, which is merely assertoric. Rational certainty refers back to the systematic scientific knowing of "The Canon of Pure Reason." In explicating empirical certainty, Kant focuses mainly on the need for reflection and empirical investigation. Thus in *The Jäsche Logic*, we read that "to be able to pass from mere persuasion to conviction, we must first of all reflect, i.e., see to which power of cognition a cognition belongs, and then investigate. . . . Many remain with persuasion. Some come to reflection, few to investigation."[38] Since this sequence from persuasion to conviction based on reflection leads up to a discussion of prejudices and preliminary judgments, we will reformulate it as a transition from the persuasion of prejudice to the reflection that can transform a prejudice into a preliminary judgment capable of orienting empirical investigation. It should be noted, however, that the reflection involved in preliminary judgments is not to be confused with reflective judgment. The reflection of a preliminary judgment merely prepares the way for a determinant judgment based on further empirical investigation.[39]

What is a stake here in *The Jäsche Logic* is the actual temporal process of empirical inquiry, which was referred to only in passing when discussing the intersubjective agreement of investigators that produces rational certainty. We could thus say that we are now moving from a general consideration of the judgmental assent and consent needed for *knowing* to the determinant judgments involved in deriving empirical *knowledge* from everyday experience.

In proceeding from prejudice to preliminary judgment to determinant judgment, Kant is looking only for empirical certainty about the content of our experience. He charts a progression from 1) the persuasive force of prejudices to 2) the reflective pause or openness of preliminary judgments and to 3) the investigative outcome of determinant judgments. The crucial member in this sequence is the preliminary judgment in that it suspends any decision about truth until investigation has done its work. A preliminary judgment requires a temporary deferral in making a determinant judgment and is to be distinguished from a permanent refraining from judgment. The former involves a neutral or, for Kant, a critical suspension of judgment, the latter a negative or skeptical suspension.

A prejudice is a claim that has come to be accepted in a noncognitive or unreflective way. Earlier, persuasion was said to have its ground in the particular psychological constitution of the subject. Perhaps there is something in the emotional makeup of individuals that inclines them to be persuaded that some assertion is true. This corresponds to the first of three main sources of prejudice given by Kant, namely, inclination. The other two sources of prejudice are imitation and custom. Whereas private inclination is an internal source of prejudice, imitation and custom point to external historical sources that can influence us. In the lectures that make up Kant's *Blomberg*

---

38. *Lectures on Logic*, 576; *Ak* 9: 73.

39. See *Lectures on Logic*, 577; *Ak* 9: 74. For more on the distinction between reflection and reflective judgment, see chapter 7.

Logic, we read that inclination leads us to investigate things "only from the side where we wish that it were so and not otherwise . . . there is simply no reflection. . . ."[40] Imitation exerts an especially significant influence on children. "In youth one does not yet have any skill in judging, hence one allows oneself to be driven by imitation, and one quickly accepts as certain and undoubted what is maintained by others. . . ."[41] Custom (*Gewohnheit*), as Kant uses it, refers both to what we assimilate from our local habitat and to the habits we ourselves develop over time. Concerning the former, Kant says: "Almost everyone, be he who he may, esteems the fashions and customs of his country or his fatherland as the best and most proper."[42] Here we tend to be very provincial, preferring what we are familiar with from our local habitat. But the preferences that we contingently inherit become prejudices only if we assume that they should be generally followed. Prejudices, according to Kant, are more than particular premature judgments in that they impose themselves as "general rules for judging."[43] These general rules derived from imitation and custom correspond in a rough way to the context of objective spirit in Hegel and Dilthey, which we have explicated as the inherited medium of commonality. But in this and the next chapter I will concentrate on Kant's terms and see how he navigates between local habitats of custom and prejudice, the wider territory of the *sensus communis*, and the universal domain of scientific inquiry.

Prejudices need to be examined because they are like deeply rooted persuasions functioning as rules that generate further premature judgments. Just as persuasion was said to be illusory in holding subjective conditions to be objective, so a prejudice can be illusory in holding something contingently local to be general. But according to Kant, not all illusions are to be dismissed. There are even unavoidable empirical and transcendental illusions. Therefore, as I pointed out earlier vis-à-vis Gadamer, it is mistaken to think that Kant expects to eradicate all human prejudices. Prejudices are so pervasive that it is unreasonable to project their eradication. The main thing is to free ourselves from the gross prejudices of superstition. Kant also admits that what "is accepted by means of a prejudice . . . is not yet on that account always false as to its matter."[44] Instead of immediately rejecting each and every prejudice,

---

40. *Lectures on Logic*, 132; *Ak* 24.1: 167.
41. *Lectures on Logic*, 131; *Ak* 24.1: 166.
42. *Lectures on Logic*, 130; *Ak* 24.1: 165.
43. *Lectures on Logic*, 130; *Ak* 24.1: 164.
44. *Lectures on Logic*, 133; *Ak* 24.1: 168.

we should "test them first and investigate well whether there may not yet be something good to be found in them."[45]

There are different kinds of prejudice that must be examined. It is possible to distinguish, for example, between the prejudice of antiquity and the prejudice of modernity. Kant does not have much to say about the prejudice of modernity. It is based on inclination, and in this case, the inclination for the new. Those who pursue the empirical sciences as well as those who value genius and wit tend to favor the idea of modernity. The prejudice of antiquity is much more pervasive and can be linked to the other two sources of prejudice: imitation as following the past and custom as continuing the past. Kant defines the prejudice of antiquity as "grounded on esteem toward the *old*. What survives of the old . . . always contains the illusion of being good, for one infers that it would be hard for it to have survived and to have come down to us if it were not good and were of no value."[46] Tradition can be the repository of important truths, but to accept any of them on authority is to make our reason passive—it is to allow reason as an active principle of conviction to be replaced by prejudice as a blind principle of persuasion. The content of any resulting judgment could be true but its form will always be false.

Human reason should not, however, reject the authority of prejudice altogether. Prejudices can be made useful by requiring that they be reflected on and thus transformed into preliminary judgments. We spoke of a prejudice as a principle that is blindly held to be true. Reflection on the meaning content of a prejudice can turn it into a preliminary judgment, which then serves as a maxim for the investigation of the truth. While a principle claims to be generally applicable, a maxim directs only a particular subject's inquiry into a particular thing. A preliminary judgment "is one in which I represent that while there are more grounds for the truth of a thing than against it, these grounds still do not suffice for a determining or a definite judgment, through which I simply decide for the truth."[47] A preliminary judgment transforms a blind principle of persuasion into a maxim that looks for evidence that is convincing. It is a neutralizing response to what is initially accepted as plausible on the basis of persuasion and transforms it into a hypothesis for investigation. As such, the preliminary judgment is like the opining we discussed earlier, and in *The Jäsche Logic* Kant actually equates them.[48] An opinion in his neu-

---

45. *Lectures on Logic*, 130; *Ak* 24.1: 169.
46. *Lectures on Logic*, 141; *Ak* 24.1: 179.
47. *Lectures on Logic*, 577; *Ak* 9: 74.
48. *Lectures on Logic*, 571; *Ak* 9: 66.

tral sense is like a "premonition of truth"[49] that serves as the basis for empirical knowledge. It suspends the "plausibility" that is merely a "quantity of persuasion"[50] to set the stage for the probability that we expect of empirical knowledge. The prejudices of which we are persuaded have a mere subjective plausibility that investigation then attempts to replace with probability, for which the grounds are "objectively valid"[51] although not objectively sufficient to amount to absolute certainty.

In examining some of the presuppositions that we bring to human inquiry, it was argued that they need to be assessed by means of judgment. We saw that when these presuppositions are conceived formally as a priori cognitive conditions, they can be schematized in terms of universally anticipated meaning-structures. But when these presuppositions involve common sense and inherited prejudices, they bring with them more local and concrete assumptions about the content of reality. In regard to the latter, Kant is willing to acknowledge the role of "historical belief" as a "source of cognition."[52] Historical belief relies on "someone else's testimony and experience" and merges it "with my own."[53] This suggests that even though belief is not considered to be rationally communicable, it may involve opinions or views that are somehow transmissible. My concluding chapter will differentiate between the communication of cognitive meaning and the transmission of informational content that has not been cognitively vetted. A similar differentiation can be located in Kant's epistemology: from the perspective of rational communication, our judgmental assent to cognitive meaning relations demands systematic verification and seeks out the explicit consent of the scientific community; experientially, however, judgmental assent often allows itself to be influenced by a preexisting consent, which derives from the way common sense views, historical beliefs, and prejudices are transmitted. Thus as we relate ordinary experience to the accumulation of empirical scientific knowledge, some of the assumptions that have been drawn from the consent based on our life situation and social involvements will need to be revised.

By giving an expansive hermeneutical account of Kant's epistemology that focuses on how universal categorial cognitive validity claims about nature as a domain are appropriated as the systematic truth claims of knowledge, it also

---

49. *Lectures on Logic*, 571; *Ak* 9: 67.
50. See *Lectures on Logic*, 583; *Ak* 9: 82.
51. *Lectures on Logic*, 583; *Ak* 9: 82.
52. *Lectures on Logic*, 483; *Ak* 24: 749.
53. *Lectures on Logic*, 483–84; *Ak* 24: 749–50.

becomes possible to consider the extent to which the prejudices of a local habitat and ordinary experiential judgments based on territorial acquaintance can be assimilated. Thus if the project of "The Canon of Pure Reason" to replace private persuasion with the intersubjective certainty of knowing is used to also frame the empirical trajectory of cognition in the lectures on logic, we begin to see how a transcendental epistemology can deal with inherited prejudices and revise them in relation to what can be empirically tested. The stages in the empirical process of truth-assessment delineate a movement beyond the mere plausibility of persuasion and prejudice through the preliminary likelihood of opinions and hypotheses to probable knowledge that provides an experiential "approximation to certainty."[54]

If Kant's judgment-based stages of truth-assessment are further related to the transition from received life-knowledge to the conceptual cognition of the human sciences and the reflective knowledge they seek, we can fill in a comprehensive hermeneutical trajectory of inquiry. In judgmental terms, the life-knowledge of ordinary experience provides an elementary understanding that can range from the fixity of prejudices to the openness of Kant's preliminary judgments. In orientational terms, elementary understanding displays the inherited commonality of objective spirit, which can draw on both the contingent factical order of a local habitat and the generality of a regional territory. These two ways of thinking about elementary understanding allow us to define it as providing a prejudgmental context for the universal cognitive judgments of higher understanding. In many cases, the higher understanding of the human sciences can arrive at results that are empirically reliable. However, the scope of determinant judgments here will be more limited than in the natural sciences. When interpretation also aims at reflective knowledge, it must give some overall perspective on historical reality. This will not provide the apodictic certainty that Kant expects of a universal rational system, but it can at least indicate a way of coordinating the disciplinary contexts needed to interpret historical life.

Interpretation as a mode of reflective judgment should use preliminary judgment not only to theoretically suspend the persuasiveness of a prejudice, but also to consider why it has had such a normative hold on us. We must be able to assess to what extent a prejudice can properly address or speak to (*an-reden*) our expectations, rather than allow it to overwhelm or persuade (*über-reden*) us. Similarly, the cognitive convincing (*über-zeugen*) that is demanded of determinant judgments will have to be moderated into a reflective

---

54. *Lectures on Logic*, 583; *Ak* 9: 82.

witnessing (*zeugen*). Here truth-assessment must take account of normative considerations that lack the self-evident standards of legitimacy established by Enlightenment reason. As indicated earlier, there is no basis for thinking that reflective judgments prematurely fix interpretation and close off further inquiry. They tend to remain provisional, but that does not mean that we cannot establish the level of commitment involved in assenting to them.

CHAPTER 5

Aesthetic Consensus and Evaluative Consent

We have shown that a theory of judgment is important for interpretation not only because it is able to differentiate the kinds of meaning contexts that can be used to organize our experience, but also because it brings out how the assent that the subject gives to meaning claims demands the consent of others. And as we shall see here, the consent will vary in scope for different hermeneutical contexts.

With reflective judgment, assent is not solely theoretical in the sense of taking something to be true, but is evaluative as well. Kant's primary example of a reflective judgment is an aesthetic judgment in which we affirm the beauty of something. Unlike the theoretical assent of knowing, aesthetic assent seems to be freely given in that there are no determinant rules or laws to bind us. Yet there is a felt sense of lawfulness associated with an aesthetic judgment that is integrally related to the consent of others. This becomes more explicit when the traditional label "judgment of taste" is applied. A case can be made that an aesthetic judgment is about appreciation and a judgment of taste about evaluation. When we say that someone has good taste we apply a normative standard, but we do not always apply a standard of goodness to aesthetic judgments. Although Kant generally equates "aesthetic judgment" and "judgment of taste,"[1] he allows for empirical aesthetic judgments that are not universal while insisting that judgments of taste must be universal.[2] In the following analysis, I will show that the latter expression is more definitive.

---

1. *Critique of the Power of Judgment*, 112; Ak 5: 228
2. *Critique of the Power of Judgment*, 108; Ak 5: 223.

To the extent that an aesthetic judgment manifests taste, we can also relate it back to prejudices of taste and other kinds of social consensus. Our tastes involve an evaluative assessment that has import for the interpretation of human life in general. In this chapter, Kant's well-known critically framed examination of taste will be considered within the historical framework that is referenced in some of his other works. This will allow us to better understand what distinguishes the judgmental assent/consent required for scientific knowing from the judgmental assent/consent implicit in an evaluative interpretation.

LEVELS OF AESTHETIC CONSENSUS IN KANT

To declare an object to be beautiful is not to assert a mere descriptive judgment (*Urteil*) about some object, but to offer an evaluation (*Beurteilung*) of it.[3] When I appreciate the beauty of something, I find it to be pleasing in a way that is not merely valid for me. The pleasure evoked is more than a private liking. In his first attempts to define the judgment of taste in section 8 of the third *Critique*, Kant twice characterizes it as *gemeingültig*, which can be translated as either "commonly valid" or as "generally valid." In his first use of *gemeingültig*, he claims that the judgment is "public (*publike*)."[4] This, together with the fact that Kant at times compares taste with common sense would seem to speak in favor of rendering the term as "commonly valid," based on public convention. But his second use is more explicit about the role of individual feeling in aesthetic judgment and the kind of agreement this allows for. In this case "generally valid" seems preferable as the translation of *gemeingültig*. In assessing whether an "aesthetic judgment" is generally valid, Kant relates what is represented as beautiful solely to the "feeling of pleasure," apart from any reference to the "faculty of cognition."[5] The general validity of an aesthetic judgment is subjective in that no claim is made about any object of experience other than how it relates to human feeling—it can be intersubjectively valid only to the extent that we reflect on feeling and abstract from its private peculiarities.

But then Kant moves from the general validity (*Gemeingültigkeit*) of feeling to a universal validity (*Allgemeingültigkeit*) ascribed to a judgment of taste based on a harmony of the cognitive faculties. This harmony is more fully

---

3. See *Critique of the Power of Judgment*, First Introduction, 15; *Ak* 20: 211.
4. *Critique of the Power of Judgment*, 99; *Ak* 5: 214.
5. *Critique of the Power of Judgment*, 99; *Ak* 5: 214.

explicated in section 9 as a reciprocal interplay of the imagination and the understanding or a reflective appreciation of a beautiful form. At times Kant goes even further in his search for aesthetic consensus by moving beyond both the general validity of feeling and the universal validity of cognitive harmony to point to a universal voice (*allgemeine Stimme*) that encompasses the concurrence of everyone (*jedermanns Beistimmung*). The latter involves the univocity (*Einstimmung*) indicative of a community.[6] By taking these varying characterizations of aesthetic consensus together, we can delineate a sequence proceeding from 1) a public commonality to 2) a general validity of aesthetic appreciation and judgment to 3) a universal validity of a judgment of taste, and finally to 4) a univocal community.

To obtain a better sense of what the relation between this initial commonality and final community might be, we need to examine some of Kant's discussions of how common sense relates to the communicability of feeling involved in taste. In sections 20 and 21 of the *Critique of Judgment*, he begins to ask what common sense means and whether we have good reason to presuppose such a sense. In the following section he writes: "The necessity of the *universal assent* that we think in a judgment of taste is a subjective necessity that we represent as objective by presupposing a common sense (*Gemeinsinn*)."[7] If we could presuppose that we all possess a sound common sense as claimed by some empiricists, then the judgment of taste would be grounded in a constitutive principle of experience that is objective. However, Kant thinks there is no justification for claiming an empirical common sense that is reliable, and in section 34 he acknowledges that an objective principle of taste is impossible.

In section 40 Kant goes on to assert that there is another kind of common sense to which taste can be referred. This is the *sensus communis* as a communal sense (*gemeinschaftlicher Sinn*). The communal sense is a possibility to be cultivated rather than something presupposed. It is not a grounding principle, but what I would call an orientational principle for reflective judgment. Rather than being an innately endowed common sense, the communal sense aims at a future community. Thus Kant's aesthetic judgment cannot be justified by some preexisting commonality such as the objective spirit appealed to by Hegel and Dilthey. Instead, aesthetic judgment projects a reflective consensus to be arrived at. At times Kant even invokes an ideal rational community, as when he speaks of the *sensus communis* as "the power to judge that in reflecting takes account (a priori) in thought of everyone else's way of

---

6. See *Critique of the Power of Judgment*, 101; *Ak* 5: 216.
7. *Critique of the Power of Judgment*, 123; *Ak* 5: 239.

representing, in order, as it were, to hold its judgment up to human reason as a whole."⁸

In light of these reflections on what is common and communal, the fourfold sequence suggested earlier can be further specified in terms of the following levels of aesthetic consensus: 1) A contingently shared pleasure that is the product of some preexisting commonality; it is a function of popular taste and limited by what Kant calls fashion. 2) A generally valid aesthetic judgment that is reflective to the extent that it abstracts from our private peculiarities. 3) A universally valid judgment of taste that links aesthetic feeling to a harmony of the cognitive faculties involving an attunement (*Zusammenstimmung*)⁹ applicable to "us human beings as such (*für uns [Menschen überhaupt]*)"¹⁰; this lies at the heart of Kant's aesthetic project. 4) A univocal approbation that directs this possible attunement of feeling among human beings toward an ideal rational community. It takes what is reflectively orientational or attuned to human beings as such and, in effect, transforms it into an a priori expectation of total agreement. This final consensus of good taste can be linked to what Kant sketches in the appendix of the "Critique of Aesthetic Judgment" as "a culture of the mental powers . . . aimed at the highest degree of perfection."¹¹ This is clearly a regulative ideal, which is then elaborated as a theory of culture in section 83 of the "Critique of Teleological Judgment."

The first kind of aesthetic consensus derives from a local commonality. It involves what Kant speaks of in *The Blomberg Logic* as a *prejudice of taste*. Whereas logical prejudices imitate custom, aesthetical prejudices of taste imitate fashion. Kant warns that "taste is quite ruined by imitation, a fertile source of all prejudices, since one borrows everything, thinks nothing of a beauty that one might be able to invent and come up with oneself."¹² Taste is a mere prejudice if we reproduce what is common or popular in our local habitat, for then we only imitate the *examples of fashion*. Nevertheless, we will see that Kant allows our background to provide us with useful prejudices that can potentially become *exemplary for taste*.

Prejudices inherited from the tradition can be useful if they open up possibilities from the past that are lacking in the present. But not until we reflect on the prejudices that we have assimilated can they be critically appropriated

---

8. *Critique of the Power of Judgment*, 173; *Ak* 5:293.
9. *Critique of the Power of Judgment*, 104; *Ak* 5: 219.
10. *Critique of the Power of Judgment*, 327; *Ak* 5: 462.
11. *Critique of the Power of Judgment*, 229; *Ak* 5: 355.
12. *Lectures on Logic*, 136; *Ak* 24: 173.

and related to judgment. The question then becomes how the prejudices of a particular cultural background stand up to the judgments of taste that are valid for all human beings.

We have seen how preliminary judgments suspend logical prejudices by introducing a reflective moment that sets the stage for investigation. The content of the prejudice becomes a hypothesis that can regulate further inquiry and represents a provisional determinant judgment. However, a pure judgment of taste modifies a prejudice of taste in a different way; it is a reflective judgment that does not aim at some further determinant judgment. It reflects on the form of what is accepted by a prejudice in order to consider whether it possesses the general validity of communicability, to which we can freely assent, as well as the universal validity of attunement that leads us to expect consent.

This can be illustrated by considering a common prejudice of Western culture. Our Western tradition has taught us to appreciate the sculptures that adorned Greek temples, so that we have inherited a prejudice of taste to that effect. This prejudice can be tested either in terms of its content, along more traditional lines, or in more Kantian, formal terms. By testing its content, the pronouncement that the Venus de Milo is a model classical statue is examined historically to discover why so many generations have interpreted it as being culturally significant. This content-focused test transforms the prejudice into a preliminary judgment or regulative hypothesis for which confirmation needs to be found. Also to be considered are the reasons that art historians and critics have given over the years for their assessments and whether they provide the basis for an eventual determinant rule about what constitutes good taste.

But such an intellectual search for an interpretive consensus about the content of taste is not the route that Kant is proposing in the third *Critique*. In this work we find the basis for a formal way of testing an aesthetic prejudice by suspending it, not regulatively, but reflectively. A pure judgment of taste tests the aesthetic prejudice that the Venus de Milo is beautiful by examining our felt response to the statue. If it enlivens feeling in a way that can be shared by others, then we can assent to its general validity. If it also stimulates the harmony of the cognitive faculties, then it is, in Kant's words, purposive for "cognition in general"[13] and implies a normative consent. Such implied consent can transform an *example* of good taste accepted through our cultural heritage into something *exemplary* for any human being. When this occurs, the rather restricted public (*publike*) sphere of commonality is enlarged into the more

---

13. *Critique of the Power of Judgment*, 136; Ak 5: 218.

expansive sphere that Kant associates with the open "public (*öffentliche*) use of human reason."[14] This open sphere is the territory of free and unrestricted debate in which we take the perspective of others seriously while exposing our own perspective to scrutiny. It is the territory of spontaneous expression and uncensored publication (*Veröffentlichung*) in which we aim at consensus rather than a final univocal approbation.

REFLECTIVE SCHEMATIZATION AND CONTEXTUAL RECONFIGURATION

Examples that are simply imitated serve us solely as external determining influences. However, when an example is subjected to the comparative evaluation of reflective judgment, it can become exemplary and function as an external guide that awakens an internal source as well. The guidance found in the exemplary does not provide some determinate rule to direct us; instead it aids us in orienting ourselves. A similar coordination of external and internal references is found in Kant's account of spatial orientation, according to which we discern our place in the world by reference both to the external position of the sun and to our internal capacity to feel the difference between left and right.[15]

Whereas examples of fashion provide determinate images with the potential to compel us, what is exemplary for taste is like an indeterminate schema that leaves the imagination more flexibility in how to respond. In section 35 of the third *Critique*, Kant states that the aesthetic imagination "schematizes without a concept,"[16] but he does not fully develop what this means.[17] The conceptual schematization of the first *Critique*, where the imagination served to subordinate particular intuitions to concepts of the understanding, is contrasted with a nonconceptual schematization, in which the imagination, as a more freely functioning faculty, is related to the faculty of the understanding by a more general "principle of subsumption."[18] So long as the aesthetic imagination does not violate the general lawfulness of the understanding, it can initiate a reciprocal play between these two faculties. Their free schema-

---

14. Kant, "An Answer to the Question: 'What is Enlightenment?,'" trans. H. B. Nisbet, *Political Writings*, ed. Hans Reiss (Cambridge: Cambridge University Press, 1991), 55; *Ak* 8: 37.

15. See Kant, "What is Orientation in Thinking?," *Ak* 8: 134.

16. *Critique of the Power of Judgment*, 167; *Ak* 5: 287.

17. In section 9 of the *Critique of the Power of Judgment*, Kant does hint that the aesthetic interplay of the imagination and the understanding involves a subjective schematization by contrasting it with the objective schematization of the *Critique of Pure Reason*.

18. *Critique of the Power of Judgment*, 167; *Ak* 5: 287.

tizing interplay is felt to be purposive and produces what Kant elsewhere calls a coordinative relation between them, rather than the subordinative relation[19] that the imagination had to the understanding in the first *Critique*. This coordinative relation can also be referred back to Kant's discussion in section 9 regarding the formal harmony of the imagination and understanding that is communicable among all human beings.

In the *Critique of Pure Reason*, schematization was the process whereby timeless concepts are explicated temporally to enable us to "read"[20] the manifold of sense as objectively meaningful. Thus the imaginative schema for the category of causation pre-figures the kind of law-bound relations to which phenomenal objects are subject, thereby allowing us to read the events of nature as a meaningful linear text. I propose that in the *Critique of Judgment* the imagination schematizes without concepts in order to con-figure possible orientational contexts for the purpose of reflective evaluation. Here we move from the cognitive textual meaning of things to the interpretation of their contextual significance. In hermeneutical terms, schematizing with a concept has a meaning-giving task, and schematizing without a concept adds a more general meaning-sharing function that creates an intersubjective human context. To schematize an aesthetic object nonconceptually is to orient our judgment to respond to it appropriately.

We noted that judgments can refer to objects while at the same time contextualizing them. Determinant judgments tend to define their subject matter in terms of lawful domains. But when a reflective judgment of taste attributes the nonconceptual predicate or mark of beauty to an object, it does not consider it in relation to the necessitation of either a cognitive or moral domain, but as part of the actual territory of what is humanly experienceable.[21] As reflective, the aesthetic judgment goes back to the "one and same territory" on which both theoretical and practical reason have their "two different legislations."[22] The new contextual configuration involved in aesthetic judgment requires a shift from perceiving an object as part of a domain to apprehending it in terms of its experiential feltness. Moreover, Kant indicates that it is only through imaginative schematization that this subjective sphere of aesthetic appreciation can be evaluated as an intersubjective human sphere of taste. In examin-

19. *Reflexionen zur Logik*, Ak 16: 119.
20. See *Critique of Pure Reason*, A314/B371.
21. See chapter 3 for a fuller discussion of the hermeneutic import of the contexts of domain, territory, field, habitat, and system.
22. *Critique of the Power of Judgment*, 62; Ak 5: 175.

ing what I have called the third level of aesthetic consensus, which pertains to the pure judgment of taste, Kant writes, "The aesthetic universality that is ascribed to a judgment must . . . be of a special kind, since the predicate of beauty is not connected with the concept of the **object** considered in its entire logical sphere (*Sphäre*) and yet it extends the predicate over **the whole sphere of those who judge**."[23] When we ascribe beauty to an object, we do not assign it another determinate objective property such as color, size, or shape. Instead, the predicate of beauty relates a work of art to the sphere of human beings who are able to evaluate it. An evaluative judgment of taste requires a contextual reconfiguration from objective to intersubjective universality.

A pure or proper judgment of taste must come through our engagement with others. The aesthetic pleasure we gain from a thing of beauty should be a communicable sentiment rather than a private sensation. Accordingly, Kant asserts that it would be self-contradictory to assign the universal communicability of a felt aesthetic pleasure directly to "the representation through which [its] object *is* **given**."[24] Instead, "it is the universal *communicability of the state of mind* in the given representation which, as the subjective condition of the judgment of taste, must serve as its ground and have the pleasure in the object as a consequence."[25] The difference here concerns the way in which the object being judged is contextualized. The directly represented object refers to the limited habitat of how I am affected, that is, my own sensuous pleasure. The aesthetically apprehended object is indicative of the larger territory of what can be humanly shared, and a reflective mental pleasure follows from my being part of this territory.

The communicability of a state of mind referred to occurs without the use of concepts to exchange information. What is communicated is not determinate cognition about the object being judged, but a cognitive disposition that makes further judgmental discourse possible from a new perspective. This is because in a proper judgment of taste, my relation to the object is mediated by the way my cognitive faculties function in attunement with those of other human beings. Insofar as the interplay of my imagination and understanding in apprehending the object also evokes the state of mind needed for cognition, Kant holds that it is in principle universally communicable. And if aesthetic pleasure arises from this communicability, I am not judging the object solely as it affects me, but in terms of an attitude of engagement with others. The

---

23. *Critique of the Power of Judgment*, 100; *Ak* 5: 215.
24. *Critique of the Power of Judgment*, 102; *Ak* 5: 217.
25. *Critique of the Power of Judgment*, 102 (my italics, translation revised); *Ak* 5: 217.

pleasure I feel has been aesthetically schematized as a shareable state of mind. This contextual reconfiguration directed at the sphere of those who judge must be conceived in terms of reflective judgment, which moves from intuited particulars to unknown universals. In *The Jäsche Logic*[26] reflective judgment is said to proceed either by induction to seek abstract universals or by analogy to conceive of generic universals that can be coordinated into systems. Aesthetic or reflective schematization can match these conceptual procedures at the level of the particulars of experience by discerning in them general features that are indicative of a fuller human context.

The hermeneutic import of reflective schematization is to show how a prejudice embedded in the habitat of local familiarity can be freed from its contingency by reorienting it to the territory of human experience as such—giving us, as it were, a greater space in which to gain our bearings.[27] This recontextualizing mode of schematization offers an *epoché* that suspends prejudices of taste to prepare us to judge things from the general perspective of human sensibility. A painting by Raphael or Vermeer may justifiably be called beautiful in an exemplary way if the feeling of pleasure it gives can be communicated among human beings. And the test for this is that the pleasure is not some private sensation but involves a formal harmony of the cognitive faculties of imagination and understanding. What makes such an aesthetic feeling normatively valuable is that it enlivens the harmony of these cognitive faculties and thereby expands the scope of what is intersubjectively meaningful.

EXEMPLARITY AND EMULATION

By regarding schematization in terms of the explication of meaning, we have been able to distinguish two modes: 1) the determinant explication of the meaning of universal concepts as rules of application and 2) the reflective explication of the meaning of intuitive particulars that locates something of significance or value in them that can be linked to some more general context. For understanding the human world, this second, reflective, mode of schematization has the capacity to reassess locally accepted viewpoints from a broader territorial perspective. Aesthetically, reflective schematization can

---

26. *The Jäsche Logic*, Ak 9: 132.

27. The communicability that extends beyond my own habitat is not unlike what Royce expects from interpretation. But for Royce the extension involves exchanging cognitive content from one standard context into another, whereas for Kant it involves transposing oneself into a broader context to open up a humanistic perspective on things.

use pleasing examples from a local cultural context to discern if any of them are exemplary and can be made relevant to the human sphere at large. But it can also induce an openness to beauty derivable from remote or unfamiliar contexts. Although good taste must be validated from within, what is exemplary for taste may involve external factors such as historical precedents and models from other traditions. Kant clearly thinks that we should take into account how others have judged—if only to learn from their mistakes. He writes: "If each subject always had to start from nothing but the crude predisposition given him by nature, [many] of his attempts would fail, if other people before him had not failed in theirs."[28] Accordingly, the development of taste is defined in terms of the human species as a whole.

This enlarged hermeneutical context locates the problem of taste in a common sphere from the start and allows us to see the force of the normative coming from both within and without. Therefore it is not enough to say that to adopt "a normative attitude" toward something beautiful is to first judge my own "mental activity to be appropriate," and then "take it that everyone ought to judge it in the same way that I do."[29] This way of relating my assent and the consent of others establishes a one-way dependence that fails to do justice to the reciprocal engagement that is involved in the communicability of aesthetic schematization.[30] To be sure, when I reach the third phase of aesthetic consensus my assent leads to the expectation of the consent of human beings as such. But as recognized by Kant, the force of what is inherited from tradition must be taken into account, and therefore we cannot rule out that individual assent already involves a tacit consent to some commonly accepted standards of taste.

Whenever judgmental assent is rooted in prejudgmental consent, precedents can become determinant influences that jeopardize the freedom of individual assent. However, the consideration of precedents need not entail the loss of individual autonomy. Kant suggests such a noncompelling kind of his-

---

28. *Critique of the Power of Judgment*, 163; *Ak* 5: 283.

29. This is how Hannah Ginsborg characterizes the normativity of taste in her essay "Thinking the Particular as Contained under the Universal," in *Aesthetics and Cognition in Kant's Critical Philosophy*, ed. Rebecca Kukla (Cambridge: Cambridge University Press, 2006), 58–59.

30. Hannah Arendt also points to the importance of the capacity to engage with others through judgment when she writes that "the unwillingness or inability to relate to others through judgment" is a scandal and a source of "the banality of evil." Arendt, *Responsibility and Judgment*, ed. Jerome Kohn (New York: Schocken Books, 2003), 146.

torical influence by introducing a distinction between emulation (*Nachfolge*) and imitation (*Nachahmung*). He writes:

> *Emulation* of a precedent, rather than imitation, is the right term for any influence that products of an exemplary author may have on others; and this means no more than drawing on the same sources from which the predecessor himself drew, and learning from him only how to go about doing so.[31]

Rather than reproducing a standard, emulation discerns what makes it normative. To regard a precedent as exemplary is not to appeal to it as a determining ground, but simply to orient oneself by it as potentially valuable or worthy of commitment.[32] This makes room for something akin to what is called "reflective endorsement" in the moral domain.[33] The emulation of reflective precedents reorients the aesthetic judgment to the sphere of normative consent as a new meaning-context.

The emulation of the exemplary requires us to consider the normative context of aesthetic judgment. Kant explores some aspects of this when he discusses how "normal ideas" of beauty relate to a normative ideal of beauty in section 17 of the *Critique of Judgment*. This often-overlooked section examines normal ideas of human beauty that are originally based on local familiarity and will typically differ for Europeans, Africans, and Asians.[34] Although our sense of the normal proportions of the human face and figure are derived from past experience, the resulting empirical average does not provide the imagination determinant rules for schematizing the normal idea

---

31. *Critique of the Power of Judgment*, 164 (translation revised); *Ak* 5: 283.

32. The question is what kind of constraint does a precedent put on the judging subject? Although Kant considers the claims of others in reflective assessment, I do not think he would be ready to acknowledge the full import of Robert Brandom's double-scorekeeping approach to our normative commitments. Because Brandom sees us as embedded in social and linguistic practices, he claims that the normative commitments that an individual acknowledges involve inferential consequences that only another scorekeeper can recognize. Thus there will always be an I-Thou gap that makes any we-perspective suspect for Brandom. But the we-perspective that Kant is aiming at in aesthetic judgment is not that of a community that has an incorrigible solution and is "globally privileged." Robert Brandom, *Making It Explicit: Reasoning, Representing and Discursive Commitment* (Cambridge, MA: Harvard University Press, 1994), 599.

33. See Christine Korsgaard, "Reflective Endorsement," in *The Sources of Normativity*, ed. Onora O'Neill (New York: Cambridge University Press, 1996), 49–89.

34. *Critique of the Power of Judgment*, 119; *Ak* 5: 234.

of human beauty. Kant regards this normal idea as the first component of an ideal of beauty, whose second component is the rational idea of the purposes of humanity. As part of the ideal of beauty, it is expected that we fashion the normal idea of human beauty to aim at "the image of the entire kind, hovering between all the singular and multiply varied intuitions of individuals."[35] What was initially a regional stereotype of beauty becomes the normal idea of human beauty in general by approximating a universal archetype. Only in relation to the archetype of human beauty can the normal as average assume a normative value. But the imagination cannot reach "the entire archetype"[36] and provides only an exemplary schema of "correctness,"[37] which is then connected in the ideal of beauty to the rational ends of humanity. The idea of beauty allows for the indirect "expression of the moral."[38]

TYPIFICATION AND THE INTUITIVE PRESENTATION OF MEANING

The ways in which Kant goes on to relate beauty to the moral sphere suggest that the reflective schematization of aesthetic play, which is purposive without a purpose, must eventually take account of the purposes that characterize the creative work of artists. Literary works in particular express meanings that arouse thought as well as feeling. The poetic imagination tends to evoke more thought than can be "comprehended within a determinate concept."[39] This surplus of thought produces "aesthetic ideas,"[40] which have the capacity to symbolize more than we can know. We saw that symbolization serves to establish relations among the various contexts needed to interpret experience. By calling beauty a symbol of morality, Kant allows aesthetic ideas to indirectly relate the "domains" of nature and freedom. The symbolic image of serene beauty can suggest features of human virtue that moral thought leaves abstract. Symbolism is a form of meaning presentation (*Darstellung*) that gives linguistic representation (*Vorstellung*) a quasi-intuitive or imaginative dimension.

It was shown in chapter 3 that meaning can be intuitively presented in

---

35. *Critique of the Power of Judgment*, 119; *Ak* 5: 234.
36. *Critique of the Power of Judgment*, 119; *Ak* 5: 235.
37. *Critique of the Power of Judgment*, 120; *Ak* 5: 235.
38. *Critique of the Power of Judgment*, 120; *Ak* 5: 235.
39. *Critique of the Power of Judgment*, 193; *Ak* 5: 315.
40. *Critique of the Power of Judgment*, 193; *Ak* 5: 315.

three ways: through determinant schematization, mathematical demonstration, and imaginative symbolization. The reflective schematization that allows for the presentation of particulars in their appropriate context can now be inserted into this sequence as an analogue of imaginative symbolization. By linking reflective schematization and the symbolic we can apply the normative considerations of aesthetic exemplarity to the task of exemplifying meaning in the human sciences.

In his discussion of beauty as a symbol of morality, Kant introduces the covering term "hypotyposis" for the intuitive presentation of meaning. A hypotype suggests the openness that characterizes a cognitive hypothesis. Just as a hypothesis is not yet a fully formed theory, so a hypotype is not a fully instantiated meaning. The preliminary nature of a hypothesis finds its counterpart in the expectant nature of the hypotype. The process of hypotyposis has to do with intuitively exhibiting the meaning of a concept or idea by an imaginative type that predelineates a set of particulars before the meaning is actually instantiated. Hypotyposis encompasses a range of operations that can be used to characterize interpretive contexts in terms of typical situations and representative individuals.

This broad account of hypotyposis sets the stage for both the real or exemplifying types used by Dilthey in delineating historical epochs and the ideal or exemplary types proposed in sociology by Max Weber. Dilthey appeals to typicality by focusing on a real human being like Lessing to exemplify what distinguishes the German Enlightenment from the French Enlightenment, namely, a tolerance concerning religious faiths rather than a rejection of religion as such. While no actual person is expected to embody Weber's ideal type of the Protestant capitalist, it points to features of a historical situation that indicate tendencies that could help explain certain results.

When aligned with some of the modes of intuitive meaning-presentation made possible by Kant's theory of judgment, hypotyposis can be specified as involving: (1) determinant categorial schemata that provide imaginative prototypes for cognizing and knowing the world; (2) demonstrations that produce intuitive archetypes for mathematical constructs; (3) reflective schemata that project exemplary contextual types for evaluating human responses to the world; and (4) symbols that produce countertypes to coordinate the various contexts involved in interpretation. Whereas Kant applied determinant schematization and mathematical demonstration to the scientific cognition of nature, reflective schematization and imaginative symbolization can coordinate the various contexts relevant to interpreting the historical world.

We have introduced reflective schemata to imaginatively specify the contextualizing function that reflective judgment contributes to the evaluation of human life. The exemplifying role of reflective schematization serves to clarify the different objective contexts that intersect in human affairs, and it can in principle add to the six kinds of interpretive context that were specified in chapter 3. Finally, we shall see that reflective schematization can facilitate the way we navigate among the intersubjective normative spheres that are relevant to historical interpretation. Symbolic presentation was considered as the imaginative process of specifying formal relations among various interpretive contexts. To also think of symbols as producing countertypes is to acknowledge that Kant speaks of symbolization as a process of *Gegenbildung*, which literally means "counter-formation."[41] A symbol cannot create a direct intuitive counterpart for any single abstract idea, but it can form an indirect imaginative countertype for relations among several ideas. *Gegenbildung* as symbolization involves a process of coordinating countertypes from different contexts so that they can illuminate each other.[42] Kant focused on the way poetic imagery can enliven our moral sensitivity, but in principle countertypes can be used to specify relations among any of the spheres of historical life.

By considering aesthetic judgment as a mode of interpretation, we have expanded the cognitive search for meaning to take into account not only truth claims, but also the exemplary role of reflective evaluation. A reflective judgment of taste does not add to our determinant knowledge of the world, yet it can have cognitive import. Aesthetic judgment has a normative validity that derives from its capacity to indirectly contribute to human understanding by exploring the communicative value of the felt harmony of the cognitive faculties. Having shown that communication among human subjects requires the capacity to schematize contexts beyond their own habitats, we can do more than seek consensus among disinterested spectators. Indeed, for reflective judgment in its more general interpretive capacity, this expansive mode of schematization is needed to make sense of other nations and cultures. Even when some of their values prove to be irreconcilable, there may be ways of recontextualizing them so that at least we can understand how they could be made to intersect. The hermeneutical task of the human sciences is to allow us to recontextualize our own lived experience and life-knowledge to find ac-

---

41. For the proper contextualization of Kant's use of *Gegenbild* = *symbolum*, see Makkreel, *Imagination and Interpretation in Kant*, 13–15, 19, 123.

42. *Gegenbildung* is one of the many variants of *Einbildung* or imagination distinguished by Kant. Other forms of our image-forming power (*Bildungsvermögen*) are *Abbildung*, *Nachbildung*, *Vorbildung*, and *Ausbildung*. See *Imagination and Interpretation in Kant*, chapter 1.

cess to the concerns of others even when they stand outside the sphere of our inherited commonality and we cannot readily engage them in a consensual dialogue.

For hermeneutic purposes then, we can say that the "reflecting power of judgment . . . of ascending from the particular in nature to the universal"[43] involves not just looking for new concepts, but also schematizing more appropriate contexts. Reflective judgment is interpretive when the available context of the given particular is considered in relation to other possible contexts. Thus what Kant called "schematization without concepts" can be more simply referred to as "reflective schematization."

*

We have argued that the cognitive results of the natural and human sciences may not be ignored when interpreting the claims of life-knowledge. But in moving on to the more integral framework that is required for reflective knowledge, it is equally important to include the evaluative considerations opened up by the arts and human creativity. What lies between everyday life-knowledge and reflective knowledge are not only the domains and systems of scientific cognition, but also the normative spheres of reference that we have considered in reflecting on aesthetic communicability. Reflective schemata are important for suggesting possible contextual reconfigurations whereby one human perspective can in principle take account of at least aspects of others.

Whenever we make interpretive judgments about reality, we need to locate a context or frame of reference for orientation. In the case of what is assimilated as life-knowledge, this context is an inherited commonality that includes prejudices and customs. The task of hermeneutics is to relate this assimilated life-knowledge to what can be scientifically acquired as universally valid cognition about the objective world. If the search for possible lawful and structural regularities within well-defined domains and systems is to have an effect on our understanding of life, quite different contexts will need to be coordinated. And for what is eventually appropriated as reflective knowledge, we will consider those more open public spheres where normative issues can come into focus.

Whereas the cognition of nature requires the formal aesthetic conditions of space and time as well as discursive conditions that delineate scientific sys-

---

43. *Critique of the Power of Judgment*, 67; *Ak* 5: 180.

tems, the reflective knowledge of history requires a more concrete sense of how we are placed in local habitats as well as the territory of the human world at large. Unlike the purely cognitive claims of the sciences, reflective knowledge claims do not abstract from the life situation of the subject. To the extent that there can be reflective knowledge of history, the systematic aspirations of reason will need to be specified in terms of individual assessments of the world. But such individual perspectives can at least be framed intersubjectively on the model of aesthetic experience.

While Kant extended a uniform cognitive ideal of universality to judgments of taste, we have located the emulation of aesthetic exemplarity within a less homogeneous worldly sphere. If the territory of the human world is to encompass the diversity implicit in the idea of a cosmopolitan perspective, works of art would seem to provide an important resource for engaging a general public composed of multiple traditions. The communicability of the arts lies in their capacity to draw us out of ourselves and exceed our own context. However, we cannot expect them to produce either the concurrence of a Gadamerian dialogue, an overall Roycean conspectus, or the univocal approbation of an ideal community. Aesthetically, the univocity (*Einstimmung*) of good taste that Kant hoped for must be scaled back to the expressive voices (*Stimmen*) of artists and thinkers who attempt to bring some overall perspective into focus. Great artists attain a characteristic style that can offer insight into a broad human theme by concentrating our attention on some typical point of impression. The interpretation of the arts teaches us that despite stylistic and cultural differences in approaching a subject matter, it is possible to generate some level of communicability and contextual accommodation.[44]

---

44. For a consideration of the complexities of the current art scene, see chapter 9 and the discussion of medial artistic contexts.

CHAPTER 6

Validity, Legitimacy, and Historical Attribution

We have examined the contextual meaning-conditions of interpretation in an attempt to make hermeneutics as open and receptive to the world as possible. And in exploring what is exemplary in the search for human consent, we have characterized aesthetic consciousness as more than a sphere of sense, feeling, and pleasure. It is not solely an inner-directed mode of awareness but inherently communicable and capable of social engagement. The normative value of the aesthetic was approached through the receptivity of sense and feeling as well as the responsiveness of judgment. Having expanded the theory of judgment to encompass not only determinant and reflective judgment, but also preliminary judgments, as the counterparts to Heidegger's pre-understanding and Gadamer's prejudices, we are in a position to consider a hermeneutical approach to the conditions of normative legitimacy in historical life.

KNOWLEDGE AND LEGITIMACY

The distinctions between cognition and knowledge that were found to be implicit in Kant and Dilthey can be developed further in terms of the normative aspects of reflective knowledge. Knowing is more than a cognitive stance; it exceeds cognition in that it also involves a normative commitment. From the hermeneutical standpoint, it was important to predelineate the reflective bounds of what can be cognized in orientational and disciplinary ways. But there are also discursive bounds on human experience that, in more Kantian terms, could be differentiated into transcendental conditions of cognition on the one hand and normative ideals of reflective knowledge on the other.

To consider a concept as transcendental is to give it primacy over other concepts as an indispensable enabling condition for finding meaning in the world. On the assumption of a unitary natural framework of inquiry, such questions about prioritizing concepts aim at universal categories. For a hermeneutic approach, priorities need to be established not only within specific contexts of inquiry, but also among them and the disciplines that represent them. The natural sciences tend to be more hierarchical than the human sciences. Since laws play a much more dominant role in the natural sciences, it is easier to differentiate levels of dependency there than in the human sciences. But even for historically informed disciplines that are hermeneutically interdependent, the question can always be raised whether the form or the content of cognition should be given priority.

Those like Dilthey who stressed the importance of structural regularities in historical life still tended to prioritize form, but they attempted to do so without sharply separating it from content. Referring to what is peculiar about our "knowledge (*Wissen*) of structural relations," Dilthey writes that "they are the so-called a priori to which objective philosophy must return."[1] Then, considering what legitimizes such knowledge of lived structural relations, he indicates that a simple appeal to mental conditions based on self-observation does not suffice. His Critique of Historical Reason requires a regress from "given knowledge" to the "regular inner relations" that can be found in "language, the understanding of other persons, and the literary manifestations of poets or historians."[2] This marks a shift from anticipatory transcendental analysis concerning the validating meaning-conditions of cognition to regressive transcendental reflection about the legitimating sources of historical knowledge.

Dilthey finds it necessary to integrate purely cognitive or intellectual conditions not only into the broader affective and volitional aspects of human consciousness, but also into the sociocultural framework that governs our life. The mental conditions of human experience must be supplemented by communicative cultural conditions. The fundamental structural relations of historical life that he considers to be binding for our understanding of it function as both formal conditions and sources with content. In order to account for these binding features of historical experience, Dilthey specifically appeals

1. Dilthey, *GS*, XXIV, 161.
2. *GS*, XXIV, 161.

to "transcendental reflection" in his 1895-96 essay on individuality.[3] Kant had used transcendental reflection to differentiate whether a representation has its source in the mind or in sensibility and to orient us to inner-outer and form-matter distinctions. This allowed him to align mind with inner and formal conditions and to refer sensibility to outer and material conditions. Dilthey, however, turns to transcendental reflection to suggest that this inner-outer distinction is not exhaustive. There are certain experiences that are not simply inner or outer experiences. Rather than use transcendental reflection to decide with Kant whether a representation has inner significance or an external reference, as we did above, Dilthey redirects transcendental reflection to the question of how some things that are external can nevertheless be recognized as having an inner significance for us. This involves a third kind of experience that makes room for "spiritual-cultural facts."[4] Some of what outer experience *perceives* as natural objects can under certain conditions be *apperceived* as also disclosing the formative influence of human agency and work.

Dilthey calls this third or apperceptive kind of experience "transcendental"[5] because it gives our life-context a spiritual significance. But since it is problematic to suggest that a transcendental condition of experience can itself be experienced, I will call it a "reflective experience."[6] This transcendental or reflective way of accounting for "spiritual-cultural facts" finds its empirical counterpart in what is assimilated as life-knowledge as we grow up. At this more basic level, we do not need to posit a reflective experience that involves a priori anticipations and need only point to a more common assimilative experience that draws on prior or pre-given sources. An assimilative experience is like outer experience in being about something other, and it is like inner experience in assenting to something I identify with. Yet it is more than either inner or outer experience by also consenting to a pre-given meaning of things. An outer experience acknowledges things as having their independent existence in nature. An assimilative experience acknowledges things as deriving their sense from a preexisting meaning-context in which we participate. Here both the thesis of chapter 3—that interpretive judgments define things by situating them in a context—and the thrust of chapters 4 and 5, that judg-

---

3. Dilthey, "Contributions to the Study of Individuality," in *Understanding the Human World, Selected Works* (*SW*), vol. 2, ed. Rudolf A. Makkreel and Frithjof Rodi (Princeton, NJ: Princeton University Press, 2010), 216.
4. "Contributions to the Study of Individuality," 217.
5. "Contributions to the Study of Individuality," 217.
6. Makkreel, *Dilthey, Philosopher of the Human Studies*, 223.

ing involves our assent/consent, are prefigured in pre-reflective or reflexive terms.

An assimilative experience can make room for what Dilthey called "spiritual-cultural facts" because it locates us within a pre-given shared context. This kind of contextualizing experience is both orientational in a spatial, worldly sense and receptive in a historical sense. Accordingly, the traditional inner-outer distinction that has been geared to nature must be rethought in light of our being part of the historical world. Similarly, form-matter distinctions must be reconceived as having been abstracted from more encompassing life-structures.

The thesis that assimilative experience is contextualizing can be used to add support to Dilthey's claim that belief in the reality of the world does not require an inference to something transcendent. With this claim, Dilthey distances himself from the Neo-Kantian Heinrich Rickert, who had argued that theoretical cognition (*Erkennen*) of the world is at every step the ideational acknowledgment (*Anerkennen*) of the transcendent value of truth.[7] For Dilthey, by contrast, any acknowledgment of the independent reality of the world must be explicable on the basis of a direct sense of what is real. It requires overcoming the epistemological prejudice that consciousness is inherently phenomenal, representational, and set apart from the world. Even when consciousness is directed at so-called phenomenal objects, it possesses its own reality and is present to itself as a "reflexive awareness (usually *Innewerden*, sometimes *Inne-Sein*)."[8] Although there is an inwardness or intimacy associated with these two German terms, they are not to be confused with inner experience. I have translated *Innewerden* as "reflexive awareness" to indicate a pre-reflective being-with-itself *(Inne-Sein)* of consciousness, whether it is directed within or without. According to Dilthey, reflexive awareness "does not place a content over against the subject of consciousness (it does not re-present it); rather, a content is present in it without differentiation. That which constitutes its content is in no way distinguished from the act in which it occurs."[9] Reflexive awareness is originally a pre-representational consciousness, but it can also come to access states of representational consciousness. Just as for Kant "the *I-think* must *be able* to accompany all my representations,"[10] reflexive awareness can potentially accompany any worldly content of conscious-

---

7. *GS*, XXIV, 297.
8. *GS*, VII, 27; *SW 3*, 48.
9. *Introduction to the Human Sciences*, SW 1, 253–54.
10. *Critique of Pure Reason*, B131.

ness, whether representational or not. It involves an implicit self-givenness that precedes an explicit or reflective sense of self. The felt self-givenness of reflexive awareness comes before any introspective observation of a self. Thus Dilthey writes that

> if we call "observation" the directing of attention to something-placed-before-me . . . then there can be no observation of reflexive awareness or its content. Attentiveness directed at reflexive awareness produces merely an intensification in the degree of consciousness connected with the exertion of effort. This intensification in the field of reflexive awareness . . . is the most simple form in which psychic life can appear.[11]

Edmund Husserl defined consciousness in terms of intentionality. Consciousness is always consciousness of something. But just as we saw that judgments are not merely *of* objects, but also *about* their context, it seems appropriate to characterize consciousness more generally by an orientational aboutness. This aboutness of consciousness can be directed at what is within or without. Reflexive awareness, by contrast, is the being-with-itself of consciousness and constitutes the real connectedness of consciousness over time. This connectedness can be articulated into cognitive, affective, and volitional structures, each of which provides its distinctive nexus to things. But Dilthey warns that however much we may want to focus on one of these structures, we should never lose sight of our overall state of mind. Thus the cognitive nexus should not be fully isolated from the affective and the volitional. Cognition is not possible without some inquisitive interest, which is a function of feeling; nor can it produce determinative results without attention, which is a function of willing.

The reflexive awareness that informs the connectedness of the processes of consciousness includes worldly content, but the latter is not explicitly recognized as belonging to an external world until an adequate sense of self is developed. On this basis, we can make the argument that reflexive awareness and assimilative experience are more primordial than what gets differentiated as inner and outer experience. Gradually, what is given as interconnected in consciousness undergoes differentiation. Dilthey illustrates this by describing the experience of musical appreciation as a sequence of "hearing and taking delight in tones," in which the taking delight becomes a constituent of the self, while the heard tone becomes "a constituent part of the external world

---

11. *Introduction to the Human Sciences*, 254.

which confronts the listening subject as something distinct."[12] The reflexive taking delight in a sequence of tones can serve as an initial reference point for the perceptual take on them as sounds stemming from a piano and the more reflective take on them as a phrase from a sonata composed by Beethoven.

Traditional epistemologists had attempted to account for our sense of the distinctness of objects and other subjects in representational terms. But what is represented in consciousness can never reach beyond itself except in hypothetical, inferential terms. What Dilthey is looking for is a non-inferential access to the world, and he finds it in the volitional nexus rather than the cognitive nexus. In "The Origin of Our Belief in the Reality of the External World and Its Justification," he writes that "the consciousness of a volitional impulse and of an intention on the one hand and that of the intention being restrained on the other, that is, *two volitional states*, constitute the core of the experience of resistance and thereby of the reality of objects."[13] We have here the reflexive awareness of the will that it has met resistance within itself.

We can carry this analysis forward in terms of our Kantian distinction between limits and bounds.[14] When resistance to our striving is felt reflexively, the will senses a diminution. But not until this experience of resistance is acknowledged reflectively as either restraining or constraining the will does a consciousness of the world as distinct from the self arise. This constitutes a transformation of the actual feeling of resistance into either the contingent *limit of a restraint* or the necessary *bound of a constraint*. We can use this to refine Dilthey's thesis about how we come to differentiate in consciousness between an experience of self and an experience of the world. On the basis of the recognition of a restraining limit, a distinction can be made in consciousness between an inner experience of the self and the outer experience of the natural world. However, the recognition of a constraining bound relates us to the world, not merely as something apart from us or contingently imposed from without, but as a pre-given, encompassing context that has a hold on us. To the extent that this hold on us conditions our behavior, it is merely at the level of inherited commonality and what Kant called the prejudices of a local public. But if we consider the context more neutrally as an orientational territory of consensus, as with the problem of educating human taste, then it can take on a normative status and make room for what Kant called the wider public sphere

---

12. *Introduction to the Human Sciences*, SW 1, 255.

13. Dilthey, "The Origin of Our Belief in the Reality of the External World and Its Justification," in *Understanding the Human World*, SW 2, 21.

14. See chapter 3.

of open debate and what Dilthey referred to as the sphere of cultural-spiritual facts made accessible through transcendental reflective experience.

Although reflective consciousness is a necessary condition for conceptual cognition of the world, being oriented to this world also requires a reference back to reflexive awareness. Kant rooted spatial orientation in a bodily feeling that discriminates between left and right as we find our way in moving among and acting upon the objects that we perceive around us. To this extent we can say that hermeneutic orientation requires the capacity to coordinate reflexive awareness with the various reflective contexts we can experience ourselves to be part of. This situated way of contextualizing experience will be hermeneutically useful as we further refine the contrast between inner and outer experience.

The traditional inner-outer experience distinction has an initial plausibility, but it is not easily defined or maintained. The awareness of my state of mind, my feelings about myself, and my attitude to my situation are obvious examples of inner experience. Perceived objects like the rocks and trees on my path tend to count as outer experience. But the perception of some external objects like a tree in my garden can also become an inner experience for me if I remember planting it and think of how much pleasant shade it has provided me. Then I see it as a valued object that belongs to my life history. A statue in a church is another example of a perceptual object that can be more than an outer experience. But in this case, it provides the basis for what we have called an assimilative experience. An assimilative experience acknowledges an outer object as possessing a value or meaning not derived from one's own life but from a pre-given public context with which one identifies. If the statue is of a revered figure from the past who embodies virtues that endow human life with dignity, it brings with it a kind of understanding that locates an inner sense in something outer.

This example of an assimilative experience can be related to Dilthey's idea of objective spirit as the inherited common context for all elementary understanding. What is inner in this context is not primarily mental or psychological. Before children learn to speak, they are already wholly immersed in the medium of commonalities. Children learn to understand the gestures and facial expressions, movements and exclamations, words and sentences, only because they constantly encounter them as the same and in the same relation to what they mean and express. This is the way individuals become oriented in the world of objective spirit.[15] Thus the inner nature of sense and meaning

---

15. Dilthey, "The Understanding of Other Persons and Their Manifestations of Life," in *The Formation of the Historical World*, SW 3, 229–30. Language is a central constituent of ob-

is rooted in contextual immersion before it can be located in introspective insight. Elementary understanding is oriented by the normative authority of a local commonality, which encompasses what is taken for granted on the basis of custom, convention, or prejudice.

For higher understanding, the human sciences introduce more differentiated universal contexts. But by moving from commonality to universality, the various human sciences often expose conflicting norms that need to be resolved. To confront this problem, we also need a reflective historical perspective to assess the overall outcome of both life-knowledge and conceptual cognition. The resulting reflective knowledge must be adjudicative if it is to produce a critical interpretation. Here we need to move the process of judging (*urteilen*) and evaluating (*beurteilen*) to a decisive assessment (*Bewertung*).

In adjudicating his antinomies of pure reason, Kant suggests that when the parties in a public dispute (*Streithandel*) cannot resolve their differences, an external judge (*Richter*)[16] may be needed to pass a rational verdict. The question raised by such a top-down resolution is whether a life-based process can cope with the tensions that arise along the way as it moves from the common sense of life-knowledge to the cognitive explication of meaning to the assessments of reflective knowledge. The question is important for determining whether reflective knowledge can provide critical understanding. The import of the hermeneutic circle is to accord reflective knowledge legitimacy only if it takes into account the entire sequence, starting with life-knowledge. But this still leaves us with the question whether reflective knowledge can itself adjudicate the conflicts that arise in elementary and higher modes of understanding or whether a distinct judge-like legitimizing source is needed.

HERMENEUTICS AND ADJUDICATION

One contemporary voice arguing for an independent legitimating source is that of Jürgen Habermas. In his volume *Between Facts and Norms: Contributions to a Discourse Theory of Law and Democracy*, he makes a sharp distinction between norms and values. The norms derived from his discourse theory of law are regarded as deontological or absolute, whereas values are defined as teleological or relative to human interests. On the one hand, "norms of action obligate their addressees equally and without exception to satisfy generalized

---

jective spirit and becomes its stand-in for thinkers such as Heidegger and Gadamer when they claim that language defines our being in the world.

16. *Critique of Pure Reason*, A529–30/B558–59.

behavioral expectations," and on the other hand, "values are to be understood as intersubjectively shared preferences."[17] According to Habermas, there is an "oughtness" that attaches to norms that sets them apart from values. Norms are universally binding whereas values represent local preferences regarding goods to be achieved.

Habermas claims that the hermeneutical assimilation of a legal tradition involves a form of value-jurisprudence that cannot properly adjudicate normative issues. He is referring to the neo-Aristotelian approach to legal hermeneutics that is championed by followers of Gadamer and by Michael J. Perry in particular. Their goal of applying the original meaning of a constitution to new historical contexts with different value interests is criticized for reducing rights to goods whose value can be measured. Accordingly, Habermas warns that "as soon as rights are transferred into goods and values in any individual case, each must compete with the others at the same level for priority."[18] Contending that such a hermeneutical approach to normative issues ultimately reduces deontological norms to the level of relative values, he concludes that the resulting "value jurisprudence raises the legitimation problem"[19] without being able to resolve it.

However, a hermeneutic approach need not result in a reduction of normative principles to an array of competing interests and values. Habermas's critique rests on his assumption of a rigid opposition between universally binding norms and values that are merely preferential and transitory. Instead of deriving all norms from the ideal conditions of discourse in general and letting them hover above what happens in history, we will also consider norms in relation to the objective systems that channel historical interaction and the intersubjective spheres that frame our understanding. Norms should not be conceived solely according to a traditional top-down model of exceptionless laws that govern a domain. Nor should values be seen as the product of a from-the-ground-up battle of competing contingent habitats. Values are inherently normative in the sense that the value judgments we make articulate the standards that we acknowledge or follow.

A reflective hermeneutical approach will place itself in the midst of the whole range of contexts that are in play in historical life and the adjudication of values that occurs within and among them. Our extended discussion of

---

17. Jürgen Habermas, *Between Facts and Norms: Contributions to a Discourse Theory of Law and Democracy* (Cambridge, MA: MIT Press, 1996), 255.

18. *Between Facts and Norms*, 259.

19. *Between Facts and Norms*, 258.

aesthetic exemplarity showed how value commitments that are initially local can be refined reflectively and validated for a larger territory. Aesthetic exemplarity in Kant allowed us to move from regional normal ideas to a normative consensus on the basis of a felt harmony that expands our horizon.

When it comes to the norms that are directly at stake in the workings of history, we cannot ignore the competing interests of everyday life. But taking elementary life values seriously does not compel us to accept them at face value and to merely report what interests happen to predominate as an actual historical outcome. A hermeneutics of history must flesh out the kinds of meaning-contexts that were delineated in chapter 3 and be able to locate actual decision-making in the most relevant of those contexts. Rather than restrict norms to regulative principles based on ideal conditions, we will also take into account normative rules that can be reflectively educed from the value judgments and standards operative in historically specifiable public contexts. The understanding of human choices is always historically mediated. It requires us to consider the institutions in which human beings find themselves and the cooperative systems they have joined. We have no choice over the family, state, and culture into which we are born. At the opposite pole are the cooperative systems that we can join voluntarily, such as a political party or a civic association. Somewhere in between would be the economic, educational, and professional systems in which we participate.

Many voluntary associations are established for a common purpose but often assume a life and validity of their own that leads them to diverge from their original telos. For this reason Dilthey changes his general concept for these historical groupings from "purposive system" to "productive system (*Wirkungszusammenhang*)."[20] The latter concept allows us to conceive of the efficacy of life and the historical world in terms of productivity before any causal or teleological analysis is applied. The carriers of history, whether they be individuals, cultures, institutions, or communities, can all be conceived as productive systems capable of producing value and meaning and in some cases realizing purposes. Each productive system of history is to be considered structurally as centered in itself and as establishing its own sphere of influence.

Every individual belongs to a number of such intersubjective systems and to that extent is influenced by their norms and subject to their rules. Most professional and cultural associations will be governed by distinct disciplinary discourses. But no individual is completely constrained by any such historical system because it engages only a part of a person's energies and

20. *The Formation of the Historical World*, SW 3, 178–82.

concerns. One can conceive individual subjects as having multiple obligations—to their family, to their profession, to their religion, to their state. Their self-understanding will be shaped by these various allegiances. The systems that intersect each other in an individual life often coexist peacefully, but if they begin to make conflicting demands, how does one set priorities among spheres that impose their distinct restraints? Here in the concrete historical context, the kind of universal legitimating procedure sought by Habermas is not possible. At best, a reflective equilibrium can be established among the individual's particular constellation of intersecting systems. By using reflective judgment to articulate this constellation, individuals can assess the legitimacy of their value commitments.

A reflective hermeneutics does not rule out the appeal to universal norms, whether moral in a Kantian sense or procedural in a Habermasian sense. But neither applies as directly or straightforwardly as is often thought. The principles of morality do not function constitutively in the productive systems of history. They can, however, provide a formal base for further normative considerations. The moral principle of equality before the law is formal and does not ensure equal access to the limited resources of the world. Just as we found that theoretical access to the world was distributed among various disciplines, so practical access is mediated by distinctive interest groups and institutions. Given this complex state of affairs, the normative rules that govern our actual lives stem mostly from the productive systems in which we participate. To be sure, we can appeal to constitutive principles of the moral domain or regulative principles of practical discourse in trying to resolve the competing demands that intersecting systems may place on us. But there comes a point where determinant moral and practical rules give way to reflective normative considerations.

Historical agents making decisions are guided by norms that are formed in accordance with the three phases previously differentiated in the movement toward reflective knowledge.[21] Initially, norms are absorbed from our habitat and its cultural heritage by assimilation. But, as we will see, there is also a more authoritative acquisition of norms, where cooperative institutional and disciplinary efforts give rise to the imputation of responsibility and to claims about entitlement. Finally, we will consider the critical appropriation of norms for the evaluation of history through processes like the reflective authentication of self-understanding and the proper characterization of self and others.

When it comes to choices among competing commitments, such as which

---

21. See chapter 4, passim.

associations and norms to prioritize in our lives, we need to consider whether the aesthetic model of reflective judgment suffices for such a decision. An obvious difference between a decisional judgment and an aesthetic judgment is that the former is rightfully interested whereas the latter is supposed to be disinterested. Aesthetic reflection may be playful and purposive without having a determinate purpose. A reflective decision about a life commitment is directed at actual purposes. Here reflective judgment will be contextual in a more constrained way, in that it cannot ignore the established historical situation to which it is applied. Reflective decisions are framed by given territorial boundaries and must take into account the legal parameters that have been established by local institutions. Individual decision makers are thus limited by the normative constraints of relevant juridical systems, but they are not fully bound by them because they can also appeal to general regulative principles about what is "right." A decisional judgment would then be a reflective judgment that incorporates determinant principles as well. Yet to the extent that the judgment remains reflective, it cannot legislate or command its normative oughtness.

When making an aesthetic judgment, I expect others to agree with me. But as Kant writes, my judgment "does not *postulate* the accord of everyone (only a logically universal judge can do that, since it can adduce grounds); it only *imputes* (*sinnt an*) this agreement to everyone."[22] I can never be sure that I have rightly imputed universal agreement in my declaring something beautiful. Similarly, as an agent making a reflective normative decision, I can never be certain that I have made the rightful choice. As we will see in the next section, reflective judgments about practical matters are imputational in a more complex way than aesthetic judgments.

ASCRIPTIVE AND ATTRIBUTIVE MODES OF IMPUTATION

The aesthetic judgment imputes its universality in a formal, ascriptive way—it cannot demonstrate its necessity conceptually. The ascriptive sense of imputation (*Ansinnung*) found in the *Critique of Judgment* reflects an anticipated consensus.[23] In the *Metaphysics of Morals*, Kant introduces stronger senses of imputation (*Zurechnung*), which point to what I will call "attributive" modes of imputation. These attributions indicate how we hold ourselves and others

---

22. *Critique of the Power of Judgment*, 101 (translation revised); *Ak* 5: 216.
23. *Critique of the Power of Judgment*, 99–101; *Ak* 5: 214–16. See also chapter 4.

accountable for our practical decisions and deeds as human agents operating within the constraints of intersubjective productive systems.

The way Kant defines imputation in the *Metaphysics of Morals* opens up some of the possible permutations of attribution and is worth citing in its entirety:

> *Imputation* (*imputatio*) in the moral sense is the *judgment* by which someone is regarded as the author (*causa libera*) of an action, which is then called a *deed* (*factum*) and stands under laws. If the judgment also carries with it the legal [*rechtlichen*] consequences of this deed, it is an imputation having a legal or rightful force (*imputatio iudiciaria s. valida*); otherwise it is merely an imputation evaluating the deed (*imputatio diiudicatoria*)—The (natural or moral) person that is authorized to impute with rightful force is called a *judge* or a court (*iudex s. forum*).[24]

We have here a complex set of imputations that will repay further analysis. Kant's first sentence is about moral imputation. It assigns responsibility to someone for an action that is attributed to be a factual deed standing under moral laws. The second sentence goes beyond attributing formal responsibility by also considering the substantive consequences of the deed and how they may affect others. If the judgment has rightful force (*rechtskräftig*), then it counts as a legal imputation that has judiciary (*iudiciaria*) legitimacy; otherwise it is an evaluation that has a dijudicative (*diiudicatoria*) status. The third sentence goes on to locate the authority to impute with rightful force in a natural person (judge) or moral person (court). The courtroom judge can thus be said to have the right to adjudicate.

Kant does not specify what is involved in evaluative dijudication (*imputatio diiudicatoria*) and seems more interested in the juridical legitimacy of adjudication. But in the following paragraph, he launches a discussion of the merits and demerits of human deeds that can be seen as allowing for the application of evaluative dijudication. One of the meanings of the word "dijudicate" is to "decide between," or weigh, alternatives. When the merits and demerits of a deed are being evaluated or dijudicated, there are for Kant three relevant alternatives among which to decide. A person can 1) do exactly what the law requires, 2) do more than what the law expects of him, which is meritorious, or 3) to his demerit, do less than the law requires. If it is determined that the agent has fallen short, there is "culpability (*Verschuldung*)," and then a "judge

---

24. *The Metaphysics of Morals*, 19; Ak 6: 227.

(*Richter*)" must adjudicate or make the final decision to direct (*richten*) what is to be done to set things right. The "courtroom (*Gerichtshof*)" establishes the authoritative context for rendering a determinant verdict concerning "the rightful consequences" of the deed.[25]

In the above sequence, dijudication was part of the legal process of correctly subsuming a deed under the law and arriving at a legitimate determinant judgment. But a few paragraphs later Kant begins to consider "the *degree* to which an action can be imputed."[26] This calls for a different kind of evaluative dijudication, one that comes closer to the attributions found in historical interpretations. In considering the degree of merit or demerit to be imputed, judgment must use reflection to compare and contrast relevant factors, such as obstacles faced and sacrifices made by agents, as well as their subjective state of mind.

When historians evaluate the behavior of human agents, their attributions concerning human deeds do not have a definitive juridical domain, such as a courtroom, for a framing context. As we saw, any historical agent participates in multiple productive systems whose competing influences need to be diagnosed. Historians do not simply consider what the law requires, nor are they in a position to judge strict culpability as a courtroom judge must. Moreover, establishing the degree of "merit or service the agent can be credited with (*zum Verdienst angerechnet werden kann*)"[27] is more difficult than Kant recognized. It requires a diagnostic use of reflective judgment because background conditions are so complex and have objective force. In addition to the constraining normative conditions that regulate the performance of human tasks, there are also restraining contextual factors that need to be assessed to determine how much of an obstacle they presented.

Since the attributive judgments of historians are oriented by larger worldly concerns than are juridical verdicts, they seldom arrive at final adjudicative

---

25. See *Metaphysics of Morals*, 19; *Ak* 6: 227. Onora O'Neill has claimed that determinant and reflective judgments are theoretical rather than practical. She argues that practical judgments are neither determinant nor reflective because they involve a decision about future action. When deciding what to do, there is not yet a given to judge, as in the case of standard determinant and reflective judgments. See Onora O'Neill, "Experts, Practitioners and Practical Judgement," *Journal of Moral Philosophy* 4 (2): 154–66. But not all practical judgments are future-directed. A legal verdict is a determinant judgment about a given deed that clearly has practical consequences. It seems equally true that certain reflective judgments about past human achievements can also have practical import.

26. *Metaphysics of Morals*, 19; *Ak* 6: 228 (emphasis added).

27. *Metaphysics of Morals*, 19 (translation revised); *Ak* 6: 228.

determinations. Thus often in a historical narrative, agents are held to account for their deeds and their consequences in a somewhat piecemeal manner by showing how they responded for good or ill to the multiple contexts in which they operated. Such attributive judgments will have to be given an overall reflective character that can incorporate more limited determinant claims. The authoritative adjudicative judgment of a courtroom judge has the aura of finality. By contrast, the attributive judgments of historians will be more provisional. But one thing they have in common is that they are both normative in considering what is required or expected of human subjects.

THE LEGITIMACY OF INTERPRETATIONS

One could attempt to model interpretive legitimacy on the public verdicts of the judge that have rightful force in executing the laws of a state. However, in discussing private rights later in the *Metaphysics of Morals*, Kant shows how it is possible to distinguish different levels of legitimacy. By differentiating such levels regarding the legitimacy of acquiring things, he indicates an approach that can be adapted to consider the legitimacy of interpretations as well. This would allow us to take ownership of an interpretation in a responsible way.

What then does the right of ownership mean? Kant claims that all human beings originally possess the earth as a common territory. This amounts to an innate a priori right of human beings "to be wherever nature or chance (apart from their will) has placed them."[28] The natural right to occupy such a contingent habitat (*Aufenthalt*) in this earthly territory (*Boden*)[29] does not however entail the further right to stay there and turn it into one's property (*Besitz*) or more lasting residence (*Sitz*).[30] Similarly, the natural right to possess corporeal things in space is provisional and can be transformed into an enduring individual right only under certain normative conditions.

Here again a geographical observation takes on a fundamental significance. Kant notes that if the earth were an "infinite (*unendliche*) plane, people could be so dispersed on it that they would not come into any community with another."[31] It is because the earth is a finite spherical surface that the problem of community must be confronted. The earth is a limited territory that must provide a supporting ground for all people. Because it is a finite common

---

28. *Metaphysics of Morals*, 50; *Ak* 6: 262.
29. See *Metaphysics of Morals*, 50; *Ak* 6: 262.
30. See *Metaphysics of Morals*, 50; *Ak* 6: 262.
31. See *Metaphysics of Morals*, 50 (translation revised); *Ak* 6: 262.

resource, the individual use of any part of it may negatively affect others. For Kant this means that if individual ownership of limited earthly resources is to attain any legitimacy, it must submit to certain bounds established by a community that has a worldly status.

The legal question here is how to justify making something one's own without depriving others of what they need. How can one's freedom to acquire something coexist with the freedom of others? According to Kant, there are three contextualizing moments in the process of legitimizing this kind of acquisition (*Erwerbung*) of property. The first moment is that of simply apprehending (*Apprehension*) "an object that belongs to no one" so that it does not "conflict with another's freedom."[32] Apprehending an object is a unilateral act of grasping it, which can claim to be a legitimate act if no one else is making a similar claim. But this can only mean that from the limited perspective of my local habitat I cannot see any counterclaim. It is a phenomenal claim where apprehension (*Apprehension*) as physical grasping would seem to be just as limited in scope as a single perspectival act of visual apprehension (*Auffassung*).

The second contextualizing moment of taking ownership involves designating it territorially as mine by an "act of choice (*Willkür*) to exclude everyone else from it."[33] Since Kant calls this an act of *Bezeichnung*,[34] phenomenal possession becomes a "designative possession" whereby I publicly declare that what was originally apprehended or taken control of should stay mine even if others may come upon it later and make a counterclaim. Designative possession can be seen as a bilateral declaration addressed to anyone who might subsequently be in a position to possess or occupy it. This second moment points to the realization that proper ownership is not merely a case of being able to hold on to something (*Inhabung*) but of having it (*Habens*) in my control (*Gewalt*).[35] To designate something as mine is less a claim on that object than a normative counterclaim against another subject.

Entitlement requires a third contextualizing moment of "appropriation (*Zueignung = appropriatio*) as an act of a general legislative will (*Willens*)"[36] that ensures external consent. Only when my choice to acquire something can be normatively justified as compatible with the general will of the overall com-

---

32. *Metaphysics of Morals*, 47; Ak 6: 258.
33. *Metaphysics of Morals*, 47; Ak 6: 258.
34. *Metaphysics of Morals*, 47; Ak 6: 258
35. See *Metaphysics of Morals*, 42; Ak 6: 233. We saw earlier that "having the world" in the sense of having it at our disposal was the aim of Kant's pragmatic anthropology.
36. *Metaphysics of Morals*, 47; Ak 6: 259.

munity will it be fully legitimate. This third or appropriative moment involves an omnilateral claim and amounts to what Kant calls an act of noumenal possession. To have an object legitimately as a "*possessio noumenon*"[37] is to have individual ownership publicly endorsed as compatible with the freedom of all. But this public legitimation presupposes a civil "domain" established by a constitution and laws reflecting a general will. The right of private ownership derives from a collective ownership, or as Kant puts it, "possession of an external object can originally be only a possession in common."[38]

Apprehending an object involves both cognizing it as a phenomenal object and grasping or treating it "as a material thing in itself (*Sache an sich selbst*)."[39] Appropriating it is to make it an "intelligible thing in itself (*Ding an sich selbst*)" on the basis of a civil constitution.[40] Kant assigns a material object a noumenal status if its availability for the free use of a subject is authorized by a constitution as being compatible with the freedom of all other subjects in the civil condition. This means that from the standpoint of his practical philosophy, the noumenal need not be transcendent. The intelligibility of legitimately appropriated objects is thought to be derivable from an omnilateral insight into their proper use in a nation state governed by laws.

By analogy, an interpretation may be regarded as legitimate if it can take its rightful place among other interpretations. If an orientational hermeneutics involves finding or creating one's place in the world, then we must expect a legitimate interpretation to defend its perspective on the world. To interpret the world is to claim ownership, so to speak, of a certain perspective on it. Ownership of an interpretation is unilaterally legitimate if it does not conflict with any of the information at hand; it will be bilaterally legitimate if it can defend itself against other local interpretations. What the omnilateral legitimacy of an interpretation would be is a more complex question.[41]

If the ideal of omnilateral legitimacy is thought to provide a Roycean conspectus, then we must reiterate our doubts about the feasibility of attaining

---

37. *Metaphysics of Morals*, 47; Ak 6: 259.
38. *Metaphysics of Morals*, 47; Ak 6: 258.
39. *Metaphysics of Morals*, 39; Ak 6: 249.
40. See *Metaphysics of Morals*, 137; Ak 6: 371.

41. The sequence of unilateral, bilateral, and omnilateral legitimacy could be compared to the sequence of being persuaded, being convinced, and the certainty of knowing that was discussed in chapter 4. Thus as interpretation attempts to move from private persuasion to conviction, which measures itself against the possible views of others, it also aims to approximate the ideal of knowledge that can actually take all others into account.

some "larger unity of consciousness."[42] Our being oriented to the world as such does not require us to lose our specific place in it and surrender our own unity of consciousness. The search for hermeneutic consent should not exclude the possibility of dissent. It is thus important to emphasize that we are not looking for an omnilateral interpretation but considering what it would mean for an interpretation to have omnilateral legitimacy. This would require, not the incorporation of all possible perspectives into itself, but taking cognizance of the "field" of possible perspectives. It should also be noted that for Kant the omnilateral legitimacy of the rightful appropriation of property does not presuppose actual approval by all fellow citizens. The civil constitution, and the general will that it represents, provide a formal consent, which in practice is executed by particular authorized functionaries.

Whereas appropriate ownership derives its legitimacy from an institutional authority representing the general will, in hermeneutics an appropriate interpretation can be said to derive legitimacy from the authority of disciplinary norms. This means that parameters can be established to delimit the field of all possible perspectives to those that meet some basic requirements of relevance and competence. Since interpretations that possess unilateral and bilateral legitimacy cannot claim to have surveyed the field of all competing perspectives made available by disciplinary standards, their authority is limited and comparable to *preliminary* judgments. By contrast, the omnilateral legitimacy of an interpretation asserts an authority approximating that of a *determinant* judgment in legal appropriation. The ideal here is to recognize the claims of all competing interpretations that have a disciplinary relevance while demonstrating the rightness of one's own interpretation and taking responsibility for it. While such a definitive outcome may be possible within a single lawful domain or discipline, it is by no means ensured if interpretation involves more than one such systematic context.

Because historical interpretations are about events that play themselves out in multiple contexts over time, the disciplinary ideal of determinant omnilateral legitimacy cannot be fully satisfied. However, the attributive imputations of historians can be expected to attain a reflective multilateral legitimacy where disciplinary authority will need to be matched by intersubjective authenticity. Here the necessary entitlement of rightful appropriation must be rethought in reflective terms to also take account of what is only contingently shared or held in common in historical life. This turn to reflective appropriation will allow us to place individual perspectives in a public framework, not

---

42. See chapter 3.

only when discussing authentic religious interpretations in the next section, but also when we go on later to consider the task of human characterization.

AUTHENTIC INTERPRETATION AND INTERSUBJECTIVE LEGITIMACY

The issue of the legitimacy of interpretations comes into focus when Kant turns to the problem of theodicy. In examining how theodicies can respond to a world filled with counterpurposive suffering and strife, Kant suggests a way of differentiating between determinant and reflective legitimacy. His initial concern in the 1791 essay "On the Miscarriage of All Philosophical Trials in Theodicy" is to distinguish between theodicies that deal with such a world by justifying (*rechtfertigen*) it from a divine perspective and those that come to terms with counterpurposiveness by interpreting (*auslegen*) what divine providence means from the human perspective.

Kant argues that theodicies using the justificatory approach would need to demonstrate "the world-author's moral wisdom in this sensible world" on the basis of "cognition of the supersensible (intelligible) world."[43] Unfortunately, we human beings do not possess that kind of cognition; thus the determinant legitimacy aimed at by justificatory theodicies cannot be attained. Therefore Kant declares that "all theodicy should really be the interpretation (*Auslegung*) of nature insofar as God manifests the intention of his will through it."[44] Interpretive theodicies consider manifestations of God's will in this world without making any speculative claims about the intelligible world. Given the futility of aiming at direct determinant proofs of God's wisdom, interpretive theodicies think of God in terms of a less direct legislative relation to this world.

According to Kant, every human "interpretation of the declared will of a legislator is either *doctrinal* or *authentic*."[45] Doctrinal interpretations consider the world as a theoretically experienceable work of God and aim to "extract from it God's final aim."[46] But there is no way we can determinately derive final purposes from a world that is cognized in terms of efficient causality. Final purposes can be made sense of only through practical reason and then related to the phenomenal world through reflective judgment.

---

43. Kant, "On the Miscarriage of All Philosophical Trials in Theodicy," in *Religion within the Boundaries of Mere Reason and Other Writings*, 24; *Ak* 8: 264.
44. "On the Miscarriage," 24; *Ak* 8: 264.
45. "On the Miscarriage," 24; *Ak* 8: 264.
46. "On the Miscarriage," 24; *Ak* 8: 264.

Authentic interpretation is then offered as an alternative that approaches God, not through how we perceive his works in nature, but through how he speaks to us as the voice of practical reason. In this way God can be thought of as the source of an "authoritative dictum or decree *(Machtspruch)*"[47] whose power is felt directly. Here Kant goes so far as to claim that to the extent that we conceive God rationally as a moral and wise Being, it is *"through our reason itself"* that God becomes the interpreter of his will as proclaimed in his creation."[48] It is through the medium of human practical reason that the divine will is interpreted authentically, so that we can become active participants in the process of giving voice to the ideal of the kingdom of ends. The prototype for this is legal or juridical hermeneutics, in which an authentic interpretation allows the authorship of a legislator to be passed on from generation to generation. In traditional philological criticism, authenticity demands evidence for something really *being* an original source, but in Kant's juridically informed philosophical critique, authenticity involves *having* an appropriate relation to an original source. This authenticating relation assigns interpretation the function of legitimating the results of exegesis.

Authentic interpretations go back to their source to make sense of counterpurposiveness in this world without relying on authoritative intermediaries, whether these be scientists who speculate about design in nature as the work of God or members of the clergy and their doctrinal power to instruct us to understand the voice of God as recorded in Biblical texts. In *Religion within the Boundaries of Mere Reason*, Kant criticizes how doctrinal interpretations have made sense of sacred texts in terms of a worldly institutional context. On this basis, churches have claimed the authority to interpret God's will through theological doctrines. However, as free human beings we have the obligation to strive for authentic interpretations of both human history and sacred texts that accord with our moral reason without appealing to institutional intermediaries. External authority must be replaced with internal authorship.

To more closely understand what Kant means by authentic theodicy we must reiterate that purposive world order can be discerned only through reflective judgment and that this must be assented to by feeling. Given the moral basis for a belief in divine providence, it makes sense that Kant stresses the role of conscience in his example of an authentic theodicy. In his reflections on the Book of Job, Kant points to the felt voice of conscience to authenticate Job's response to his suffering.

---

47. "On the Miscarriage," 24; *Ak* 8: 264.
48. "On the Miscarriage," 24 (translation revised); *Ak* 8: 264.

In trying to come to terms with the unexpected reversal of his fortune, Job turns to his friends for consolation. They are sure that he is being punished for past sins and advise him to plead for God's forgiveness even though neither he nor they were aware of any such sins. Their advice can be said to rely on either dogmatic assertions of a straightforward justificatory theodicy or doctrinal interpretations of institutional authority. By falling back on either a *dogmatic determination* that would require us to know God's will or a *doctrinal determinacy* rooted in belief in church teachings, they short-circuit the role that reflective judgment should play in interpreting his life situation.

After considering these pseudodeterminant explanations of his friends, Job has the courage to resist their advice and refuses to feign contrition for sins about which his conscience has not reproached him. In place of his friends' glib explanation of suffering as divine punishment, Job comes to a more reflective stance based on his own conscience and what his moral faith in God might reveal. Theoretically, the relation between God and his creation remains largely inscrutable, but Kant admires Job's honesty and truthfulness in openly admitting his doubts. He finds in Job's morally grounded faith the basis for an authentic theodicy because what matters is "the uprightness of the heart" in making sense of his life and "the shunning of feigned convictions that one does not really feel."[49] Only a genuinely felt moral interpretation of one's life can provide authentic self-understanding. The authenticity of how we interpret life is more about trueness to self than about determinate objective truth. Similarly, an authentic theodicy does not seek to divine the spirit of God's intentions for this world, but merely gives some "sense (*Sinn*) to the letter of his creation."[50] This is because when it comes to worldly purposes we cannot make determinant attributions but must content ourselves with more restrictive, morally based reflective ascriptions. Using the idiom of the *Critique of Judgment*, we can say that an authentic theodicy is an attempt to use our moral idea of God regulatively to orient our reflective judgments about purposiveness in nature and providence in history. An authentic interpretation is a reflective interpretation that aims at a legitimacy that is both true to the interpreter and open to intersubjective or public scrutiny.

Kant's best-known attempt at interpreting the meaning of human history is his essay "Idea for a Universal History with a Cosmopolitan Purpose" (1784). Here his reflections about human struggles and conflicts emerge from the idea that competitiveness is beneficial in that it can produce historical prog-

---

49. "On the Miscarriage," 26; *Ak* 8: 266–68.
50. "On the Miscarriage," 25; *Ak* 8: 264.

ress. What is needed is a cosmopolitan framework to keep competitiveness confined within lawful bounds. States must uphold the supremacy of law to protect individuals against criminal excess and should be organized as part of a worldwide confederation to preserve us from the excesses of war. This essay and another entitled "An Answer to the Question: 'What is Enlightenment?'" have provided significant points of reference for the discussion of the public use of our reason. In contrast to the attempt by theodicies to discern the original intent of a transcendent creator, the cosmopolitan intent is this-worldly and future-directed. But to the extent that Kant's cosmopolitan goal is governed by the idea of the sovereignty of law, reflection about history is bound by a framework, which, though not dogmatic, is determinant. There is thus a doctrinal aspect to Kant's cosmopolitan reflections about history. To move closer to an authentic secular history, we will specify Kant's views on immanent purposiveness and cultural development in the *Critique of Judgment* before considering what his *Anthropology from a Pragmatic Point of View* can contribute to the idea of human development.

PRAGMATIC CHARACTERIZATION

The immanent purposiveness that Kant ascribes to organisms is not intended to be explanative, but to make their workings reflectively intelligible to ourselves. This idea of immanent purposiveness can also be applied to the reflective interpretation of the complex interactions involved in history. The productive social systems of history, whether they be economic, political, or cultural, manifest differentiated contexts of immanent purposiveness within the overall nexus of history. Instead of accounting for what happens in a social system by some external end or higher telos, we can describe its behavior in the functional terms of an inner cooperation or adaptation of its parts to each other and their whole. This kind of functional description provides reflective "elucidation" (*Erörterung*) rather than determinant "explanation" (*Erklärung*).[51] When we turn to the human understanding of historical life based on our participation in productive systems, there is an imputation of inner connectedness that not only relates parts to a larger whole, but also recognizes this whole in the parts.

The productive interdependence elucidated in historical life need not remain heuristic and indeterminate as in the case of organic functional descrip-

---

51. *Critique of the Power of Judgment*, 281; *Ak* 5: 412-13. In Diltheyan terms, this distinction translates into that between structural understanding and law-based explanation.

tions, but can be articulated in terms of declared and explicit human ends. Here there will be a constant interplay of reflective and determinant judgment. We can see this in section 83 of the *Critique of Judgment* when Kant discusses the civilizing tasks of the culture of skill together with the emancipatory tasks of the culture of discipline. He arrives at the reflective judgment that human beings can be considered the ultimate purpose (*letzter Zweck*) of nature if they are primarily concerned with contributing to culture rather than to their own happiness. But this ascriptive imputation of reflective judgment is then strengthened into what I consider an attributive imputation by making it intersect with the moral determinant judgment that human beings are those creatures of nature who are inherently capable of setting themselves final purposes (*Endzwecke*) independently of nature. To the extent that we attain the capacity to become self-determining and partially independent of nature, we can cultivate whatever reflective purposiveness is discernible in nature and apply it to our own cultural ends.

It is through this reflective self-specification of our social and moral vocation that the defining theme of Kant's pragmatic anthropology comes into play. For many this will raise the question, what does Kant mean by the term "pragmatic?" In contemporary popular usage, the pragmatic has come to be commonly associated with expediency and the subordination of moral principle to present prudential concerns. Kant had lent credence to such a view in the *Critique of Pure Reason* when he placed the pragmatic at the rather lowly level of the prudential by writing that "the practical law from the motive of happiness is the pragmatic rule of prudence."[52] But subsequently, in his *Anthropology from a Pragmatic Point of View*, the pragmatic is reconsidered within the broader context of what man "can and should *make* of himself" as a free, responsible being. Now he stresses the "*pragmatic predisposition* to become civilized through culture, particularly through the cultivation of social qualities."[53] Insofar as the culture of skills is involved in the development of social life, the pragmatic still brings with it the prudential interest of the individual "to use other human beings skillfully for his purposes."[54] But to the extent that social development also includes the emancipatory tasks of the culture of discipline, the pragmatic moves beyond the prudential concern for individual happiness and becomes identified with the good of the human spe-

---

52. *Critique of Pure Reason*, A806/B834.
53. *Anthropology*, 228; Ak 7: 323.
54. *Anthropology*, 226; Ak 7: 322.

cies. Now the pragmatic cultivates "social relations"[55] and aims at a cultural "concord . . . among the living inhabitants of the earth."[56] Although culture is not yet truly moral, it allows for a mutual use of human beings for their common good.

Kant's pragmatic anthropology is meant to instruct us to become capable of "playing our part (*mitspielen*)"[57] in the world. It can also prepare for interpreting and evaluating the historical world by setting forth a normative characterization of its human participants and their ends. The *Anthropology* proceeds from the "Didactic" of Part I, which describes the capacities and practical qualities of human beings in general to the "Anthropological Characteristic" of Part II, which asks how the peculiarity of each human being is to be cognized. There Kant looks for distinctive human characteristics at the level of persons, the sexes, peoples, and the species. Of special interest is the way he correlates the character of individual persons with his final "portrayal (*Schilderung*) of the character of the human species."[58] What I will call "pragmatic characterization" interprets the predispositions of human nature as they are found in individuals in light of their full and "appropriate development"[59] in the human species. Characterization goes beyond description and exposition by looking for an individual's mode of thinking and feeling as indicative of what his or her "vocation" will be.[60] It is normative by promoting the vocation of the human species "with all prudence and moral illumination."[61] Kant summarizes his "characteristic of full human development (*Ausbildung*)" as a process in which "the human being is destined by his reason to live in a society with human beings and in it to *cultivate* himself, to *civilize* himself and to *moralize* himself by means of the arts and sciences."[62]

The projective quality that makes pragmatic characterization both interpretive and normative recalls Kant's statements in Part I about the faculty of using signs as connecting the given with the nongiven and the empirical with the intelligible. This is then taken up at the very beginning of Part II: "From a pragmatic consideration, the universal, *natural* (not civil) doctrine of signs (*semiotica universalis*) uses the word *character* in two senses," namely, to re-

---

55. *Anthropology*, 228; *Ak* 7: 323.
56. *Anthropology*, 226; *Ak* 7: 322.
57. *Anthropology*, 4; *Ak* 7: 120.
58. *Anthropology*, 235; *Ak* 7: 330.
59. *Anthropology*, 234; *Ak* 7: 329.
60. See *Anthropology*, 234; *Ak* 7: 329.
61. *Anthropology*, 233; *Ak* 7: 329.
62. *Anthropology*, 229–30; *Ak* 7: 324.

fer to "physical" and "moral" characters.[63] Physical character is man's way of sensing (*Sinnesart*), or the temperament that nature has given him; moral character is his mode of thinking (*Denkungsart*),[64] or what he has made of himself. A person's natural temperament has been traditionally characterized as dominated by one of four different traits,[65] but moral characterization is "singular (*einziger*)"; according to Kant, "a man either has it or has no character at all."[66] Individuals develop character in the morally relevant sense if their mode of thinking is derived from their own reason, rather than from without.[67]

Character formation does not involve imposing some external form on oneself, but results from finding one's inherent form and thoroughly working it out. We see here again that, contrary to widely received opinion, Kant does not always impose form from without. Indeed, his transcendental principle of reflective judgment seeks form from within by articulating what is given. Similarly, pragmatic characterization involves a mode of reflective articulation that projects the overall vocation of individual human beings. Like reflective specification it aims to transform merely ascriptive imputations into attributive imputations. But whereas reflective specification begins with universal determinations and works, as it were, from the top down, pragmatic characterization proceeds from the ground up. Instead of specifying or restricting objective systematic contexts, pragmatic characterization projects the completion of a subjective context.

Although Kant claims that character is "originality in the way of thinking,"[68] it would be naïve to assume that character develops purely by a process of completion from within. Thus the projection of the overall mind-set of an individual cannot be disassociated from external worldly influences, whether they be simply assimilated, cognitively acquired, or reflectively appropriated. To characterize someone's way of thinking is to project an interpretive idea for reflective attribution. Accordingly, Kant's goal of pragmatic characterization, as a "way of cognizing the interior of the human being from the outside,"[69] can

63. *Anthropology*, 185; *Ak* 7: 285.
64. See *Anthropology*, 185; *Ak* 7: 285.
65. The sanguine, melancholic, choleric, and phlegmatic. See *Anthropology*, 186-91.
66. *Anthropology*, 185 (translation revised); *Ak* 7: 285.
67. See G. Felicitas Munzel, *Kant's Conception of Moral Character: The Critical Link of Morality, Anthropology, and Reflective Judgment* (Chicago: University of Chicago Press, 1999) for an excellent study of the relevance of character formation.
68. *Anthropology*, 192; *Ak* 7: 293.
69. *Anthropology*, 183; *Ak* 7: 283.

only be approximated. There is no direct observational path to the attribution of character. The task of understanding others must proceed indirectly by interpreting their verbal and behavioral expressions.

Kant proposes that to interpret someone's character is to find the unifying principle of that person's way of thinking. Positively, this defines "an inner principle of conduct"[70]; negatively, it demands of persons that they "not dissemble."[71] Persons of moral character will express themselves by communicating truthfully. However, Kant is realistic enough to recognize that few if any individuals have fully attained this moral ideal of truthfulness. Thus the moral task of the *ars characteristica* of interpreting human beings by their voluntary expressions may be supplemented by a study of involuntary expressions. We should also consider "expressions that unintentionally betray one's inner life while intentionally lying about it."[72] What cannot be directly cognized about others because of their penchant for privacy, or directly communicated because of their urge to dissemble, may still be indirectly discerned or interpreted from their outward manifestations.

CONSCIENTIOUSNESS AND TRUTHFUL INTERPRETATION

The problem of judging the character of others and coping with their dissemblance leads back to an even more fundamental issue related to self-knowledge, namely, our capacity to deceive even ourselves. Kant is much concerned about this, especially in connection with his moral philosophy. In the *Critique of Pure Reason*, when he was most skeptical about self-knowledge, he wrote: "The real morality of our actions (their merit and guilt . . . remains entirely hidden from us."[73] Doubt about the possibility of access to our intelligible, moral character leads him to conclude that "attributive imputations (*Zurechnungen*) can be referred only to the empirical character."[74] If only an omniscient God can determinantly judge our intelligible, moral character, how are human beings to make any moral judgments about themselves on the basis of their empirical character?

Not until the *Metaphysics of Morals* of 1797 does Kant acknowledge that

---

70. *Anthropology*, 194; *Ak* 7: 294.
71. *Anthropology*, 193–4; *Ak* 7: 294.
72. *Anthropology*, 201 (translation revised); *Ak* 7: 301.
73. *Critique of Pure Reason*, A551/B579.
74. *Critique of Pure Reason*, A551/B579.

empirical character can provide a clue to our intelligible character. There he speaks of conscience and the feeling of respect as providing "an aesthetic receptivity (*ästhetische . . . Empfänglichkeit*)"[75] on the empirical level for the intelligible. These modes of aesthetic receptivity are important because practical reason requires us to judge our internal as well as external conformity to the moral law. The feeling of respect induced by moral reason is an indicator of an inner conformity to law. Conscience monitors the correlation between empirical and intelligible character and judges their conformity in our thought and action. What is felt by conscience cannot direct us determinately in deciding what to do, but it can orient us reflectively in how we interpret the world. Hermeneutically, conscience can be involved in assessing the fairness and justness of our historical attributions. The truthfulness of our interpretations will be the result of the conscientiousness of our dijudication in weighing the multiple factors and contexts in understanding historical events and situations.

For Kant our conscience (*Gewissen*) can be said to provide an ultimate subjective baseline for human judgment. He writes: "I can indeed be mistaken at times in my objective judgment as to whether something is a duty or not, [but] I cannot be mistaken in my subjective judgment as to whether I have submitted it to my practical reason (here in its role as judge) for such a judgment; for if I could be mistaken in that . . . there would be neither truth nor error."[76] Paying heed to one's conscience is an act of truthfulness that underlies the ability to distinguish between truth and falsity. We saw that an authentic theodicy aimed at a truthful interpretation of the meaning of our historical existence may make no pretense to know more than what is humanly possible. Any appeal to providence in history is obviously subject to doubt and could at most be ascriptive in its attempt to reconcile the field of the divine with the territory of the human. Only when we work at the more pragmatic level of human characterization can we hope to attain legitimate reflective attributions.

For a reflective perspective on history, it is important to correlate Kant's theoretical quest for objective certainty (*Gewissheit*) about a system of true knowledge (*Wissen*) with his worldly quest for wisdom rooted in the felt truthfulness of subjective conscientiousness (*Gewissenhaftigkeit*). Conscientiousness would then have the same indexical function in a normative sense

---

75. *Metaphysics of Morals*, 159 (translation revised); *Ak* 6: 399.
76. *Metaphysics of Morals*, 161; *Ak* 6: 401.

that reflexive awareness has for Dilthey in a hermeneutical sense.[77] The test of conscience provides the reflexive self-reference that can validate reflective interpretations. Kant directly links truthfulness and his appeal to conscience by calling truthfulness the "formal conscientiousness (*Gewissenhaftigkeit*)" of "not pretending to hold anything as true (*Fürwahrhalten*) that we are not conscious of holding as true."[78] For him this means that while it is not always possible to continue to "stand by the *truth* of what one says to oneself or to another (for one could be mistaken) . . . one can and must stand by the *truthfulness* of one's declaration or confession because one has immediate consciousness of this."[79] This tension between objective truth-content and subjective formal truthfulness is most evident when individuals make assertions and attributions based primarily on their own experience and their local surroundings. For the historical knowledge we are aiming at, however, the truth claims being asserted require more than formal validation; they require intersubjective legitimation. Here inward concerns about authenticity and truthfulness must be balanced with thorough anthropological characterizations that look outward. This means that, hermeneutically, conscientiousness also requires a more explicit worldly orientation.

In our discussion of the amphiboly of moral reflection, we spoke of conscience as offering a self-interpretation oriented by the limit of an ideal interpreter.[80] Then, in exploring what kind of meaning can be ascribed to human life on the basis of an authentic religious interpretation, conscience stood for honesty about the self and being open to public scrutiny. In the context of making attributive imputations about historical agents on the basis of pragmatic characterization, conscientiousness will need to take into account the standpoint of others through a kind of reflective equilibrium.

Kant's most general definition of conscience is "practical reason holding the human being's duty before him for his acquittal or condemnation."[81] Here the feeling of respect for moral law is reinforced by using the language of a court of law. Conscience creates a virtual courtroom in which it passes a verdict on itself. But it is not a unilateral judgment, for Kant adds that "to think of a human being who is *accused* by his conscience as *one and the same person* as

---

77. See above, 140–44. For more on how reflexive awareness functions and how it differs from reflective consciousness. see chapter 7.
78. "On the Miscarriage," 27; *Ak* 8: 268.
79. "On the Miscarriage," 27; *Ak* 8: 267.
80. See chapter 3.
81. *Metaphysics of Morals*, 160; *Ak* 6: 400.

the judge is an absurd way of representing a court."[82] Juridically, conscience will involve a multilateral interpretation, for it must consider the standpoints of the accusing self and the accused self as well as of their representatives as "prosecutor" and "defense counsel."[83] Conscientious dijudication demands a reflective equilibration that should be thorough in taking account of all the virtual courtroom participants and in rendering a verdict that represents more than a personal self.

As in the case of authentic interpretation, what makes possible a relation to other interpreters is Kant's idea of a publicly shared practical reason. Although conscience is about ourselves, it must be oriented toward a worldly forum. In examining our sense of what is right or just, Kant indicates that our capacity to transpose ourselves into the standpoint of others will be crucial. Actions that are all too easily found blameworthy in others may lead us to reconsider similar actions that are all too easy to condone in our own case.[84] To be conscientious in characterizing the decisions made by self and others is to place interpretation in a public and worldly framework of reflective appropriation. While we must consider the standpoint of others, the amphiboly of moral reflection reminds us that these references are initially mere external limits. It is the task of conscientious characterization to transform these negative limits into positive bounds that legitimate the priorities we establish among the relevant contexts for making responsible historical attributions.[85]

*

The quest of historians to gain a truthful and critical understanding of human and social affairs has been shown to proceed through the phases of assimilation, acquisition, and appropriation. Mindful of the immediacy and self-evidence of what has been assimilated about common life through elementary understanding, historians also tend to consider the cognitive findings of relevant human sciences about their subject matter for validation. Because the higher understanding acquired this way draws on disparate general contexts, it is important that it also be properly integrated into the structural nexus

---

82. *Metaphysics of Morals*, 189; *Ak* 6: 438.

83. *Metaphysics of Morals*, 189; *Ak* 6: 439.

84. See Kant, *Bemerkungen in den "Beobachtungen über das Gefühl des Schönen und Erhabenen,"* Herausgegeben und kommentiert von Marie Rischmüller. (Hamburg: Felix Meiner Verlag, 1991), 262.

85. See chapter 3.

of the historian's narrative. The aim then will be to produce a critical understanding whereby cognition is appropriated and legitimated as reflective knowledge.

To attain all this, it is necessary to delimit the already available disciplinary contexts of understanding by specifying the distinctive worldly circumstances that can legitimately bring particular historical attributions into focus and place them in a normative framework. The task of such supplemental specification is to provide the bearings that make it possible to transform merely ascriptive imputations based on individual reflective judgment into attributive imputations that tie into more generally testable determinant judgments. This intersection of the reflective and determinant must be referred back to the general systematic contexts of the human sciences and referred forward to the normative space of public deliberation that is necessary for critical understanding. Accordingly, the formal hermeneutic virtues of conscientiousness and truthfulness will apply to historical interpretation, not as mere modes of subjective self-assent, but as necessary for the judgmental consent to what has been reflectively appropriated.

CHAPTER 7

A Reflective and Diagnostic Critique

So far we have explored the tasks of hermeneutics largely in relation to a Kantian conception of philosophical critique, which exposes the conditions and sources of experience and at the same time defines the scope of our cognitive powers. Recalling distinctions made regarding the conditions and sources of hermeneutics, we can reiterate that any interpretation of human experience must take into account not only the formal and categorial conditions that make valid meaning-claims possible, but also the legitimating evidential sources of the content of actual truth claims. In examining the critical scope of our capacity to understand and assess the world, we spoke of the need to test the actual and contingent limits of experience in order to consider the boundaries of possible inquiry as well as the necessary bounds of intelligibility. In this chapter these analyses will be carried further and lead us to delineate three kinds of critique that can be applied to hermeneutics: constitutive, regulative, and reflective.

CRITIQUE AS CONSTITUTIVE AND CATEGORIAL

Kant conceived of critique as being constitutive or foundational for human experience. Accordingly, all scientific inquiry of nature must submit to a priori categorial rules established by the understanding. Kant also appeals to rational principles in projecting the overall organization of experience. This means that within the bounds of intelligibility set by reason, it can be stipulated, for example, that in the search for systematic order in nature, continuity among the species can be posited even when actual experience points to gaps between them. This constitutive and categorial critique has served as the background for developing our analysis of the kinds of judgment that need to be applied in hermeneutics. But if we are to work out more fully what a critical hermeneutics can be, we must also consider later relevant conceptions of critique. One of these will be a variant of Kant's constitutive approach as found in Dilthey. Another, to be discussed in the next section, will be a regulative kind of critique as exemplified by Habermas and Ricoeur. Finally, I will propose a reflective and diagnostic mode of critique.

Over against Kant's *Critique of Pure Reason* for the natural sciences, Dilthey designates his own project as a Critique of Historical Reason that is more encompassing in also investigating the human sciences and the categories needed for understanding historical life. He writes: "Kant's a priori is fixed and dead, but the real conditions of consciousness and its presuppositions, as I grasp them, constitute a living historical process, a development; they have a history, and the course of this history involves their adaptation to the ever more exact, inductively cognized manifold of sense-contents."[1]

In delineating his own enlarged critique of historical reason, Dilthey criticizes Kant for failing to take account of the conditions of consciousness in their full scope as they "are found in willing and feeling as well as in thinking."[2] A critique of historical reason will require moving beyond an epistemological standpoint, which only attends to the cognitive conditions of thinking. Dilthey admits that the "apparently fixed . . . conditions under which we think . . . can never be abrogated, because we think by means of them."[3] But he suggests that the import of these a priori conditions can change if we consider their relation to the other constituents that contribute to our knowledge of the world. The cognitive conditions that Kant put ahead of all empirical inquiry must be reconsidered in relation to the affective and volitional conditions that factor into our overall knowledge of the world. The real conditions of human knowledge are rooted in life itself.

For Kant the cognition-knowledge distinction was used to establish objective, formal categorial conditions, which are then followed up by the intersubjective testing of content. In place of such a synthetic or progressive epistemic critique that begins with validating cognitive conditions, Dilthey provides an analytic or regressive historical critique that retraces the legitimating presuppositions of human knowledge. We referred to this as an assimilative search

---

1. *Introduction to the Human Sciences*, SW 1, 500–01.
2. *Introduction to the Human Sciences*, SW 1, 501.
3. *Introduction to the Human Sciences*, SW 1, 501.

for the legitimating sources that inform the understanding of historical life. This search requires more than a philological critique of historical materials that tests whether these materials accrued over time are reliable and true to their origins. Philosophical critique must move from this kind of authentication of evidence to probe whether the way we assimilate historical sources will ultimately produce authentic understanding. That is, can the cognitive disciplines of the human sciences analyze and reorganize the assimilated content of life-knowledge into an acquisition that can be counted on to do justice to our historically funded world?

Just as past experiences contribute to the formation of the acquired psychic nexus that guides an individual's present and future experiences, so communities assimilate their inheritance in ways that inform our present. What is gathered from the past is a function of what we value and is organized and systematized in terms of its meaning for us. Thus we gradually filter out certain aspects of reality that are no longer useful or purposive for our lives. But what assurance do we have 1) that our acquired psychic nexus is representative of the larger world and 2) that the commonality of our background can be mined for something potentially universal? Dilthey's response is to look for mediating categorial structures as we move from the core life-concerns of individuals and established communities to the broader span of historical development.

In a world that is conceived in terms of external cause and effect relations, any purposive convergence among the events associated with individuals, communities, and historical movements would be as hypothetical as the purposiveness that Kant ascribes to organic nature. In the *Critique of Judgment*, Kant accepts purposiveness as merely a regulative supplement to the mechanical causality that is constitutive of nature in general. While Dilthey concedes that purposiveness may be ascribed to organic nature only in a regulative way, he maintains that the historical world that we help to shape manifests actual purposive connections. In history, as distinct from mere nature, we can experience an immanent purposiveness that is constitutive rather than regulative.

But this constitutive immanent purposiveness must be distinguished from the Hegelian trajectory of reason that continues to posit some final unifying goal for history. For Dilthey, human history is too complex to justify either a traditional external telos or the unfolding of some internal unitary narrative. Since we can come to terms with history only midstream, attributions of immanent purposiveness must be restricted in scope to specific historical formations and the sociocultural systems to which human beings contribute.

In interpreting history, the human sciences may appeal to causal conditions as well as to purposive relations. According to Dilthey, the natural science category of causality as manifested in outer experience and the human science category of purposiveness taken from inner experience are both rooted in a lived sense of efficacy that comes with our participation in the world as such. This leads him to posit efficacy as one of three underlying "categories of life" that inform our experience before any judgment is made whether it is to be contextualized as part of the domain of nature or part of the human territory of history.

Dilthey delineates his three basic life-categories of selfsameness, efficacy, and essentiality in the essay "Life and Cognition" (1892/93).[4] The term "life" refers to the overall givenness of reality. As the ultimate context of Dilthey's interpretive critique, life encompasses not only vital processes and historical forces, but also the mechanical causality of classical physics. The essay makes it clear that his concern is not merely to validate cognitive categories of the human sciences, such as purposiveness, over against the already accepted categories of the natural sciences, such as causality. His real project is to legitimate both kinds of cognitive categories by indicating their rootedness in categories of life that grasp the connectedness of experience before it is articulated in terms of the conceptual connections of either the natural or the human sciences. Categories of life designate points of convergence within experience rather than formal relations of thought.

Dilthey speaks of the categories of life as "the nexus of the given presupposed by all cognition."[5] The first of them, selfsameness (*Selbigkeit*), refers to a "togetherness" that "persists through time" and is characterized as a lived experience of "convergence."[6] The traditional philosophical substance-attribute relation is rooted in this life-category of selfsameness, which then finds its cognitive expression in either the objective unity of a natural substance or the subjective identity of an ego.

The life-category of efficacy (*Wirksamkeit*) referred to earlier involves a reciprocal nexus of doing and undergoing (*Wirken und Leiden*). This reciprocity of doing and undergoing experienced in life is then cognitively explicated in two more formal ways. In the natural sciences it is conceived as the external relations of cause and effect (*Ursache und Wirkung*) among objects and in the human sciences as internalizable relations of acting and suffering (*Tun und Leiden*) among subjects.[7] It is in the latter context of acting and suffering

---

4. Dilthey, "Life and Cognition," in *Understanding the Human World*, SW 2, 85–112.
5. See "Life and Cognition," SW 2, 85.
6. "Life and Cognition," SW 2, 88–91.
7. See "Life and Cognition," SW 2, 94–95.

that an indeterminate sense of purposiveness can emerge. The concept of a determinate purpose will come into play in relation to the final category of essentiality.

This third fundamental life-category of essentiality focuses on what is central in the overall context of life. As Dilthey writes, "life itself forces us to distinguish between what matters, what is decisive . . . and what can be dispensed with."[8] All lived experience manifests an inherent selectivity aimed at the essential, which in turn leads natural scientists to search for the elemental constituents of nature and philosophers to look either for the general marks of substances or the specific thisness of things. Yet the category of essentiality points to "an obscure core that is unfathomable for the intellect"[9] and needs to be further explored by the human sciences. It has a special relevance for the way we focus our understanding of history in separating what is transiently desirable from what has lasting value. In human practice it leads us to distinguish what is a mere means from what counts as an intrinsic end. Therefore we can say that the category of essentiality is more directly related to the human sciences than to the natural sciences. It lies at the basis of the three main categories of the human sciences, those of value, purpose, and most importantly, meaning. Essentiality brings out a convergence between certain core moments of life and its overall meaning.

Relative to our earlier statement that all of Kant's categories provide experience with meaning, it may seem unnecessary for Dilthey to propose a special category of meaning for the human sciences. However, we should note that for Kant the categories exhibit their meaning only indirectly through schemata that give them an objective reference. This schematic meaning or *Bedeutung* involves a *deuten* or pointing at objects. The *Bedeutung* of the human sciences does more than project a validating cognitive reference; it aims to provide a legitimating assessment of the value of things. Here meaning invokes the selectivity or sense of importance that marks the life-category of essentiality and has a clear bearing on the task of hermeneutics to establish priorities among relevant interpretive contexts.

In that both Kant and Dilthey conceive categories to be constitutive for experience, they can be said to make critique foundational for hermeneutics. They establish parameters of intelligibility that place bounds on the possible functions of interpretation. Whereas Kant's categories structure the cognitive understanding of the discursive intellect (*Verstand*), Dilthey's life-categories

---

8. "Life and Cognition," *SW* 2, 101–102.
9. "Life and Cognition," *SW* 2, 108.

already apply to prediscursive lived experience and are operative at all levels of understanding (*Verstehen*), including the elementary understanding of everyday life-knowledge. The life-categories of selfsameness, productivity and essentiality lay out (*aus-legen*) the overall nexus of life before the human sciences interpret (*auslegen*) and specify its historical manifestations. Since Dilthey's categories are not just about cognitive validity and are also considered for their import for the reflective knowledge of historical life, he does not delimit a fixed set of human science categories.

CRITIQUE AS REGULATIVE AND EMANCIPATORY

Another approach to the relation between critique and hermeneutics views critique as regulative rather than constitutive. Kant at times used reason regulatively to further the idea of an overall systematic or purposive order, and we saw that concepts can be applied regulatively when they are extended beyond the bounds of their proper domain in order to project ideal limits. Thus when the category of causality is extended beyond the bounds of the mechanical order of nature and directed at some ideal final end or future telos, it no longer functions as a constitutive concept, but as a regulative idea. Even when a telos is not external, but regarded as the immanent purposiveness of an organism, there is a projection of an ideal limit. Kant initially characterizes each part of an organism "as existing for *the sake of the others and of the whole*."[10] But by itself this characterization can apply as well to the parts of a clock or other humanly designed mechanisms, so that we must also think of each part of an organism as an organ capable of coproducing the other parts. An organism is thus redefined as both "an *organized* and a *self-organizing* being"[11] that can sustain itself. There being no known living being that can indefinitely organize itself, it follows that the regulative idea of a self-organizing being represents a limit for thought.

Traditionally, critique was concerned to define the bounds of our cognitive faculties in terms of the ideal medium of reason. But once critique is also related to some life-based medium, it begins to assume a more practical role. We saw Dilthey turn to the historical medium of objective spirit as the repository of human practices and achievements.[12] To the extent that this medium nurtures human development, it constitutes an important resource for historical

---

10. *Critique of the Power of Judgment*, 245 (translation revised); *Ak* 5: 373.
11. *Critique of the Power of Judgment*, 245; *Ak* 5: 374.
12. See chapter 1.

knowledge. This inherited medium provides the local context of commonality relative to which we can understand how human beings come to define their individuality as well as generate more universal goals.

Jean-Paul Sartre's "practico-inert"[13] as the background of social and political life represents in effect a reformulation of Dilthey's objective spirit and provides for the transition from a constitutive to a regulative critique. The practico-inert serves as a more concrete inherited medium against which to exert critical leverage in light of a regulative idea or ideal. Whereas constitutive critiques delimit what is possible on the basis of universal conditions applicable to all contexts, regulative critiques tend to project what is possible over against actual contexts that have proved to be limiting. In relation to social and political theory, regulative critique calls for the capacity to distance oneself from one's limiting situation and to seek emancipation from alienating circumstances. The link between regulative critique and emancipation has its background in Marx's critique of the inequalities and divisions of a capitalist society and his call for a more equitable communal order. The Marxist focus on the economic medium of human exchange may be socially useful, but it leaves little room for philosophy and hermeneutics. As Marx himself put it: "Philosophers have *only interpreted* the world, in various ways; the point, however, is to *change* it."[14]

Jürgen Habermas and Paul Ricoeur are important in this regard because they reaffirm the contributions of hermeneutics to the task of emancipating human beings from repressive forces. By turning to an early programmatic work by Habermas and a series of essays by Ricoeur, we can see how they reconceive an emancipatory regulative critique in light of twentieth-century developments in the human and social sciences. They focus especially on advances in linguistics and psychoanalysis to argue for the possibility of supplementing traditional hermeneutics with a depth hermeneutics.

In *Knowledge and Human Interests,* Habermas examines three ways in which human beings have exerted and expressed themselves to advance the human species, namely, through work, language, and power. We see here both a further specification of what is inherited as a medium of commonality and a move beyond the practico-political interests of Marx and Sartre that is able

---

13. See Jean-Paul Sartre, *Critique of Dialectical Reason*, trans. Alan Sheridan Smith, vol. 1 (London: Verso, 1991), 319.

14. Karl Marx, *Theses on Feuerbach*, XI, in Robert Tucker, ed. *The Marx-Engels Reader* (New York: W.W. Norton & Co., 1972), 109.

to differentiate among the various human interests that aim to transform the lifeworld. This early book by Habermas serves as a useful point of reference because it assigns distinctive cognitive interests to the medial efficacy of work, language, and power. Work is aligned with the theoretical and technical interests to control nature that characterize the project of the natural sciences. Language is aligned with the practical interest to facilitate communicative action that is considered to be central to the hermeneutical or human sciences. Finally, power is aligned with the critical interest to emancipate ourselves from the institutional constraints that have diminished our lives and alienated us from each other.

These technical, hermeneutical, and critical human interests invoked by Habermas are not conceived reductively, but as having their source in human reason. The industrial revolution made it possible to extract work from its local empirical context and refashion it as a mode of technological control over nature's resources in general. Consequently, the natural sciences are technical as well as theoretical by encompassing the "learning processes of socially organized labor."[15] Although the rules of inquiry of these sciences are no longer purely transcendental, they nevertheless "have a transcendental function" that arises from the technological "structures of human life."[16] For their part, the hermeneutic human sciences "are directed toward the transcendental structure of various actual forms of life" that are relevant to "action-orienting mutual understanding."[17] Here the practical-hermeneutical interest in communicative action demands inquiry into "the grammar of ordinary language, which simultaneously governs the non-verbal elements of a habitual mode of life-conduct or practice."[18]

But neither the technological natural sciences nor the hermeneutical human sciences explore the overall framework uniting interest and reason in what Habermas calls the "self-formative process"[19] that defines the human species as such. In considering the power to shape our own history, Habermas moves away from methodology in the epistemological mode to critical self-reflection. A similar transition from epistemology as a theory of cogni-

---

15. Habermas, *Knowledge and Human Interests*, trans. Jeremy J. Shapiro (Boston: Beacon Press, 1972), 194.
16. *Knowledge and Human Interests*, 194.
17. *Knowledge and Human Interests*, 195.
18. *Knowledge and Human Interests*, 192.
19. *Knowledge and Human Interests*, 197.

tion to the knowledge of self-reflection (*Selbstbesinnung*) had already been proposed by Dilthey.[20] There is even a resemblance in their rationale for such a turn to self-reflection. For Dilthey, self-reflection "seeks not only the conditions that give our statements about what is real their evident certainty, but also the conditions that guarantee the will and its rules their rightness or justness."[21] For Habermas self-reflection is the critical process in which "knowledge for the sake of knowledge comes to coincide with the interest in autonomy and responsibility."[22]

To the extent that the subject can become "transparent to itself in the history of its genesis,"[23] Habermas considers self-reflection to be an "emancipatory" experience. When it is applied to actual situations, self-reflection is said to hold the promise of releasing us "from dependence on hypostatized powers."[24] This leads Habermas to delineate a third set of "critical" sciences that share with philosophy an emancipatory cognitive interest. Whereas the interests of the natural and human sciences are about the preservation and reproduction of life, the interests of the critical sciences are radically reconstructive.

Habermas identifies the critical social sciences and the "depth hermeneutics" of psychoanalysis as dealing with situations where human action and communication are constrained by the power relations of repressive institutions. These disciplines analyze instances of pathological behavior and deformed communication in light of the regulative idea of unconstrained communicative action. In his effort to exemplify emancipatory regulative critique, the major focus is on how psychoanalytic theories and techniques respond to crisis situations where normal understanding has broken down. Psychoanalytic interpretations provide an interesting model because they involve both causal explanation and reflective understanding. They appeal to explanative hypotheses about the unconscious and repressed instinctual drives to account for pathological and antisocial behavior. But these explanations cannot have a curative effect unless they are translated through dialogue between the analyst and the patient into a form that can be reflectively appropriated and understood by the patient in relation to the narratives of his or her everyday life. To that extent psychoanalysis is a kind of meta-hermeneutic.

20. See chapter 1.
21. *Introduction to the Human Sciences*, SW 1, 268.
22. *Knowledge and Human Interests*, 197–98.
23. *Knowledge and Human Interests*, 197.
24. *Knowledge and Human Interests*, 310.

Liberation from pathological obsessions involves breaking patterns of repetitive behavior that impede the maturation of the full self. Marxists have argued that such vicious cycles do not occur solely in our private lives. Since many modes of public behavior, whether economic or political, often reveal similar pathologies, Habermas claims that the depth hermeneutics of psychoanalysis offers a new critical paradigm that the social sciences can adapt for their own ends. For the public sphere, Habermas revives the Marxist language of "ideologically frozen relations of dependence"[25] that sustain illusions about our social institutions. Ideological critique is considered necessary to separate those stable institutions that legitimately express "invariant regularities of social action as such"[26] from those that merely reify existing privileges and produce alienation.

Habermas's multileveled approach to interpreting the self-formative processes of human history in *Knowledge and Human Interests* contains many provocative insights. However, it still leaves us with a deficient conception of hermeneutics and the human sciences. To characterize the human sciences as centered solely on the practical concerns of communicative action and to align their hermeneutics primarily with the precritical "reflexivity of ordinary language" and "nonverbal life-expressions" of habitual practice is to relegate the hermeneutical human sciences to the level of elementary understanding. But the human sciences are not confined to the concerns of "habitual life conduct" and ordinary discourse. They must survey the full scope of human activity and achievements, and hermeneutics must address the complexities and ambiguities that arise in all human life with the methodological tools of higher understanding provided by disciplinary theoretical analysis.

Self-reflection and critique are not unique to Habermas's "critical" sciences and their exposure of distorted communication. Critical reflection also plays a role in the human sciences as they probe possible sources of transformative insight and alternative practice. But Habermas renders the hermeneutics of the human sciences merely preparatory and precritical by declaring the need for a special depth hermeneutics to initiate critique. His extensive explorations of the emancipatory function of psychoanalysis point to a depth hermeneutics that draws its critical credentials from "meta psychological basic assumptions about linguistic structure and action."[27] In acknowledging

---

25. *Knowledge and Human Interests*, 310.
26. *Knowledge and Human Interests*, 310.
27. *Knowledge and Human Interests*, 272.

that his self-reflective critique appeals to "meta-theoretical"[28] claims, Habermas offers an essentially speculative model of regulative critique. In his later writings, these meta-psychological speculations about a depth hermeneutics are replaced with more formal procedures for regulating communicative action. More emphasis is placed on the differentiation of social systems, but the hermeneutics of the human sciences remains at the level of pre-theoretical knowledge.[29]

Paul Ricoeur differs from Habermas in providing a more encompassing view of the hermeneutics of the human sciences. Going beyond the elementary analysis of habitual life and ordinary discourse, Ricoeur stresses the theoretical advances of hermeneutics made possible by psychoanalytic theory, linguistic analysis, and structuralism. However, the relation between ideological critique and hermeneutics remains somewhat problematic in Ricoeur. On the one hand, he sees critique as arising from the experience of alienation. Thus he agrees with Habermas that critique is emancipatory and derives its universality from a "regulative ideal of an unrestricted and unconstrained communication."[30] On the other hand, Ricoeur characterizes hermeneutics as stemming from the experience of belonging. This reflects his acceptance of the Gadamerian position that hermeneutics is based on the experience of belonging to a tradition and establishes its own claim on universality through dialogue and a fusion of horizons. Thus Ricoeur argues that hermeneutics and critique will always remain distinct but must not be totally separated.

Although he seems content to regard critique as a supplement outside the purview of hermeneutics, Ricoeur speaks of the "recognition of a critical instance" in interpretation as a "vague desire constantly reiterated within hermeneutics."[31] One of the counterparts of emancipatory critique that Ricoeur finds in hermeneutics is the technique of distanciation, which focuses on the objectifications of human experience. He credits Dilthey's late hermeneutics with anticipating this technique of distanciation by having "located the specificity of interpretation . . . in the phenomenon of fixation by writing, and more generally, of inscription."[32] However, he faults Dilthey

---

28. *Knowledge and Human Interests*, 272.

29. Habermas, *The Theory of Communicative Action*, vol. 2, trans. Thomas McCarthy (Boston: Beacon Press), 1987, 153.

30. Paul Ricoeur, *From Text to Action, Essays in Hermeneutics*, II, trans. Kathleen Blamey and John B. Thompson (Evanston, IL: Northwestern University Press, 1991), 286.

31. *From Text to Action*, 295.

32. *From Text to Action*, 297.

for instituting a dichotomy between understanding and explanation that excludes explanation from the human sciences. This must be overcome, he argues, if "hermeneutics is to account for a critical instance in terms of its own premises."[33]

Ricoeur's criticism alludes to the fact that in an early essay on descriptive psychology, Dilthey had opposed explanation to understanding, and by implication to interpretation as well. With the motto "Nature we explain, but psychic life we understand,"[34] Dilthey asserted that the basic structures of psychic life can be described and understood without first appealing to explanative causal hypotheses based on the natural sciences. But in the same essay he makes it clear that explanations do have a role in psychology and other human sciences so long as they are not considered foundational. Ricoeur also mistakenly ascribes to Dilthey the "conviction that any explanatory attitude is borrowed from the methodology of the natural sciences and illegitimately extended to the human sciences."[35] A more appropriate way to characterize Dilthey's approach is to say that in the human sciences, the reflective concerns of understanding must provide the framework for seeking explanations. Any natural science-type causal explanation could accordingly be restricted in its scope. Thus while Dilthey rejects the possibility of there being overarching historical explanative laws like those of nature, he thinks it proper to explore laws of development within specific social, economic, and cultural spheres. At times he even broaches the idea of sui generis human science explanations.

Regarding his own hermeneutical position, Ricoeur states that "the appearance of semiological models in the field of the text...."[36] convinced him that all explanation is not naturalistic or causal but may be structural instead. Thus he proposes that linguistic interpretation is itself a structural form of explanation. Moreover, he goes so far as to suggest that structural explanations can dispose of the need for understanding. Through such explanations we can interpret linguistic texts without appealing to psychological understanding.[37]

Ricoeur's criticisms overlook the structural potential of Dilthey's theory of understanding as it was developed beyond its psychological beginnings. The understanding that Ricoeur would remove from interpretation is the psycho-

33. *From Text to Action*, 299.
34. Dilthey, "Ideas Concerning a Descriptive and Analytic Psychology," in *Understanding the Human World*, SW 2, 119.
35. *From Text to Action*, 299.
36. *From Text to Action*, 299.
37. *From Text to Action*, 112.

logical act of attempting "to coincide with the inner life of the author."[38] However, Dilthey himself came to renounce the view that understanding is about reproducing the subjective intention of the author, and made it clear that to understand authors is to determine the meaning of their output. Even what he calls "reexperiencing" (*Nacherleben*) in his late writings does not involve a reproductive coincidence with other states of mind. Reexperiencing is conceived as a supplement to understanding that makes possible the transition to interpretation. Like Kierkegaard, Dilthey claims that understanding as such is retrospective. It requires the capacity to stand back and expand the structural context of one's present experience to take into account other positions. Understanding involves a "transposition" or a kind of contextual reorientation of our experience. What differentiates reexperiencing from understanding is a forward interpretive movement. The contextualizing hermeneutical circle that first curves backward now moves forward. Reexperiencing is not the literal reliving of someone else's experience, but a kind of completion of our own understanding that interprets the other's experience. Both understanding and interpretation can be described as ways of structurally articulating meaning in relation to various contexts. But because these different contexts engender quite discrete discourses, the hermeneutical circle will inevitably develop jagged edges that require judgmental assessment to be smoothed out.

When Ricoeur contends that structural interpretation conceived as a mode of explanation can dispense with understanding, he is looking to the structuralist explanations associated with linguistics. Instead of focusing on the meaning structures of sentences, linguistics analyzes elements such as phonemes and morphemes, about whose meaning nothing need have been established. Or as he writes, "linguistics considers only systems of units devoid of proper meaning, each of which is defined only in terms of its difference from all the others."[39] Such differential structures abstract from content and provide not meaning but an intelligibility that concerns formal, often polar, relations. One commentator on structuralism has claimed that its structures are labyrinthic networks in which each node is itself a network.[40] Every relation leads away from itself and needs to be translated or remapped.

By moving toward this kind of structuralism, Ricoeur seems to be departing from his own Husserlian phenomenological writings in which he had

---

38. *From Text to Action*, 112.
39. *From Text to Action*, 113.
40. See Michel Serres, *Hermes: Literature, Science, Philosophy* (Baltimore: Johns Hopkins University Press, 1982), 16.

adopted a more Diltheyan conception of structure compatible with the understanding of meaning. Phenomenological and meaning structures articulate the overall nexus of our experiences and are explicated from what is given in life. A phenomenologically informed hermeneutics conceives structure holistically, but Ricoeur's turn to structuralism leads him to posit binary oppositions and generate a dialectical play of structural polarities. His hope here is to find that "under certain conditions . . . units of language of a higher order than the sentence, display organizations comparable to those of . . . units that are of a lower order than the sentence."[41] The higher units that are to be illuminated by such analogical transference are narrative and mythic structures. Ricoeur admits that some analogies generated here may be sterile and artificial. Structuralist analysis must thus be contained and relegated to a "working hypothesis" stage in the movement from surface to depth interpretation.[42]

The opposition between surface and depth is one of Ricoeur's primary hermeneutic polarities and is displayed in another way when he delineates an opposition between two modes of hermeneutics: 1) a restorative hermeneutics, which enriches understanding by going back to historical sources and 2) a demystificatory hermeneutics, which seeks explanations that expose hidden motives and forces.[43] He locates the primary exemplars of restorative hermeneutics in the works of Dilthey, Heidegger, and Gadamer and the best instances of demystificatory interpretations in the unmasking efforts of Marx, Nietzsche, and Freud. The latter group is also characterized as offering a hermeneutics of suspicion. Ricoeur proposes that the binary opposition of demystification and restoration drives interpretation as such and speaks of the "double motivation" of hermeneutics: the "willingness to suspect "coupled with the "willingness to listen," a "vow of rigor" with a "vow of obedience."[44] However, by pairing listening with obedience on one side as opposed to rigor and suspicion on the other, Ricoeur creates the impression that true listening lacks rigor, and by implication, is uncritical. But it is possible to listen critically with an open and disciplined mind. Moreover, it limits our understanding of rigor to conceive it negatively as a mode of demystification.

Ricoeur's hermeneutics of suspicion shares some features with emancipatory critique, but in the essay "Hermeneutics and the Critique of Ideology,"

---

41. *From Text to Action*, 114.

42. *From Text to Action*, 121.

43. See Ricoeur, *Freud and Philosophy*, trans. Dennis Savage (New Haven, CT: Yale University Press, 1970), 27.

44. See *Freud and Philosophy*, 27.

he attenuates that relation by speaking of a "gulf" between the hermeneutical project that "puts assumed tradition above judgment" and the critical project that "puts reflection above institutionalized constraint."[45] With this formulation, he goes beyond the general idea that hermeneutics comes from the experience of belonging to a tradition and in effect aligns himself with Gadamer's stronger claim that hermeneutics is a mode of service to tradition. Hermeneutics is now regarded as the retrospective handmaiden of tradition, while critical theory is viewed as governed by future-directed regulative ideas. According to Ricoeur, they cannot be encompassed by some overarching system, for "each speaks from a different place."[46]

To say that tradition stands above judgment is to overlook the hermeneutic potential of judgment to expose traditional institutionalized constraints. At one point, Ricoeur does make an effort to lessen the alleged gap between hermeneutics and social critique. He asserts, quite rightly, that emancipatory critique is not just a regulative idea still to be realized, but has already been practiced in the past. There is, according to Ricoeur, a tradition of critique, which he traces back not only to the Enlightenment, but also to the Bible. Thus he muses that "perhaps there would be no more interest in emancipation, no more anticipation of freedom, if the Exodus and the Resurrection were effaced from the memory of mankind."[47] However, this only illustrates how an awareness of past events and movements may provide inspiration for the critical project, not yet how hermeneutics itself can contribute to critique.

In sum, the emancipatory critique proposed by Habermas and adapted by Ricoeur goes beyond a constitutive critique and is regulative by projecting an ideal field of nondistorted communication as the condition of political liberation. It takes the idea of the autonomy of the moral individual in Kant, who still operates within the constraints of established laws and institutional powers, and expands it into an ideal public freedom unconstrained by arbitrary authority. As with all regulative uses of reason, the projection of nondistorted communication is speculative and can only make as-if determinations. However desirable the ideal of nondistorted communication and its correlate of "undeformed public spheres"[48] may be, it needs to be supplemented by hermeneutic considerations about the feasible alternatives in a given situation. This requires judgment.

---

45. *From Text to Action*, 290.
46. *From Text to Action*, 294.
47. *From Text to Action*, 306.
48. Habermas, *Between Facts and Norms*, 148.

CRITIQUE AS REFLECTIVE AND JUDGMENT-CENTERED

A third possibility to be proposed is that of a reflective critique that focuses on the role of judgment in interpretation. This kind of critique is neither pre- nor post-hermeneutical but will be thoroughly hermeneutical in that no function of understanding is assumed to be either fully grounded from below, as by a constitutive critique, or rationally directed from above, as by a regulative critique. A hermeneutic critique will not search for a priori categories constitutive of all experience but reflect instead on priorities among possible interpretive contexts for a given experience. Thus the overarching framework still implicit in Dilthey's Critique of Historical Reason will need to be specified as a series of reflective contexts relevant to understanding and interpretation in a Critique of Historical Judgment.[49]

Judgment must play a central diagnostic role in hermeneutics as we move from our initial orientation to the world in order to critically assess the historical situation and our possible actions. The diagnostic function of reflective critique is essential for the mediation of theory and practice needed to apply regulative or emancipatory critique. While theory may keep a hypothetical or speculative distance from reality and practice may impose our will on things, judgment and reflection give us the capacity to take the measure of a situation and consider an appropriate response.

In moving toward a judgment-centered hermeneutics, we can reformulate some of Kant's ideas regarding the regulative use of reason in light of their relevance for a reflective critique. Since many of Kant's assertions about purposive order are both "regulative" and "reflective," it has been commonly assumed that these two terms mean roughly the same thing. However, it should be noted that the regulative nature of a claim pertains to its objective reference and its reflective nature to its subjective status. By itself the regulative use of a concept makes hypothetical explanative claims about objects. Thus Kant's teleological idea of purpose counts as a regulative expansion of the explanative concept of causality. But when he describes organisms as having the immanent purpose of self-development and preservation, they are made sense of from the standpoint of human reflection without a determinant explana-

---

49. These contexts can be said to center in on themselves like immanently purposive systems. But because they intersect with other contexts, these centered contexts may not need to be deconstructively decentered if a reflective hermeneutics can heuristically recenter them.

tion. This reflective sense of purposiveness is intersubjectively legitimate but makes no objective explanative claim.

All this raises a significant point of difference for how regulative ideas and the power of reflective judgment are to be applied to hermeneutics. Whereas regulative ideas project broad speculative claims, the task of reflective judgment is to consider whether certain contextual specifications can make these claims less hypothetical. Thus the reflective specification of the idea of purpose should make no claim to be legislative for the domain of nature, but restrict itself to providing functional descriptions about the territory of human experience. As applied to individual organisms or social systems, the general idea of teleology can be reflectively specified in terms of how they organize themselves to develop over time and to confront challenges to their survival. When reflective judgments expand our mode of thinking in this more cautious way they can be appropriated as legitimate interpretations by hermeneutics.

Earlier we made reference to regulative critiques that project what is possible over against an actual limiting situation such as alienation in capitalist economics. A reflective critique must be even more specific by also taking account of the particular circumstances involved in human alienation. Whereas the solutions to economic and political conflicts proposed by regulative critique are still universalistic in kind, reflective critique must offer solutions that take into account the specific worldly locus of those who suffer from alienation. Ultimately, expansive regulative ideas and self-binding reflective judgments must be made to work together to serve hermeneutics in adjusting its focus as it searches for the appropriate meaning contexts for interpreting historical phenomena. A reflective hermeneutical critique must make the best of the fact that what is to be understood historically is embedded in a series of social, cultural, and regional contexts, some of which can be examined in systematic disciplinary terms and some of which cannot. Working in medias res, diagnostic judgment will have the task of distinguishing these historical and disciplinary frames of reference and indicating points of their possible intersection.

What is needed for hermeneutics is a judgment-based critique that can be reflectively oriented to regulative ideals without being determinantly directed by them. If historical and disciplinary frames of reference are related to such a regulative horizon, then one of the tasks of a critical hermeneutics will be to specify universal ideals into reflective exemplars for judgment, just as reflective schematization was used to specify a normative ideal of beauty into individual exemplars. Reflective schematization, which explores the most appropriate context for particulars, is hermeneutically relevant in allowing us to transpose traditional cultural products from their contingent local habitat to the larger territory of the human community from which we can evaluate whether or not they are worth emulating.

We also indicated that critical philosophy is reflective insofar as it focuses on the setting of priorities. Accordingly, a critical hermeneutics will have to coordinate various spheres of discourse and to consider if any priorities can be set among them for examining a specific theme. One could argue, for example, that it is necessary to understand the discourse of juridical duties before we can make sense of the language of duties of virtue, because legal rules establish the minimum standard of what is right as the basis for reflection on the good.

The task of legitimating hermeneutics has been explored by means of an expanded theory of judgment in which normativity displays itself in acts of evaluative dijudication and determinant adjudication. Within a given determinant context, evaluative dijudication can simply decide between the available alternatives. But when it comes to historical attributions, reflective judgment becomes important in considering what other contexts are relevant. We have spoken of reflective judgment mostly as searching for not yet available universals. However, as Kant makes clear in *The Jäsche Logic*, the search for universality involved in reflective judgments can proceed "either 1) from *many* to *all* things of a kind, *or* 2) from *many* determinations and properties, in which things of one kind agree, *to the remaining ones, insofar as they belong to the same principle*."[50] The first mode is an inductive inference, the second an inference from analogy in accordance with a "principle of specification."[51] Whereas induction argues from the premise that many x's are y to the conclusion that all x's are y, specification by analogy reflects on the partial similarity of things to test for further similarity. Although both reflective inferences are oriented to reason, they are empirical and move beyond abstract universality. It follows then that an inductive reflective judgment really moves from particularity to "general rather than universal propositions"[52] and that reflective specification really proceeds from some parts of a contextual whole to other parts. Reflective specification can test for the systematic relevance of a context and lead to the judgment that another interpretive context is needed to more fully account for the evidence.

It is this empirical reach of reflective specification that can prove to have systematic import for reinterpreting experience. Kant himself supplemented his determinant *architectonic* project of subordinating particular laws to

---

50. *Lectures on Logic*, 626; *Ak* 9: 132.
51. *Lectures on Logic*, 626; *Ak* 9: 133.
52. *Lectures on Logic*, 627; *Ak* 9: 133.

higher universal principles with a reflective *tectonic* project of adjusting systematic part-whole relations to search for generic relations among laws.[53] Initially, the reflective specification of universals may produce a tectonic adjustment among some of the parts of a whole, but it can also force a revision of the higher-level laws of a system to take account of newly established lower-level regularities. Thus Kant allows a universal concept to be made more specific "by adducing or taking into account (*anführen*) the manifold under it."[54] This goes beyond the commonly held assumption that specification applies solely to the particulars that may be subordinated to a universal. Instead, the reflective specification involved in systematization can transform an abstract universal into what Hegel would call a "concrete universal."

If the universal sought by reflective judgment proves to be an already available principle that needs to have its own content specified, reflective specification becomes a *reflexive* self-specification. We will see that this idea of the reflective going over into the reflexive can provide critical leverage for reassessing accepted principles and historical precedents.

FROM REFLECTION TO REFLEXIVITY

Reflective specification involves not only a correlation of universals and particulars, but also a coordination of parts and wholes. For historical interpretation, which is inherently an indirect mode of understanding, these processes are mediated by a variety of contexts. The complexity of history makes it necessary to frame our historical understanding in terms of distinct interpretive contexts, some of which are established by disciplinary or systematic considerations while others are based on temporal and regional circumstances. When relevant contexts, such as social and cultural systems, are reflectively coordinated and shown to intersect in a specific historical occurrence, we obtain the diagnostic focus needed for a legitimate interpretation and a critical assessment.

As indicated above, no hermeneutical meaning claim should be exempt from considering all available empirical evidence and appropriate contexts in the search for its truthfulness. This normative demand for truthfulness involves the expectation that individual assent be coordinated with public consent.[55] However, all efforts to acquire public consent for an interpreta-

---

53. See *Critique of the Power of Judgment*, First Introduction, 17; *Ak* 20: 213–14.
54. *Critique of the Power of Judgment*, First Introduction, 18; *Ak* 20: 215.
55. See chapter 5.

tion must be placed in relation to one's own overall judgmental assent to it as appropriate. Thus the critical mode of judging that is required for hermeneutics is not only reflective in being open to other points of view, but also reflexive in being drawn back to oneself. The capacity to authoritatively adjudicate among different perspectives must be rooted in the authentic and conscientious self-scrutiny discussed in chapter 6. In order to affirm this self-referential or indexical aspect of hermeneutical considerations, it is important to carefully distinguish between our use of the terms "reflection," "reflective," and "reflexive."

Reflection (Überlegung, Reflexion) is the simple comparative procedure of noting commonalities among particulars, which in Kant's view even animals are capable of performing.[56] It can be added that for human beings such comparative reflection is also one of the conditions for empirical concept formation. While reflection can contribute to the conceptual order of empirical apprehension, *reflective (reflektirendes)* thought goes further in aiming at interpretive comprehension of experience in general. Judgment first becomes reflective when it proceeds as an orientational and ultimately inferential mode of thinking that searches for generic principles of integrating experience and systemizing empirical laws.[57]

In some of the more recent Kant literature, it has been claimed that the "merely reflective judgment"[58] is no more than a condition for empirical concept formation, thereby reducing reflective judgment to only an anticipatory mode of determinant judgment.[59] Such a position tends to conflate the reflection (*Reflexion*) needed for concepts and the reflective (*reflektirende*) power of judgment. But the hermeneutical task of reflective judgment is more global than to initiate empirical cognitive inquiry. It orients all our ways of responding to reality, whether they are cognitive, affective, or volitional. Whereas reflection contributes to thoughtful apprehension, our thinking be-

---

56. See *Critique of Pure Reason*, A260/B316, and *Critique of the Power of Judgment*, First Introduction, 15; *Ak* 20: 211–12.

57. In *The Jäsche Logic*, reflection is discussed in section 6 in relation to concept formation, and reflective judgment not until sections 81–84 on inferences.

58. *Critique of the Power of Judgment*, First Introduction, 15; *Ak* 20: 223.

59. See Beatrice Longuenesse, *Kant and the Capacity to Judge*: Sensibility and Discursivity in the Critique of Pure Reason (Princeton, NJ: Princeton University Press, 2001), 164, and Henry Allison, *Kant's Theory of Taste* (Cambridge: Cambridge University Press, 2001), 16–30. For a more extended questioning of this position, see Makkreel, "Reflection, Reflective Judgment and Aesthetic Exemplarity," in *Aesthetics and Cognition in Kant's Critical Philosophy*, ed. Rebecca Kukla (Cambridge: Cambridge University Press, 2006), 223–44.

comes reflective when it also examines its scope and assumptions. And from the perspective of orientational thought, the reflective attitude that leads us into the world must eventually bring us back to ourselves in a *reflexive* or self-referring moment.

Although the reflexivity that we have derived from Dilthey is initially the self-awareness that is inherent in any act of consciousness, it can also become a more inclusive self-awareness that reflects various states of mind. This would be a second-order reflexivity made possible by reflective judgment. Kant was able to link reflective judgment with the capacity to feel aesthetic pleasure precisely because it can produce a reflexive awareness of our overall state of mind. When reflective judgment is geared to the normative considerations involved in interpretation, the reflexivity of self-awareness is broadened into an evaluative attitude.

Focusing mainly on the reflexive and the reflective, we can now correlate them with our three levels of historical understanding as follows: Elementary understanding involves a first-order *reflexive mode of assimilating* what is already there for us in experience. This includes what we inherit from the past through our local community and produces what we have called life-knowledge. Higher understanding applies conceptual reflection to transform what was experientially assimilated into the more universal cognitive mode characteristic of the sciences. This higher or cognitive understanding constitutes a kind of *reflective acquisition,* which, like all discursive representation, is piecemeal and dispersed over various disciplines. Finally, in critical understanding, experience and conceptual cognition are appropriated to form an integral mode of knowledge that produces a second-order reflexivity in which representational cognition moves to the level of a representative normative judgment capable of attaining some overall assessment or interpretation. Whereas reflexive assimilation makes us part of human history, *reflective-reflexive appropriation* makes history a part of us in our critical evaluations. The reciprocity between the reflective and the reflexive in critical appropriation will be an important factor in recognizing that hermeneutics is more than a theory of examining rules and methods of interpretation.

A RESPONSIVE HERMENEUTICS AND A TRANSFORMATIVE CRITIQUE

There can be procedural guidelines for interpretation in any discipline, but that does not make them hermeneutical. On the procedural level, the methods of the natural and human sciences partly overlap and partly diverge. Even in the natural sciences, interpretation becomes necessary when the evidence for inductive generalizations is insufficient to determine the outcome. When we cannot appeal to general laws to explain the behavior of natural or historical phenomena, we can apply detailed descriptions and statistical correlations to generate interpretations. Here procedural theories of interpretation expand the scope of conceptual reflection to bring up alternative reflective contexts for consideration. But this reflective contextualization does not yet define what characterizes hermeneutic understanding and how the human sciences can contribute to it.

What differentiates hermeneutics from simple procedural theories of interpretation and defines it as orientational is its capacity to relate reflection about the world back to reflexive awareness. Thus an interpretation of history will not be hermeneutical unless it also influences self-understanding. Ideally, the process of interpretation will move from the first-order reflexivity of elementary understanding to the reflection of higher understanding to reach the second-order reflexivity of critical understanding. These two levels of reflexivity introduce a circularity that involves not only a reciprocity of parts and wholes, but also an eventual reversal of the temporal order in which the reflexive and reflective function. Experientially, reflexive awareness involves an *implicit* understanding that must then be reflectively explicated. But at the level of critical hermeneutic understanding, all that has been reflexively assimilated and reflectively acquired also needs to be legitimately appropriated. Here the reflexive follows the reflective as the *implicative* moment that takes responsibility for an interpretation. The reflective operates on the level of judgment and compares possibilities of ever wider scope. The reflexive is indexical or self-referential without necessarily providing transparent access to some inner self. But when second-order reflexivity also encompasses what has been reflectively acquired, our sense of our standing in the world also provides the basis for a stance toward it.

Our orientational capacity to take a stance requires a responsiveness to particular circumstances as we gain our critical bearings. As an essential characteristic of life, responsiveness indicates openness not only to what is given in experience, but also to the possibility of transforming those givens. The responsiveness of life is a mode of activity that is neither simply self-active in the way that Kant defines the spontaneity of the understanding, nor is it merely passively receptive.[60] Life, which is often identified with the capacity to initiate movement, must also be conceived broadly enough as responsive to

---

60. See Makkreel, *Imagination and Interpretation in Kant*, 105–106.

the various ways of being moved and stirred. In the life of consciousness, this can be registered in terms of aesthetic feelings that lead one to embrace and prolong pleasurable or harmonious states of mind as a way to compensate for or overcome painful and conflicted ones.

Hermeneutically, responsiveness in interpretation must employ the receptivity of sense in resisting any willful urge to impose an alien form on the content to be understood. Whatever form we discern in a text must preserve some reference back to the circumstances of its original context. Previously, in stressing the need for hermeneutics to bring various contexts to bear in interpreting a subject matter, we sketched a reflective topology that relates concepts to objects by specifying their relevant contexts.[61] Our reflexive turn also contextualizes the interpreting subject, who must be responsive to a situational context while at the same time taking responsibility for assessing the appropriateness of the disciplinary contexts brought to bear.[62]

If a critical hermeneutical approach is to be charted between Gadamer's reliance on the authority of traditional precedents and Habermas's social critique it would seem to begin at the point where aesthetic responsiveness becomes diagnostic and cultivates interpretive responsibility. There may be a continuum linking what tradition delivers to us as being normal and what can be projected as normative, and yet we must be able to discern the difference. This capacity to pause and respond to our background is crucial for a critical appropriation of tradition. Thus it is not enough to say that tradition engenders its own modes of change.[63] The question is what kind of changes will be admitted by tradition? Will it make room for the responsiveness of critical engagement and be open to fundamental change? In order to decide what changes are desirable, the general procedural criteria provided by Habermas

---

61. See chapter 3.

62. See Makkreel, "An Ethically Responsive Hermeneutics of History," in *The Ethics of History*, ed. David Carr, Thomas R. Flynn, and Rudolf Makkreel (Evanston, IL: Northwestern University Press, 2004), 222–23.

63. This is what Allen Hance claims in his essay "The Hermeneutic Significance of the *Sensus Communis*," *International Philosophical Quarterly* XXXVII, no. 2 (June 1997): 146. Hance notes correctly that my hermeneutical use of reflective judgment and common sense is meant to leave more space for criticizing the tradition than Gadamer has left, namely, by allowing us to appeal not only to tradition but also away from it. But Hance likens my position vis-à-vis Gadamer to that of Habermas's "procedural account of critical rationality" (145) and thereby misses what is distinctive about my approach. Habermas's challenge to Gadamer has its own legitimacy but fits more readily into the foundational and regulative modes of analysis that I have tried to supplement with orientational and reflective modes.

need to be supplemented with a more judgment-focused approach. Instead of characterizing the intersection of hermeneutics and social reality in the abstract language of communicative action or the utopian rhetoric of emancipatory regulative ideals, we must rethink this intersection in terms of the more concrete diagnostics of a reflective critique.

The call for emancipation involves the need to escape some limiting situation, a need made especially urgent if the relevant limits undermine participatory parity or are inherently inhumane. But the regulative ideal of emancipation will remain an empty promise until it is matched by a reflective diagnosis that assesses the actual situation for what can and should be changed or overcome. For hermeneutics to succeed in configuring and reordering the various contexts needed to interpret historical phenomena, diagnostic judgment must distinguish between contingent and necessary conditions as well as relate change to the human capacity for development and transformation.

Perhaps reflective critique is best linked with the idea of transformation as encompassing the interplay of internal and external developmental change. Emancipatory critique suggests a sweeping negation or liberation from repressive institutions and codifications. But a more affirmative conception of critique geared to transformation will be compatible with a wider range of options, including more limited negations that push established practices in new directions. We saw a precedent for this in the way Kant refused to dismiss authoritative prejudices but suspended them reflectively as hypotheses to be tested and potentially revised or modified. Transformation will involve an altered relation to a limiting situation so that the conditions that function negatively as an obstacle can also be used positively as an opening for creative conversion. The greatest artists are often the ones who do not throw past conventions and rules to the wind but select from them what can be rethought and given new life through a process of emulation.[64]

COMPLETENESS IN CRITICAL HERMENEUTICS

Having examined how critical hermeneutics must consider both the validating conditions of cognition and the legitimating sources of knowledge, we can also address the demands for completeness and comprehensiveness that are often assigned to critique. Although at times Kant rather modestly insisted that critique is preliminary to the actual doing of philosophy, he was always bold enough to expect it to provide a complete and comprehensive preview

---

64. See chapter 5 on emulation as a process of surpassing a model.

of the proper ends of philosophy. One of these overarching ends is to establish what can be cognized independently of experience. Another is to determine how reason can reconcile its theoretical and practical needs. These ends are "not proposed arbitrarily," he declares, but stem from the very nature of "reason itself and its pure thinking."[65] For Kant the problems of reason are so integrally related that if a philosophical principle leaves even a single end unaccounted for, its reliability relative to the others must also be questioned. Completeness must project "*each* of the ends" to be reached, and comprehensiveness concerns "reaching *all* of them together."[66]

The completeness of the hermeneutical project will differ from Kant's philosophical project in not claiming the comprehensive sweep whereby all ends are reached together. Such a pre-articulated togetherness would collapse the specificity of the various relevant contexts and hinder the ongoing refinement of historical understanding. Instead of being centered on the two legislative domains of theoretical and practical reason, hermeneutics adjusts to and negotiates the more varied contexts that are relevant to the proper understanding of human life and the historical world. It is important to keep in mind the different ways in which actual territories, contingent habitats, necessary domains, and possible fields provide orientational contexts for interpretation. To ignore these differences is to risk the contextual confusions that were discussed as amphibolies of reflective orientation. In examining historical events such as wars, one can frame them in the context of actual territorial claims made by governmental institutions as well as the contingent circumstances that provoked specific conflicts and declarations of war. When their outcomes and settlements are also considered, relations among the legal domains established by the respective nation states and the field of international law become relevant. Finally, systematic disciplines such as economics and sociology may be able to provide some general explanations for the causes and effects of such developments.

A reflective critique is not bound by the demand for integral systematic unity that drives standard constitutive critique. Constitutive conditions are no longer regarded as supplying an overall unity for interpretation. Instead, they primarily inform the reflexive aspects of experience as it assimilates the commonality of local prejudices and customs. These contextual conditions of life-knowledge are relevant to our elementary understanding of the factual and contingent circumstances that influence human action and historical events.

---

65. *Critique of Pure Reason*, Axiv.
66. *Critique of Pure Reason*, Axiv.

Higher understanding then contributes disciplinary cognition, in which the constitutive conditions of experience are refined by the regulative ideals of the sciences. Here, political, economic, and legal considerations are applied to what was already understood on an elementary level about the main features of a historical situation. Thus, higher understanding is not merely assimilative; it involves the reflective acquisition of methodical means of conceptual analysis and systematic reconstruction to validate the meaning of experience. But each systematic discipline has a relatively fixed scope and will increase our understanding in only limited ways. The extent to which constitutive and regulative conditions of experience shape human understanding therefore remains open to question.

How far to apply the cognitive tools of the natural, social, and human sciences to our interpretation requires a diagnostic use of reflective judgment. An interpretation will be reflectively complete when it encompasses not only the validating conditions for meaningful interpretation, but also the normative considerations that legitimate its truthfulness. With this, we enter the *reflective-reflexive appropriative* phase of interpretation, where an individual takes responsibility for the evaluative perspective brought to bear in making attributive imputations about the merits of human practices and their outcomes. It is essential here to have a broad or worldly orientation that can adequately frame both the situational context of the interpreter and the specific circumstances being interpreted.

Hermeneutical completeness will therefore be more in line with reflective interpretations based on pragmatic anthropological characterizations governed by the norms of authenticity and conscientiousness. Although these norms were invoked in order to focus on the responsibility of the individual interpreter working in medias res, they should not be taken as an endorsement of subjectivism. Both authenticity and conscientiousness have been shown to involve an intersubjective engagement that could be considered the reflective diagnostic counterpart of the more speculative ideals of dialectical reconciliation and dialogical communication.

The engaged judgmental assent needed for hermeneutic legitimacy was examined in relation to three regulative ideals: that of scientific communal consent in chapter 4, that of univocal aesthetic approbation in chapter 5, and finally that of omnilateral justification in chapter 6. But reflective critique focuses on situated individual knowers for whom these Kantian regulative ideals must be specified at the same time that the contexts relevant to their inquiry are delimited. Accordingly, the certainty of Kant's communal consent will be modified into the conviction of consensus, the finality of univocal approbation into the process of reciprocal engagement, and the legality of omnilateral justification into multilateral legitimacy. As hermeneutics calls upon the sources provided by the tradition, it must aim to complete them critically by approximating comprehensiveness through a reflective coordination of the relevant disciplinary contexts. The way in which any interpretation allows these contexts to intersect must be subject to scrutiny so that connecting threads can be adequately woven together into what is established to be the most appropriate context. The aim will be to attain a multilateral completeness without claiming an omnilateral or final completion.

The idea of philosophical hermeneutics has been used by some to insist on a dichotomy between a basic ontological understanding of human existence on the one hand and the epistemic and methodological results of the human sciences on the other. A reflective critique can work to bring together these two approaches to hermeneutics by showing the incompleteness of each by itself.

To critically address our hermeneutic situation is to probe life-knowledge based on who we are—not only to consider what conceptual cognition can add by way of elucidation, but also to attain a well-rounded reflective interpretation. In underscoring the complexities of the hermeneutical task, we have appealed to the differentiating power of judgment to keep clear of reflective amphibolies. Beyond that, the crucial, positive contribution of judgment stems from its capacity to reorient interpretation as it moves from discursive cognitive considerations to the more normative concerns of critically appropriated reflective knowledge.

3

Applications and Adaptations

CHAPTER 8

Genealogy, Narrative History, and Hermeneutic Transmission

I will now turn to genealogical and narrative theories of history and assess them in light of our hermeneutical approach. The orientational and critical hermeneutics presented in this work makes a diagnostic use of reflective judgment to assess the human world. In proposing this more central role for judgment, we considered the extent to which historical attributions are imputational and how they can be legitimated. Such attributions raise questions about the traditional fact-value distinction and the objectivity of interpretation.

Some of the most radical challenges to the objectivity of historical interpretation derive from Friedrich Nietzsche's genealogical conception of history. This genealogical approach regards "events" not as facts, but as subduing forces that invent "a new interpretation, a corrective reshaping (*Zurechtmachen*) through which any previous 'meaning' and 'purpose' must necessarily be obscured or even obliterated."[1] Whatever may seem to be a fact and is described with some expectation of lasting validity will prove to be a momentary interpretation that can be replaced by another.

Nietzsche, like his contemporary Dilthey, expects historical interpretation to contribute to finding meaning in this life apart from any higher telos. Both thinkers approach history from the perspective of life and look to interpretation to provide an alternative to deterministic, causal explanation, but arrive

---

1. Friedrich Wilhelm Nietzsche, *On the Genealogy of Morals*, trans. Walter Kaufmann and R.J. Hollingdale (New York: Vintage Books, 1989), 77 (translation revised). See *Zur Genealogie der Moral*, in *Kritische Studienausgabe* (*KSA*). Band 5. Herausgegeben von Giorgio Colli und Mazzino Montinari. Berlin/New York/ Munich: DTV/Walter de Gruyter, 1988.

at different solutions. Nietzsche rejects the very idea of causal connectedness; Dilthey develops methods of understanding that still leave a limited place for causal explanation. Each will be shown to prefigure a distinct kind of narrative history.

NIETZSCHE'S CHALLENGE TO THE OBJECTIVITY OF HISTORICAL INTERPRETATION

For Nietzsche, historical interpretation is neither a cognitive act that attributes lasting meaning to events nor a reflective knowing, but a willful assertion of control over a situation. To interpret is to exert the will to power—something that already occurs at the level of life itself. Life as the exertion of the will to power "draws its ultimate consequence at every moment."[2] And in its drive for survival, life will overpower all opposition and continue to reinterpret itself by "doing violence (*Vergewaltigen*), setting right by force (*Zurechtschieben*), abbreviating, omitting, padding, inventing, falsifying."[3]

For Nietzsche's philosophy of life, it is the moment that counts above all. Anything from the past that does not contribute to the energy of the present moment can be dispensed with. Accordingly, Nietzsche's genealogical history thrives on shifts in meaning and has no patience with a search for enduring trends. It undermines the idea of universal history, especially in the teleological terms conceived by Kant and Hegel. History for Nietzsche does not have an inherent telos, and its narration will display contingent emergences that defy causal explanation. And because good can arise from what is bad, absolutist normative divisions between good and evil are made suspect. Genealogy is meant to liberate historical narratives from an excessive concern with facts and traditional norms. It questions the very idea of law-based explanation as a symptom of the modern disease of submitting to egalitarian standards. What could be more anti-Kantian than this? And yet the idea that the historian must make critical judgments survives in Nietzsche.

Genealogical history appears to be a variant of Nietzsche's idea of critical history advocated in his early essay "On the Uses and Disadvantages of History for Life." As distinct from a monumental history that invents a future goal and an antiquarian history that reveres the past, critical history serves the present by "destroying" those parts of the past that result in human suf-

---

2. Nietzsche, *Beyond Good and Evil*, trans. Walter Kaufmann (New York: Vintage Books, 1989), 30 (translation revised). *KSA* 5: 37.

3. Nietzsche, *Zur Genealogie*, *KSA* 5: 400.

fering. Nietzsche's critical history sits in judgment of the past and condemns its aberrations. Like Kant, he speaks of a "tribunal (*Gericht*)"; but instead of appealing to lawful and conceptually mediated verdicts of the court of reason, Nietzsche invokes the immediate "verdict (*Urtheil*)" of life itself. Critical history is not merely judgmental and evaluative (*beurteilend*), but condemnatory (*verurteilend*) and destructive (*vernichtend*).[4]

Both Nietzsche and Dilthey were transitional figures who appealed to the idea of life to reinterpret reality. They recognized the inadequacies of traditional philosophy for assessing the complexities of life.

Nietzsche made biological life and its harsh contingencies his point of departure. For him life is a power that ruthlessly eliminates what it no longer needs. Being healthy requires us to forget much of the past, and what does deserve to be remembered often needs to be reassessed. This is why his narratives stress genealogical discontinuities and new beginnings. Interpretation for Nietzsche is always reinterpretation.

Dilthey, as we have seen, focused more on human historical life and its sociocultural constellations. For him, life is a force that sustains and restores. This is why Dilthey stresses the possibility of finding meaning in history on the basis of generative continuities. These continuities can be located at the level of individuals as the nexus of lived experience and at the level of social interaction as structural systems. Change is conceived as a function of processes of differentiation, and historical interpretation requires the further articulation of what is already implicitly understood. To be sure, there also historical discontinuities, but they are often a function of mere sedimentation that allows us to forget what has been covered over.

In what follows, I propose to consider some of the narrative conceptions of history developed since the life-philosophies of Nietzsche and Dilthey and take their measure on the basis of a reflective hermeneutical critique and the interpretive potential of contextual orientation. The narratives we are provided in historical works can provide insight into history only if we recognize how they interweave the distinctive meaning contexts relevant to human interaction. Negotiating these formal contexts requires a constant narrative reconfiguration. Similarly, historical narratives will need to be analyzed to determine how much the contents that they have assimilated from the past have also been subjected to the test of cognitive acquisition and critical appropriation.

4. See Nietzsche, *Untimely Meditations*, trans. R. J. Hollingdale (Cambridge: Cambridge University Press, 1986), 76; *KSA*, 2: 270.

NARRATIVE APPROACHES TO HISTORY

According to narrative theorists, the historian's account of past events is best conceived as developing a story line or narrative. Without appealing to historical laws or assuming some overall end of history, they claim that historical narratives have their own order and intelligibility that dispenses with deterministic explanations. The question then arises, how does a narrative obtain its special intelligibility? Dilthey had already spoken of the historical nexus as an articulation of the life nexus in which we participate and of understanding the connectedness of events from within. This approach is developed by such narrative theorists as William Dray and David Carr, who are representative of what I will call the generative or continuity narrativists.

The continuity view is opposed by theorists like Hayden White and Louis Mink, who regard narrative structure not as rooted in the events of life, but as having an invented origin. I consider them reconstructive or discontinuity narrativists. For them, the intelligibility of narratives is not found in what can be characterized as an educed sense of form. They reject the idea of an inner form that unfolds from the content and see narrative as imposing a fictive form on a formless life. With form considered as a literary construct, White's *Metahistory* analyzes the reconstructive styles of the great historians of the nineteenth century by discerning four basic literary tropes at work in their writings: metaphor, metonymy, synecdoche, and irony.[5] The relation between history and a literary conception of narrative was also explored in a series of essays by Mink. I will focus on those essays by Mink that were collected in the volume *Historical Understanding* because they clearly engage the important philosophical discussions from the brief period that the analytic philosophy of history blossomed.[6]

For discontinuity narrativists such as Mink, "stories are not lived but told. Life has no beginnings, middles and ends.... Narrative qualities are transferred from art to life."[7] This literary conception of narrative, which makes

---

5. See Hayden White, *Metahistory: The Historical Imagination in Nineteenth-Century Europe* (Baltimore: Johns Hopkins University Press, 1973), 31–42.

6. See also Arthur Danto, *The Analytic Philosophy of History* (Cambridge: Cambridge University Press, 1968).

7. Louis Mink, "History and Fiction as Modes of Comprehension," in *Historical Understanding*, ed. Brian Fay, Eugene O. Golob, and Richard T. Vann (Ithaca, NY: Cornell University Press, 1987), 60.

any storyline a product of the imagination, goes back to Sartre's existential attitude toward storytelling as expressed in *Nausea*. In this novel, Sartre writes that everyone "tries to live his life as if he were telling a story. But you have to choose: live or tell." When you live life, "nothing happens,"[8] for life is a monotonous sequence of events proceeding without beginnings and ends. Only when you tell about a life does it become an adventure that engages the imagination: "everything changes. . . . Events take place in one direction, and we tell about them in the opposite direction."[9]

Although we may not be able to simultaneously live and tell in any one existential moment, surely the lives we lead are not perceived as passively as Sartre suggests. To the extent that I act with some result in mind, I am anticipating some storyline for my life. Things may turn out differently than what I expected, but this only means that the story I would have told will now have to be revised. We should not forget that narrators, too, are always revising their stories as the retrospective endpoints from which they tell them change.

For continuity narrativists such as Carr, the practical decisions that we make in life mark the beginnings and projected endings of the prethematic narratives of the Husserlian lifeworld. If narrative beginnings require imagination, it is the imagination at work in ordinary life and accessible through phenomenological description. Carr writes that stories "are told in being lived and lived in being told."[10] This reflexive telling of a life story is of course what makes autobiography possible. Autobiography should be problematic for theorists such as Sartre and Mink, because in this kind of history "the person who understands [the course of life] is the same as the one who created it."[11] The reflexive perspective of autobiography is important for the possibility of writing sound history in general, because it shows the basic way in which human life intuitively grasps itself. Even when a story is not complete, we have opportunities to pause and reflect on what we have so far done, and articulate some connections. Speaking of autobiography in general, Dilthey claims:

---

8. Jean-Paul Sartre, *Nausea*, trans. Lloyd Alexander (New York: New Directions, 1969), 39.

9. *Nausea*, as cited in an earlier version of the Alexander translation in *The Philosophy of Jean-Paul Sartre*, ed. with an introduction by Robert D. Cumming (New York: Random House, 1965), 58–59.

10. David Carr, *Time, Narrative, and History* (Bloomington, IN: Indiana University Press, 1986), 61.

11. Dilthey, *The Formation of the Historical World*, SW 3, 221.

The same person who seeks the overall coherence of the story of his life, has already produced a life nexus according to various perspectives, namely, in the ways he has felt the values of his life, actualized its purposes, worked out a life plan, either genetically when looking back or projectively when looking forward to a highest good. These various ways of producing a life nexus must now be articulated as a life history. The person's memory has highlighted and accentuated those life-moments that were experienced as significant; others have been allowed to sink into forgetfulness. Momentary mistakes about the meaning of his life are corrected by the future. Thus the initial tasks involved in apprehending and explicating a historical nexus are already half-solved by life itself.[12]

To be sure, the initial meaning that we find in our lived experience can be illusory and may need to be corrected. But our own life already corrects many of these mistaken impressions and leads us to revise our narrative. As a result, Carr writes, "events that were lived in terms of one story are now seen as part of another."[13] Although the autobiographer inevitably lacks the time to reflect on and narrate his or her whole life from the point of view of its end, even subsequent biographers can never find a point beyond which the value and significance of an individual cannot be reinterpreted. If an individual was influential, then the productive history (*Wirkungsgeschichte*) that follows his or her death can never be definitively closed off. Even artists or scientists whose reputations wane can never be completely dismissed so as to rule out a revival of interest in them. A historian who is convinced of the ultimate insignificance of a subject might nevertheless choose to reflect on why that subject was considered significant by his or her contemporaries. This would have the paradoxical result of giving their subjects a continued half-life—not to assign them genuine importance, but merely to recognize their representative significance. This is not unlike what Peter Shaffer's play *Amadeus* did for the all-but-forgotten composer Antonio Salieri. But to recognize that Salieri was considered an important composer in his own time does not ensure that his fame will be restored. Instead Shaffer's play has promoted Salieri's infamy through speculating about his plotting against Mozart.

12. *The Formation of the Historical World, SW* 3, 221.
13. *Time, Narrative, and History*, 76.

INCOMMENSURABLE CONTEXTS AND THE POSSIBILITY OF UNIVERSALIST HISTORY

A hermeneutic approach to history can encompass aspects of both the continuity and discontinuity conceptions of narrative theory. Even though historical narration occurs from a retrospective point of view, we have maintained that historical experience is originally assimilative by drawing from the continuity of tradition what is relevant to our current context. Assimilation provides the primary historical context within which we frame our understanding. This chronologically generated or inherited context of elementary understanding can then be reconfigured retrospectively by means of the disciplinary contexts that we acquire through higher understanding.

However, narrative discontinuity theorists like Mink point to a possible incommensurability when concepts that have their basis in a contemporary cognitive context are used to explicate concepts that stem from an earlier context. He writes:

> Concepts belong to narratives of human action in two ways: there are the concepts which inform *our* understanding of past events, and there are the concepts which at least in part were *constitutive* of past actions, in the sense that they were necessarily involved in the agent's understanding of what they were doing. We could not understand Greek civilization without the concept of *moira*, which is not part of our conceptual systems, and without a concept of culture, which was no part of theirs.[14]

Mink uses this kind of incommensurability to argue against the idea of universal history. But while there may indeed be no neutral or universal perspective from which the ancient concept of moira or fate and the Enlightenment-inspired idea of culture can be directly compared, we can move beyond simple incommensurability if we consider how and in what contexts the concept of fate actually conflicts with our modern conception of causality. We can at least compare and contrast what is involved in the concepts of fate and causality. Although the modern theory of causality can dispense with fate, historical understanding of the Greek experience still needs to take their belief in fate into account.

---

14. Louis Mink, "Philosophical Analysis and Historical Understanding," in *Historical Understanding*, 141.

Our analysis of aesthetic evaluation and interpretation expanded the idea of communicability to include not only conceptual mediation but also contextual reconfiguration.[15] This means that even when the concepts appealed to in different contexts cannot be directly reconciled, it may nevertheless be possible to redefine and reconfigure contexts to allow for interpretive transposition between them and make some sense of a pagan conception of fate. The appeal to fate may not be scientifically defensible, but we can still relate to it through some aspect of our experience. Indeed, in terms of our three ways of processing and organizing experience—from life-knowledge to conceptual cognition to reflective knowledge—we can say that "fate" refers to life-knowledge and "causality" to conceptual cognition, while "culture" hovers between the latter and reflective knowledge.[16]

The language of fate is still meaningful today because our own lived experience allows us to make sense of what it means to feel that something is unavoidable. This is not to suggest that the life-knowledge of the Greeks was the same as ours. To the extent that the common sense informing life-knowledge reflects basic scientific changes, most of us recognize today that the sun does not really rotate around the earth, even though it still looks that way. Thus the earth can no longer be assumed to be the center of the universe as it was for the Greeks. Theirs was a more limited universe, with finite gods, where the inscrutable fates loomed larger. In our expanded universe, the idea of blind fate affecting us in inscrutable ways has been diminished on the one hand because of our increased confidence in scientific explanation and on the other hand because of the Judeo-Christian-Muslim legacy that still leads many to believe that nothing happens in defiance of the providence of an infinitely powerful God. Yet we cannot deny that there are moments in our lives when we feel powerful and unfathomable forces at work. In this sense our life-knowledge may provide an original access to the Greek conception of fate, which the cognitive methods of the human sciences can then attempt to analyze and explicate.

Historians may be able to challenge aspects of the original Greek understanding of an event if it conflicts with what contemporary science knows to be causally possible or impossible. But however much they reinterpret the significance of the past, they should not ignore the self-understandings of the original agents and participants. Even if these subjects were deluded or inadequately informed, their viewpoints influenced what they did and did not do.

15. See chapter 5.
16. See chapters 1 and 4.

How these strands in any historical narrative fit together needs to be judged from the various systematic perspectives made possible by the human sciences. The concept of culture referred to by Mink can be specified historically in terms of distinct cultural systems, which provide the framework for understanding the actions and projects of human beings. The success or failure of these projects may in turn be explained by reference to natural factors. Thus the victory of one army over another may not just be due solely to the brilliance of the military tacticians, but also to some unpredictable factors such as the weather or other environmental conditions.

If the intelligibility of the various strands of a narrative is to be convincing rather than merely persuasive, every potentially relevant background condition must be factored in. These background conditions may point to either the historical world of understanding or to the natural world, where causal explanations are often available. In both cases we appeal to something beyond the narrative itself. On this score it would be self-defeating for narrativists to rule out causal explanations altogether. This is taken into account when Dilthey wrote in the Addenda to "The Rise of Hermeneutics" that "when pushed to its limits, understanding is not different from explanation, insofar as the latter is possible in this domain."[17] Having first distinguished understanding and explanation, he now sees them as also capable of converging in certain situations.

This linkage of understanding and explanation can be conceived in two different ways. The first or weaker version of linkage merely acknowledges that the full understanding of human life must also take into account the explanation of the external contextual factors involved. Here explanation can continue to mean what it normally means for Dilthey: the derivation of particular instances from the general causal laws found in the natural sciences. However, it is also possible that Dilthey is considering a mode of explanation sui generis to the human sciences. Explanation in this light would be the process of bringing what we know about the external contextual factors to bear on the inner processes to be understood. This is what is suggested when Dilthey goes on to write: "There, where general insights are consciously and methodically applied in order to bring what is singular to comprehensive cognition, the expression 'explanation' finds its proper place in the cognition of the singular. It is only justified insofar as we remain aware that we can never allow what is singular to be fully submerged into what is universal."[18]

---

17. Dilthey, "The Rise of Hermeneutics" in *Hermeneutics and the Study of History*, SW 4: 253.

18. *Hermeneutics and the Study of History*, SW 4, 257.

The first mode of explanation subordinates the particular to the universal but remains an external supplement to the process of understanding the meaning of human activities and their objectifications. The second, hermeneutically instigated mode of explanation would bring specific systematic disciplines like economics or sociology to bear on local circumstances. Part of the difference here may lie in the nature of the context involved. Explanations of the first type are causal explanations where the universal is a law or inductive generalization that governs the domain of nature as such. Explanations of the second type would refer to reflectively specified functional systems. Thus when Dilthey speaks of universal history, he means a study of the main systematic aspects of life that can be coordinated within a certain time span.

From the hermeneutic perspective, we can speak of a universalist rather than a universal history. This would involve not a speculative all-inclusive study of the totality of world history, but the application of general systematic reflection to delimited spheres of history. Such a universalist history does not appeal to overarching historical laws, but allows more restricted lawful correlations established within specific social and cultural systems to be brought to bear diagnostically in order to approximate the ideal of making interpretation as objective as possible.

The possibility of universalist history does not require that there be univocal consent about some overall context within which everything can be evaluated. If we have the capacity to transpose among various contexts, and if hermeneutics can provide the reflective guidelines for ordering the way those contexts should be understood to intersect, then a limited form of universalist history may be defensible. Moreover, hermeneutics need not rule out the application of causal analysis at certain points.

DELIMITING THE APPEAL TO CAUSES IN HISTORICAL INTERPRETATION

Nietzsche challenges the standard conception of causality by questioning the underlying assumption that the cause-effect relation is law-governed and mechanistic. He deconstructs the scientific legitimacy of mechanistic causation by questioning the idea that any law can guarantee that the same effect will follow the same cause. In *Beyond Good and Evil*, he writes: "one should use 'cause' and 'effect' only as . . . conventional fictions for the purpose of designation and communication—not for explanation. In the 'in-itself' there is nothing of 'causal connections' of 'necessity'... there is no rule of 'law.'"[19]

According to Nietzsche, the very idea of natural laws has a moral origin, not a scientific one, and is something we impose on ourselves as part of the misguided modern ideology that all humans should be treated as equal. The parallel scientific claim that a cause must be equal to the effect creates the illusion of a continuous temporal nexus in which we expect a cause to "press and push until it 'effects' its end."[20] In the world of genealogy, by contrast, every power draws its consequences instantaneously. In such a world no cause can guarantee an enduring outcome. We saw this in the way that the will to interpret attempts to overpower prior interpretations.

Instead of rejecting causality, others have reassessed the role of causality in history by limiting the scope and applicability of natural laws. Dilthey claims that lawlike relations among historical phenomena could only exist within specific social and cultural systems. This means that standard causal explanations can have only a limited place in human history. In his magisterial study of the role of narrative,[21] Ricoeur looks for a kind of causal analysis of historical events that can offer a middle ground between universal causal laws and idiographic description. Ricoeur's account of historical causality takes note of Max Weber's thesis that a religiously inspired work ethic was necessary for the rise of capitalism. Since there is no way of generalizing about happenings such as the rise of capitalism in the Protestant countries of England, the United States, and the Netherlands, Ricoeur speaks only of "singular causal imputation."[22] And because history does not provide alternatives to what happened, the procedure of singular causal imputation necessitates the ideal construction of possible alternatives as ways of testing its results. Thus the dependence of capitalism on a religious work ethic can be tested only by considering counterfactual scenarios based on different relevant factors such as technological, legal, political, and commercial advances in order to argue that by themselves they would not have been sufficient to cause the formation of capitalism. This kind of causal imputa-

---

19. *Beyond Good and Evil*, 29.
20. *Beyond Good and Evil*, 29.
21. Paul Ricoeur, in *Time and Narrative*, 3 vols. (Chicago: University of Chicago Press, 1984), provides a wide-ranging treatment of narrative theory that resists an easy classification into the two camps distinguished earlier.
22. *Time and Narrative*, vol. 1, 192.

tion is, according to Ricoeur, a comparative claim involving a probability calculation.

Being based on a comparative claim, Ricoeur's singular causal imputation can be likened to a reflective judgment. The use of the term "imputation" puts what seems like a causal explanation in relation to the kind of ascriptive and attributive evaluations that we underscored as being characteristic of cultural and historical understanding. Clearly, singular causal imputations lack the demonstrative rigor of classical causal explanations, but can contribute to historical narratives when limited to the diagnosis of specific situations. Thus it must be stressed that singular causal imputations can have an explanative power only to the extent that they are framed by a hermeneutic understanding that orients reflective judgment toward the relevant interpretive contexts. It is this adjudication among contexts that allows reflective judgment to assume a diagnostic function.

CAUSES AND INFLUENCES

Causal explanations are regarded as demonstrably objective and universally valid if the number of variables involved is limited. Natural scientists establish laboratory systems and experiments in which many variables are excluded to allow the results to be controlled and repeated. This is not feasible when it comes to understanding the changing complexities of history. The many strands of influence that intersect in historical events require what Dilthey called "genetic understanding."[23] The language of influence and genesis could be seen as linking historical understanding to a consideration of causal factors without necessarily expecting a full determinate explanation. But Louis Mink regards any form of causal imputation as incompatible with his ideal of narrative history.

Mink aims to reconstruct historical narratives by replacing the scientific system of *"causation, law, event, explanation, prediction* . . . and *change* in the sense of repeatable successions" with a historical system of *"series, action, disposition . . . understanding, intelligibility, narrative, genesis . . .* and *change* in the sense of development."[24] Mink's two systems revive the explanation-understanding distinction, not hermeneutically, but closer to the absolute dualistic way in which Dilthey's predecessor Gustav Droysen had attempted

---

23. Dilthey, "The Eighteenth Century and the Historical World," in *Hermeneutics and the Study of History*, SW 4: 363.

24. Mink, *Historical Understanding*, 216.

to rule out determinism from what he considered the moral domain of history.[25] However, instead of dialectically opposing history and nature as two domains, it is more useful to think of history diagnostically as a territory that intersects with the lawful domain of nature and other specifiable social and cultural contexts.

Mink contends that terms like "influence" and "genesis" should be used in historical narratives without assigning them any causal import. This leads him to give a very narrow account of how the term "influence" is applied when considering the importance that Friedrich Schlegel attached to his having read an essay by Schiller. Mink writes: "strictly speaking, it was not Schiller's essay which influenced Schlegel, but Schlegel's own reading of it; nor was it the ideas in Schiller's essay which influenced Schlegel, but Schlegel's understanding of those ideas."[26] Here Mink betrays his Collingwoodian heritage by conceiving influence idealistically as an internal mental relation. But one cannot speak of being influenced by an essay without acknowledging an external dependence, an influx from that outside source. The process of understanding the meaning of Schiller's sentences and assessing their truth may be conceived idealistically, but that is not the same as establishing what influence Schiller might have had. Understanding is about the essay's content; establishing influence is to measure the essay's force by considering whether it introduced Schlegel to new ideas or led him to change earlier views he held. Only after considering both factors can one know whether an author has been influential. To be sure, an influence does not determine its outcome in the way that a cause determines its effect. One can be influenced by reading Schiller without fully sharing his views. To acknowledge an influence is merely to accept that one has been affected in some way.

Causality cannot be banished from historical narratives merely by redesignating history as a domain of spiritual development where the language of necessitated events is replaced with what Mink calls "advents" that "emerge into the light of actuality from the darkness of possibility."[27] It is impossible to demarcate a clear boundary line between causally determined events and consciously understood advents. Mink, however, claims that "the chain of causation ends with perception" and that "influence begins . . . at the border

---

25. Mink admits that his two systems may not be "completely independent," but for purposes of historical understanding there need be no reference to causes, laws, and events. *Historical Understanding*, 216.

26. *Historical Understanding*, 221.

27. *Historical Understanding*, 115.

between perception and consciousness."[28] He suggests that perceiving a page in a book is causal, but that reading it as a text initiates a new series of influences and genetic development. But in fact reading involves simultaneously perceiving the material letters of a text and understanding them as having an intelligible meaning. It is a responsive way of understanding that acknowledges that meaning is not just a private mental construction, but something pre-articulated in a public language. Words have both a meaning and a force to influence the thinking of others. Mink ignores the contextual conditions of how meaning gets passed on, which makes reading more than a merely mental occurrence. Reading is a way of understanding that is not fully autonomous but open to outside influences. Like elementary understanding, reading is an assimilative process where sharp inner-outer, self-other distinctions do not make sense.

The contextualizing nature of the process of assimilation was explored when we analyzed how Kant addresses the cognitive and aesthetic prejudices that influence us. We can now make a further distinction between what is assimilated through inheritance and what is more actively assimilated, as through reading and education. Hermeneutically, we can come to terms with any assimilated influence by also recontextualizing it through cognitive acquisition and critical appropriation.

INTENTIONALIST EXPLANATION AND HERMENEUTICAL CONTEXTUALIZATION

In *Explanation and Understanding*, G. H. von Wright points to two ways of distinguishing between explanation and understanding that leave open the possibility of their cooperation. When standard causal explanations cannot be obtained in history and the social sciences, we can still look for teleological explanations, based on the beliefs of human agents that they can intervene in a situation to produce some end. Such teleological explanations are not about some overall historical telos, but merely appeal to the intentions of agents to make what von Wright calls a practical inference. He provides the following schema for such an inference: "*A* intends to bring about *p*. / *A* considers that he cannot bring about *p* unless he does *a*. / Therefore *A* sets himself to do *a*."[29]

---

28. *Historical Understanding*, 221.

29. Georg Henrik von Wright, *Explanation and Understanding* (Ithaca, NY: Cornell University Press, 1971), 96.

The explanative force to be found in a practical inference is that A considers a necessary for p. A may also think that this a is causally sufficient to produce p. But it could turn out that a is neither necessary nor sufficient; if it was not necessary, then A could have chosen another means. An important aspect of a good teleological explanation is to show why A chose a and not b or c. In fact, those who use the philosophy of language to argue for an "erotetic" or question-based model of explanation would demand to know the reasons why alternatives to a were not pursued.[30]

To teleologically explain specific events in history presupposes that we can understand what has happened as action rather than behavior. Von Wright distinguishes two kinds of understanding: a *descriptive understanding* of what something "is like" and an *intentionalist understanding* of what something "means or signifies."[31] He then argues that the first or descriptive kind of understanding "is a characteristic preliminary of causal . . . explanation,"[32] and that the second or intentionalist kind of understanding prepares for teleological explanation. The intentionalist-teleological approach allows historians to offer narrative accounts that replace causal language with the language of action. But von Wright, like Dilthey, does not absolutely exclude causal conditions: it is always possible that my intention to *raise* my arm coincides with a physiological state that causes my arm to *rise*.[33] Nor is he willing to rule out that "desires or wants could have a causal influence on behavior."[34]

Von Wright's attempt to reconcile understanding and explanation is useful, but it ends up making understanding merely preliminary to explanation. The reason for this is that he conceives understanding as providing either a description that sets the stage for a causal explanation or an intention that initiates a teleological explanation. In both cases he assumes that understanding can be replaced and surpassed by explanation.

While it is true that intentions are preliminary, it need not be the case that they provide the basis for a teleological explanation. Attempts to reconstruct intentions tend to be highly speculative. Historical agents rarely articulate their true intentions, and when we do find them expressed, they are often

---

30. See Mark Risjord, *Woodcutters and Witchcraft: Rationality and Interpretive Change in the Social Sciences* (Albany: SUNY Press, 2000), 66–72.
31. *Explanation and Understanding*, 135.
32. *Explanation and Understanding*, 135.
33. See *Explanation and Understanding*, 129.
34. *Explanation and Understanding*, 95.

self-serving and may even be based on self-deception. However, the greatest problem with focusing understanding on intentions is that even when they are sincerely expressed, they have psychological roots that tend to be only partially actualized in social settings. There are often countervailing intentions and resistant institutional forces that the historian must also take into account. In those cases a more inclusive descriptive understanding may be the solution, rather than a special teleological explanation.

We saw von Wright explicate the intention of an agent in terms of a projected means-end relation. But this abstract understanding of an intention needs a fuller description that brings in the circumstances that frame its formation. The descriptive understanding that is called for should be more than preliminary in the sense of merely establishing the initial terms for, and assumptions of, inquiry. Once one has decided to describe the closing of someone's eye as a blink, it seems to be behavior that needs to be explained causally; if it is described as a wink, it is assumed to be an intentional action where someone is trying to signal something. But much of the value of descriptive understanding comes from being more open ended and encompassing throughout the interpretive process. The narrator should describe a human deed without making a preliminary decision about its being a free action or determined behavior. But most importantly, descriptive understanding must be provisional by also including the contextual circumstances that will continue to provide the framework for assessing the validity of any explanation that is provided.[35] An explanation can only be as good as the understanding that goes into the ongoing description of what is to be accounted for.

As with many other attempts to defend the role of explanation in the social sciences, von Wright has not demonstrated that a teleological explanation is sufficient to account for a historical outcome. It mainly serves to clarify why agent A sets out to do a in order to bring about p. A similar limit can be assigned to Dray's efforts to distinguish historical explanations from Carl Hempel's covering-law explanations. Hempel had argued for the thesis that all historical explanations must follow the lead of explanations in the natural sciences. Historians are expected to find the laws that relate events so that an outcome can be explained by deducing it from the relevant laws and antecedent events. Acknowledging that appropriate historical laws have not yet been found, Hempel also proposed an inductive-probabilistic variant of his deductive-nomological ideal.

35. See the way the terms "preliminary "and "provisional" were distinguished in chapter 4.

However, Dray believes that both the deductive and inductive models miss what historians actually do. His counterthesis is that historical narratives need not appeal to laws and thereby *explain why* things happened. This is because their primary concern is to *explain what* really happened. In doing so, they offer "an explanation of the form, 'It was a so-and-so.'"[36] When historians classify a specific uprising as a "bourgeois revolution," they supply a concept rather than a cause. Dray's historical explanations are in effect conceptual explanations.

Both von Wright's teleological explanations and Dray's conceptual explanations are limited in that they do not fully account for a historical outcome. I see them as narrative attempts to focus understanding by providing intelligible schemata. Hermeneutic understanding cannot content itself with such reductive schematization; it must aim at attributive characterizations that can locate human intentions within larger contexts and provide a normative orientation for historical reflection and judgment. Hermeneutical contextualization allows us to diagnose historical events as the concatenation of many factors, including those that may have been assumed to be irrelevant. If explanation tends to be exclusive and subordinative by ruling out factors not relevant to the search for generalizations, understanding should be inclusive and coordinative by diagnosing how various strands of influence interact in a specific situation. Explanations are primarily theoretical proposals that can be tested like specific hypotheses. Understanding, however, is not something that is proposed like a hypothesis. It is something we possess, either as an inherited assessment rooted in life or as a subsequent reflective achievement. Explanation produces connections at a clearly defined level; understanding exposes interconnectedness at many levels.

As we have seen, a hermeneutic approach to history must develop a reflexive-reflective understanding of interconnectedness to provide the framework for more focused disciplinary explanations. Even when merely describing what happened, it is always necessary to diagnostically frame the actions and results of historical agents in terms of the contexts within which they operate. Human beings often attempt to satisfy multiple interests, concerns, and loyalties in a course of action. Even the intentions of one and the same subject cannot be properly understood through psychology alone, for they are shaped by a variety of interrelated background conditions.

---

36. William Dray, "'Explaining What' in History," in *Theories of History*, ed. Patrick Gardiner (New York: The Free Press, 1959), 403.

NORMATIVE JUDGMENT OR NORMALIZING GENEALOGY

We have stressed the reflective aspects of historical understanding and underscored the normative aspects of historical attribution. Attributive characterizations of historical actions will look to various disciplines to make sense of human agency, for to judiciously attribute responsibility to historical agents requires that a historian be responsive to all the relevant cultural and social systems that may have influenced them.

The normative judgments of attributive imputation were initially compared with courtroom verdicts that derive their authority from strictly defined legal bounds. Their legitimacy was then reconfigured and adapted to the broader contexts of the human sciences. Michel Foucault, however, in his analysis of how justice has come to be administered in society, argues that the human sciences have actually eroded the normative legitimacy of courtroom verdicts by the practices they have introduced to execute these decisions. In *Discipline and Punish*, Foucault presents a "genealogy of the present scientifico-legal complex from which the power to punish derives its bases, justifications and rules."[37] This genealogy surveys how the execution of legal judgments and verdicts has been transformed by the human sciences into a disciplinary penal system that ultimately controls the fate of those who have been punished for violating the law. The ideal of normative legitimacy that we have applied and adapted to the attributive judgments of the human sciences is claimed to be undermined by human science practices that enforce institutional standards of normality. Foucault correlates this erosion of what is normative to what is merely normal with the rise of the human sciences at the end of the eighteenth century. He links these new human or anthropological sciences with the emergence of modern techniques of disciplining and controlling human beings. But how thoroughgoing is this linkage to be understood?

Whereas Kant saw his pragmatic anthropology as fostering a spirit of human cooperation, and Dilthey conceived the human sciences as broadening our understanding of life and deepening our appreciation of individuality, Foucault views these new sciences as primarily a set of techniques for surveying people as case studies, with the intent of making deviants normal. The legal punitive judgment of the courtroom is transformed into

---

37. Michel Foucault, *Discipline and Punish: The Birth of the Prison* (New York: Vintage Books, 1979), 23.

"a technical prescription for a possible normalization"[38] by those who administer penal institutions, so that normative legal constraints are reduced to normalizing restraints. Our expansive *disciplinary* topology of hermeneutic judgment would thus have its institutional counterpart in the narrowing *disciplining* techniques of normalizing judgment. Whereas the reflective disciplines we have relied on are often oriented by emancipatory ideals, the administrative disciplining of deviants (whether they be criminal or insane) reduces what is expansively *regulative* to techniques of controlling *regulations*.

One of Foucault's aims is to show that the system that administers and supervises punishment uses a disciplining power to which even courtroom judges must bow. Thus he writes that "the judge . . . requires a compulsory and rectifying supervision of his assessments."[39] The verdict of the courtroom judge accordingly loses its aura of finality and must be reassessed by a system of "medico-judicial treatment."[40] The human sciences are assigned a new technical and "prognostic"[41] power to judge, which is no longer concerned with evaluating responsibility and justice, but with how best to manage the prisoner. The original legal decision about how long a sentence someone should serve may be revised by psychiatrists and other anonymous experts who decide how to discipline prisoners. Thus Foucault sees the prescriptive power of the courtroom judge being undermined by extrajuridical prognostic considerations about whether it is best to reintegrate deviants into society or to keep them permanently isolated.

An orientational and critical hermeneutics can provide a diagnostic way of restricting the primordial authority of juridical verdicts without necessarily having to undermine them through prognostic techniques. Foucault's genealogical claims provide a further way to underscore the complexity of arriving at historical judgments, and they should constrain the human sciences to acknowledge the impersonal ways in which administrative institutions function as systems. But the contributions of the human and social sciences are not limited to such operations as surveillance and disciplining. Similarly, the normative legitimacy that we articulated for legal and historical judgments is not reducible to normalizing techniques, even if they occasionally become conflated in real life.

38. *Discipline and Punish*, 21.
39. *Discipline and Punish*, 247.
40. *Discipline and Punish*, 22.
41. *Discipline and Punish*, 19.

HERMENEUTICS AND HISTORICAL TRANSMISSION

Genealogical accounts like Foucault's point to ways in which past practices are eviscerated by being accommodated to current policies and practices. They stand counter to Gadamerians who take the idea of tradition (*Überlieferung*) literally as the past being delivered over (*überliefert*) to us as something that continues to nurture us. What is needed to mediate between these opposites is a more robust hermeneutical conception of transmission that can account for the give-and-take of historical interpretation. Whereas narrative theories of history can still claim to be explanative when they appeal to influences rather than causes, hermeneutical approaches to history must make room for a more responsive account of what Jacques Le Goff calls the "transmission of 'memory' from generation to generation."[42]

The idea of narrative influence was used to bring the events or "advents" of history to the level of experiential time. Hermeneutically, however, historical transmission must be conceived as occurring at the deeper level of a "receptive process" that reflexively absorbs and selectively digests its sources. Just as reflexive awareness is the being-with-itself of individual consciousness, the hermeneutic transmission of memory is the being-with of historical consciousness, where what is taken in is also recognized as being taken over. We have anticipated a conception of hermeneutical transmission by thinking of experience as a nexus that preserves the past in the present. Now we can apply our concepts of assimilation, acquisition, and appropriation[43] to further explicate them as three stages of transmission, where gradually the role of being influenced or determined is lessened and taken over by our capacity to respond.

We assimilate what conditions and influences us, whether this involves inheriting customs and beliefs or a more active process like the ongoing participation in our community. Assimilation as a mode of hermeneutic transmission preserves from the past what is still relevant to present experience. Assimilation can be considered a generative process that allows us to experience history as a forward-moving nexus that orients present and future action. But the acquisition that is involved in the higher cognitive understanding of the human sciences will be more focused and is often directed by specific meaning concerns. It is this more attentive process that transforms implicit memory into an explicit remembering.

---

42. Jacques Le Goff, *History and Memory* (New York: Columbia University Press, 1992), 92.
43. See chapter 4 and chapter 7.

Instead of making sense of a present experience by referring it to discrete past items stored in a special place called memory, a hermeneutical approach sees each new experience as framed by an overall meaning context that is acquired over time. Such an acquired framework can function like a program that continually takes in, orders, and reorganizes data and their relations. More than a passive accumulation or storehouse of separate data, the acquired nexus of an individual's consciousness consists not only of experiential contents, "but also of the connections which are established among these contents."[44] Dilthey emphasizes that "these connections are just as real as the contents. The connections are lived and experienced as relations between representational contents, as relations of values to one another, and of relations of ends and means."[45] Individuals develop a distinctive acquired experiential nexus that provides the frame of reference for their response to the world. It is a selective network that informs the significance assigned to subsequent experiences.

What is selectively acquired serves as a regulative cognitive system providing the background for the reflective knowing that is involved in hermeneutical appropriation. It is at this third stage that we recognize the reciprocal nature of such an acquired nexus—allowing us not only to assess the significance of past experience for subsequent experience, but also to reevaluate past experience on the basis of present experience. In addition to being true to what is preserved from the past, historians should consider its significance as we live our present lives and face the future. They must not only represent the past through narratives that can integrate the distinct synchronic systems of the human sciences, but also strive for a representative judgment about the import of human history.

One historical context proposed by the early Dilthey and used to frame his own attempts to arrive at representative historical assessments is that of a "generation." A generation is marked by a shared receptivity, not only to intellectual influences from the past, but also to contemporary conditions. Dilthey's biography of Schleiermacher places the life and work of this theologian in the context of his important philosophical and literary contemporaries. Schleiermacher was born in 1768, but Dilthey treats him as central to a new generation that does not crystallize until 1796, when Schleiermacher arrived in Berlin. This is the point in time when he and contemporaries such as Hegel, Schelling, and the Schlegels began to engage each other and define

---

44. Dilthey, *Poetry and Experience*, SW 5, 72.
45. *Poetry and Experience*, SW 5, 72.

themselves over against the previous generation of Lessing, Kant, and Fichte that they had already assimilated. Dilthey's massive *Life of Schleiermacher*[46] ensured that the contributions of this earlier generation were incorporated as part of a continuing process of transmission and revision.

In addition to differentiating the various contexts that can frame historical meaning, a reflective hermeneutical theory of history must recognize the distinct ways in which assimilation, acquisition, and appropriation transmit the content of the past to new generations. We can employ these ways of taking ownership of our heritage to sketch a generative conception of history that can account for at least limited continuities, despite some of the legitimate doubts that have been raised about universal history.

In light of our three ways of conceiving historical transmission, we can see that the most direct continuity applies to assimilation, which is rooted in a less extensive commonality of a local tradition. Assimilation refers to what a generation inherits from the past on the basis of local customs, practices, and means of communication that nurture it. For elementary understanding, everything is from the we-perspective of commonality and can still include prejudices inherited from previous generations. What is assimilated from the past tends to provide the simple certainty of life-knowledge or of common know-how and seldom attains the differentiated recognition characteristic of what is acquired cognitively.

Cognitive acquisition then analyzes the common nexus of life into special systems, each of which establishes a potentially universal horizon. When common life is differentiated into the social, cultural, economic, political, and legal structures that intersect in it, elementary understanding makes way for the higher understanding characteristic of the human sciences. This transition to conceptual cognition and higher understanding can occur when something in the inherited medium of common life does not match our normal expectations. A feature that does not seamlessly fit into the familiar patterns of our life may need to be accounted for by reorienting us to another or broader context for understanding it. Higher or cognitive understanding is not confined by the contingent parameters of a generation's inherited life-context and attempts to realign the possible frameworks for conceptualizing historical reality in universal terms. But as important as universal disciplinary contexts

---

46. Dilthey's extensive *Leben Schleiermachers* has not yet been translated into English, but his manuscript entitled *Schleiermacher's Hermeneutical System in Relation to Earlier Protestant Hermeneutics,* which was planned to become part of the second volume of the biography, has been translated in Dilthey, *Hermeneutics and the Study of History,* SW 4, 33–227.

are for arriving at a more explicit understanding—even explanations—of what is at work in history, they do not naturally or rationally cohere to produce an integral system of comprehension. This leads us to reiterate that the perspective of universalist history cannot be that of a totalizing history, but of a history that is elucidated in terms of a series of delimited but universally applicable disciplinary contexts.

Finally, the hermeneutical appropriation of historical situations or events requires a diagnostic use of reflective judgment to bring the most relevant contexts to bear on what is being interpreted in historical narratives. It is at this third level of appropriation that we can attempt to achieve a critical understanding of historical life. But here hermeneutical reflection is also reflexive, making it the responsibility of the individual interpreter. What is hermeneutically transmitted through assimilation and acquisition tends to be shared with one's generation, but the reflective appropriation that completes the hermeneutic project ultimately calls for individual judgment. It is at this level that paradigm shifts in interpretation can occur.

CHAPTER 9

Contextualizing the Arts: From Originating to Medial Contexts

Orientational hermeneutics as presented so far has analyzed the basic reflective conditions and schemata of interpretation. It has proposed a template of typical contexts that serve to orient practices of critical interpretation relating to general historical and cultural phenomena. In this concluding chapter, I will turn from these general contextual forms to consider the more specific contexts that come into play in the interpretation of particular works. This is especially relevant for the understanding of works of art, which tend to have a distinctive form and content. To account for this individuating form, interpreters of art have most often looked for an originating context, usually centered on the artist.

A relatively simple instance of such an originating context is invoked by those who hold that the meaning content of a text is determined by authorial intention. The standard of an originating intentional context has been upheld by thinkers as far back as Georg Friedrich Meier in the eighteenth century and as recently as E.D. Hirsch. Attacking Gadamer in *Validity in Interpretation*, Hirsch writes that "meaning is an affair of consciousness [which] is, in turn an affair of persons, and in textual interpretation the persons involved are an author and a reader."[1]

At the other end of the spectrum, the recipients of content—from critical readers to mass audiences—are made the arbiters of meaning. This is increasingly prevalent today, when information is digitized and disseminated

1. Hirsch, E.D., *Validity in Interpretation* (New Haven, CT: Yale University Press, 1967), 23.

with few restrictions, so that we can easily lose sight of original sources and contexts. For Gadamer, however, neither the artist nor the recipient determines the meaning of a work of art. Instead this meaning is said to develop through the productive or effective history (*Wirkungsgeschichte*) of the work itself. Gadamer points to the ongoing performances of a classical tragedy as the meaningful presence of the work. "Neither the being of the creative artist, nor that of the performer, nor that of the spectator has any legitimacy of its own."[2] They are all absorbed into an open-ended temporal context of an unfolding tradition.

Having characterized orientational hermeneutics as a reflective art of appropriate contextualization, our present task is to configure a more distinctive context for the interpretation of works of art. Traditionally, these efforts have been largely directed at the meaning content of individual works, whether conceived by Meier in representational terms or by Kant through a theory of expression. With this theory of expression, Kant moves beyond his more general concern with the aesthetic communicability of feeling to the problem of how artists can communicate their idiosyncratic emotions and ideas. Then by reconceiving expressions as manifestations of life, Dilthey points out that the process of expression also involves the articulation of some more general worldly medium. Subsequently, Heidegger rejects the primacy given to worldly meaning and claims that equal attention should be given to the earthly materials that ground the arts. To properly locate and contextualize artistic objectifications, we will revisit the earth-world distinction found in Kant and see how it stands up to the way Heidegger confronts earth and world in his interpretation of works of art.

The last sections of this chapter will focus on what the material medium of artworks contributes to their contextualization. Artists and their audience are related in terms of what I will call "medial contexts." In contemporary culture, the materiality of the medium has been expanded to include technological means of transmission that have important ramifications for meaningful communication. Artistic medial contexts will therefore be considered for their more general relevance for understanding how information is exchanged. Since today's media also manifest the effects of the digital revolution, medial contexts cannot be ignored by hermeneutics.

---

2. Gadamer, *Truth and Method*, 128.

MEIER ON REPRESENTATIONAL SIGNS AND THEIR INTENTIONAL CONTEXT

Meier provides a useful starting point by expanding hermeneutics to include aesthetic interpretation.[3] In his *Attempt at a Universal Art of Interpretation* (1757), Meier makes a distinction between rational and aesthetic interpretation that parallels the distinction his teacher Alexander Baumgarten had made between conceptual and sensible cognition. Baumgarten claims that sensible cognition is not simply an imperfect form of conceptual cognition but can have its own kind of aesthetic perfection. The distinctness that Descartes had assigned to conceptual cognition is rethought by Baumgarten as an "intensive clarity" that involves the internal differentiation of representations of things into their general marks. The perfection of sensible cognition consists of an "extensive clarity" that brings out the overall individuating form of representations and gives them a contextual determinacy.[4]

Based on this new analysis of cognition by Baumgarten, the task of Meier's hermeneutics is to consider the distinctive modes of cognitive clarity that can be assigned to signs. A sign is defined by Meier as "a means whereby the reality of something else can be cognized."[5] When the relation between a sign and what is designated is natural, Meier assigns it a place in a rational, systematic context. When the relation is based on a voluntary choice of a thinking being, then we have an arbitrary sensible sign within a more limited human context. It is the latter relation that needs to be clarified aesthetically and given contextual determinacy.

The hermeneutic task of gaining extensive clarity about the meaning of human texts leads Meier to place great stress on the individuality of the author as the source of the signs being interpreted. Meier defines the hermeneutically true meaning of a voluntary sign as "the intention or purpose for which the author of the sign uses it."[6] The author's main purpose defines what Meier calls "the immediate sense" of a sign or speech (as distinct from a mediate sense defined by a more remote purpose). This all-important immediate

---

3. For a more general discussion of Meier's place in the history of hermeneutics, see Jean Grondin, *Einführung in die philosophische Hermeneutik* (Darmstadt: Wissenschaftliche Buchgesellschaft, 1991), 73–78.

4. See Makkreel, "The Confluence of Aesthetics and Hermeneutics in Baumgarten, Meier and Kant," *The Journal of Aesthetics and Art Criticism* 54: 1 (1996), 66.

5. Meier, *Versuch einer allgemeinen Auslegungskunst* (Düsseldorf: Stern-Verlag Jannsen & Co., 1965), 4.

6. *Versuch einer allgemeinen Auslegungskunst*, 9.

sense is distinguished from the literal sense, which is based on the common usage of language. But the common usage of the author's habitat can leave open several possible meanings that are proper within that objective context. An interpretation may be proper *(eigentlich)* in using the linguistic and historical means available, but it will not be authentic *(eigen, authentisch)*[7] unless it discloses the immediate subjective sense of the author. Authenticity, which was initially a concern of philological criticism about the genuineness of ancient texts, is now used by Meier to define the correct interpretation of any text. Empirical inquiry into the original existence of a text is replaced with a concern about correctly representing its originally intended meaning.

The main principle of Meier's sensible hermeneutics is that of "fairness or reasonableness *(Billigkeit)*."[8] Reasonableness can be regarded as the aesthetic counterpart of rationality. According to this principle, one must interpret humanly created signs as appropriate to their subject matter until the opposite can be proved. Just as natural signs are known to be perfectly appropriate in a rational world, so invented human signs must be assumed to have been chosen reasonably if we are to draw clarity of meaning from them.

According to Meier, there is initially "sufficient ground" to focus on the author's intention. Not to do so would be "unfair *(unbillig)* because it would presuppose that the author spoke and wrote without using his intellect or has not understood himself. Accordingly, an interpreter must regard the authentic interpretation as true until it becomes evident that the author has changed his meaning and had another meaning than he says."[9] Meier's appeal to reasonableness is a call for fairness and establishes something like Quine's and Davidson's principle of charity,[10] but instead of being an acknowledgment of the indeterminacy of meaning, it is used as an aesthetic standard for interpretive clarity.

The idea of authentic interpretation is meant to resist reading too much into a text. It stands in opposition to doctrinal interpretations that have allowed religious texts to accrue meanings in accommodation to traditional institutional perspectives. But Meier's attack on the practice of "thinking more

---

7. *Versuch einer allgemeinen Auslegungskunst*, 52.
8. *Versuch einer allgemeinen Auslegungskunst*, 107.
9. *Versuch einer allgemeinen Auslegungskunst*, 75–76.
10. See Willard Van Orman Quine, *Word and Object* (Cambridge: MIT Press, 1960), 59n., and Donald Davidson, *Inquiries into Truth and Interpretation* (Oxford: Oxford University Press, 1984), 153.

than the author understands"[11] could undoubtedly also be extended forward to the Kant-inspired maxim of Herder, Schleiermacher and Dilthey that the task of hermeneutics is to open up the possibility of understanding authors better than they understood themselves.

Since Meier makes the author's intention the primary determinant of what a text means, he can be said to commit the intentionalist fallacy. However, he does not rule out subsequent counter-determinations by the interpreter, for he recognizes that someone other than the author may be better able to follow out the text's implications. Moreover, Meier admits that for an author "to be understood correctly, it is not also necessary for the interpreter to think what the author has thought in the same way as the author thought it."[12] The thought must be the same, but the mode of thinking it may be different. An interpretation may not endow a text with more meaning than the author gave it, nor with less.[13] If the literal sense allowed by common linguistic usage provides more than the immediate sense that represents the intention of the author, we must institute a restrictive interpretation. Only in the unusual case that the literal sense provides less meaning is there a need for an "expanded interpretation *(erweitende Auslegung)*."[14]

KANT AND EXPRESSING WHAT WAS INEXPRESSIBLE

Kant's idea of authentic interpretation may have been influenced by Meier, but differs in being less directly tied to individual subjects and their local habitat. Authenticity is still conceived subjectively but as we saw in chapter 6 cannot be defined without reference to others and must have a wider territorial scope. Another important change is that Kant is more concerned with understanding what is expressed than what is represented. We should also note that the idea of expanded interpretation that Meier considered a special or remedial case becomes for Kant a desideratum for all interpretation. The reflective or interpretive power of judgment is correlated with an "expanded mode of thinking *(erweiternde Denkungsart)*"[15] that serves to make authentic-

---

11. *Versuch einer allgemeinen Auslegungskunst,* 70.
12. *Versuch einer allgemeinen Auslegungskunst,* 70.
13. Hirsch makes a more useful distinction here between the meaning that the author intended a text to have and the significance that the language of the text may have for others.
14. *Versuch einer allgemeinen Auslegungskunst,* 100.
15. *Critique of the Power of Judgment,* 175 (translation revised); *Ak* 5: 295.

ity an intersubjective ideal. Accordingly, an interpretation's authenticity cannot be adequately measured by the subjective standard of authorial intention. Moreover, when we turn to Kant's theory of artistic genius, the very idea of conscious intentions is called into question. He writes that "the author of a product that he owes to his genius does not know himself how the ideas for it come to him," and cannot produce them "at will."[16] The specifically artistic task of genius is to express meanings that were previously inexpressible and could not have been intended.

Kant developed his theory of expression as part of his effort to account for the way the unprecedented and inexplicable ideas of genius can nevertheless be communicated to a more general audience. Genius is the originating context or "inborn predisposition of the mind"[17] that leads the imagination to playfully expand a given concept of the understanding to uncover "extensive undeveloped material for the understanding, of which the latter took no regard in its concept."[18] The product of this imaginative expansion of a *concept* of the understanding is called an aesthetic *idea*. In section 49 of the *Critique of Judgment*, Kant defines an aesthetic idea as a "representation of the imagination that occasions much thinking without it being possible for any determinate thought, i.e. *concept*, to be adequate to it, which, consequently, no language fully attains or can make intelligible."[19] As an indeterminate representation of the imagination, the aesthetic idea has no available conceptual or linguistic expression to communicate it.

But if the power of genius is to be more than subjectively idiosyncratic, it needs to be made communicable to others by expressing its seemingly inexpressible aesthetic ideas. Or as Kant writes, genius must draw on spirit or the animating principle of mind to "express (*auszudrücken*) what is unnamable" in its mental state and "make it universally communicable."[20] This capacity of spirit for expression consists in "apprehending the rapidly passing play of the imagination" involved in the aesthetic idea and "unifying it into a concept."[21] Genius can be more fully defined as the capacity to imaginatively expand an available concept of the understanding by "finding" an aesthetic idea that suggests a field of possibilities, some of which are then expressed in a new con-

---

16. *Critique of the Power of Judgment*, 187; *Ak* 5: 308.
17. *Critique of the Power of Judgment*, 186; *Ak* 5: 307.
18. *Critique of the Power of Judgment*, 194; *Ak* 5: 317.
19. *Critique of the Power of Judgment*, 192; *Ak* 5: 314.
20. *Critique of the Power of Judgment*, 195; *Ak* 5: 317.
21. *Critique of the Power of Judgment*, 195; *Ak* 5: 317.

cept. The resulting concept is "original and . . . discloses a new rule, which could not have been deduced from any antecedent principles."[22] Thereby, what was previously inexpressible can now "be communicated without the constraint of rules."[23]

Here the art of creative expression anticipates a new concept in a way that is similar to how reflective judgment proceeds from particulars to an as-yet unavailable universal. The resulting concept can be called a *reflective concept*. Such a concept goes beyond the constraint of already available concepts and rules, and introduces what Kant elsewhere calls a sense of lawfulness without a determinate law.

Earlier, we distinguished between 1) the normal communication that makes use of discursive concepts and 2) the aesthetic communicability involved in a judgment of taste that expands our felt state of mind so that it can be shared without appealing to any of our available concepts. Normal concept-based communication is governed by logical rules when the relevant hermeneutical context is the field of the possible; it is also governed by transcendental rules when we seek agreement about the territory of actual experience. Empirical rules or conventions may suffice when communication is limited to a more local habitat.

The most determinate mode of conceptual communication exists within a scientific community when it is able to legislate laws to the domain of nature—laws that any potential rational intellect must acknowledge as objectively binding. Aesthetic communicability aims at intersubjective validity and concerns only those rational beings who possess human feeling. Through the reflective engagement of feeling, we can generalize what is valuable in our own limited context and claim it to be valid for the larger territory of all human beings. Kant's subsequent discussion of genius and the artist's spirited state of mind supplements normal communication and aesthetic communicability with expressions that make it possible to communicate in a new, reflective way about what matters to us. Whereas aesthetic judgment expands the contextual scope of our thinking, the artistic function of expression is to name or spell out the analogical relations used to relate what we know about familiar contexts to those that we can only represent abstractly.[24] The indirect reflective analogy that Kant suggested between an integral organic system and his ideal of a republican form of government can be more directly expressed by

---

22. *Critique of the Power of Judgment*, 195; *Ak* 5: 317.
23. *Critique of the Power of Judgment*, 195; *Ak* 5: 317.
24. See chapters 3 and 5.

artists through symbolization. We can thus call the third way of communicating "symbolic."

DILTHEY ON MANIFESTATIONS OF LIFE AND THEIR INTERPRETIVE CONTEXTS

To further explore the contextual scope of expressions, we will consider how expressions as objectifications can be subsumed under the more encompassing category of what Dilthey calls "manifestations of life." Because expressions are often assumed to be governed by conscious intentions, Dilthey uses the term "expression (*Ausdruck*)" sparingly in his late writings and refers more often to "manifestations (*Äußerungen*) of life."[25] Manifestations are less personal than expressions per se and thereby lead further away from the focus on consciousness in Meier and Kant. With life considered as the overall context of reality, "manifestations of life" becomes the generic covering term for all the historical materials that require reflective interpretation and contextual orientation.

Dilthey distinguishes three classes of life-manifestations. The first class consists of propositional judgments and other pure thought-formations. They manifest life in the most abstract way, and their relevant orientational context will be, in our terms, either a logical field or a law-governed natural domain.[26] "Here understanding is directed at . . . mere logical content, which remains identical in every context, and is more complete than in relation to any other manifestation of life."[27] Theoretical judgments are intended to communicate conceptual thought, but they are not expressive of the individuals who put them forward. Thought-formations "have been detached from the lived experience in which they arose, and they possess the common basic trait of having been adapted to logical norms. This gives them a selfsameness independent of their position in the context of thought."[28] A propositional judgment aims to objectively represent universally valid relations about the world: its meaning is not to be located in the subjective representations of the person uttering it.

The second class of life-manifestations consists of practical actions. In

---

25. Dilthey, "The Understanding of Other Persons," *SW* 3, 226.
26. "Field" and "domain" were defined in chapter 3, as were the terms "territory" and "habitat" used in the next paragraph.
27. "The Understanding of Other Persons," *SW* 3, 226–27.
28. "The Understanding of Other Persons," *SW* 3, 226.

themselves, actions are not initially intended for ordinary communication, but the way they relate to purposes can disclose something about those who perform them as well as manifest the values and goals of their communal life. If an action does disclose anything about the state of mind of the agent, it is only as "situationally conditioned," not as expressive of the overall "life-nexus itself in which the state of mind is grounded."[29] When the historian interprets practical actions, the most relevant meaning context will be either the habitat of what is locally familiar or a more generally shared territory of human life. The task of reflective judgment is to locate intermediary contexts such as the social and cultural systems that specify the public roles of human beings and frame the interpretation of historical events.[30] For ethically controversial deeds, Kant's universal domain of moral laws should also come into play.

Only the third class of life-manifestations, which include works of art, are called "expressions of lived experience." It consists of expressions that draw on the full scope of lived experience and can be found in letters, memoirs, religious writings, philosophical meditations, as well as artistic creations. They offer not only the greatest challenge to understanding but also more occasions for misunderstanding. Expressions of lived experience are more difficult to interpret than the other two kinds of life-manifestations because they are directed neither by the universal aims of theory nor by commonly shared practices. Dilthey makes this especially clear for the interpretation of works of art. Here judgment must establish to what extent the biography of the artist may or may not be a relevant interpretive context and consider what other situational factors require us to consider more encompassing life-contexts. This is important because the individuating styles of works of art reflect both artists and their times. The style of a work is expressive of the lived experience of the artist, but it also articulates the nexus of the world that inheres in that experience.

When speaking of musical compositions, Dilthey indicates that the feelings composers express in their music are not first found through introspection and then translated into sounds. Their feelings are musical from the start and are generated in a tonal sphere. Here expression is not to be conceived as the externalization of psychological states of mind. There is no musical work, he declares, "that does not speak of what has been experienced, and yet everything is more than expression. For this musical world with its infinite possibilities of tonal beauties and of meaning is always there . . . in history,

---

29. "The Understanding of Other Persons," *SW* 3, 227.
30. See chapters 3 and 6.

capable of endless development. And it is in this world that the musician lives, not in his feelings."[31]

Musical genius lies not in expressing a mental aesthetic idea and giving it a communicable form as Kant had conceived it, but in giving expression to what any inhabitant of the tonal sphere is implicitly capable of feeling. Artistic creativity, as the power to give determinacy to what others feel indeterminately, leads expression to go over into the articulation of meaning. What was assumed to be primarily an intentional process of externalizing an inner state is here recognized to be a process of also articulating a work so that its parts can be understood as having an inner relatedness to each other. As two aspects of one process, expression relates inner to outer, and articulation relates parts to wholes.

An artistic expression of lived experience does not simply mirror the mental life of the creator but, as noted, it pushes toward an outcome that can be "truthful in itself."[32] A poetic work that is truthful in this deeper sense attains its own kind of coherence and constitutes a nexus that is "separable from"[33] the inner processes of the poet. The connectedness produced does not involve the domain-like necessity (*Notwendigkeit*) that Aristotle demands of a dramatic plot with an inevitable denouement. Instead the inner development of the work results in a sense of things "having-to-be-thus (*Soseinmüssen*)."[34] This nontheoretical sense of rightness discloses itself as "the actualization of an aesthetic value"[35] whose development could not have been predicted but is felt to be inherently fitting. In the case of musical development, this sense of having-to-be-thus is the contextual coherence or felt appropriateness that arises when the musical themes of a sonata are varied and recapitulated and finally brought back to the tonic key.

THE EARTH-WORLD CONFLICT IN HEIDEGGER'S "THE ORIGIN OF THE WORK OF ART"

In moving from Meier to Kant and Dilthey, we have shown a declining hermeneutical concern with the originating context of works of art. And Heidegger continues this trend by downplaying psychological considerations

---

31. "The Understanding of Other Persons," *SW* 3, 242.
32. See chapter 2.
33. The Formation of the Historical World, *SW* 3, 107.
34. "The Understanding of Other Persons," *SW* 3, 242; *GS* VII, 211.
35. "The Understanding of Other Persons," *SW* 3, 242.

in interpretation. In *Being and Time* (1927), he conceives his hermeneutical philosophy as a further development of Kant's orientation to the world as well as Dilthey's project of understanding our historical situation. The understanding of being is clearly focused on our being-in-the-world, and *Being and Time* even thematizes the project of articulation as the way interpretation makes intelligible what is already pre-understood about our worldly involvement. The primary concern of *Being and Time* is our existential situatedness, but no indication is given there that artworks can draw their inspiration from this worldly involvement and yet point to an origin that undermines this very world.

However, in his later philosophy of art, Heidegger sets up a struggle (*Streit*) between the world and the earth as two opposing frames of contextualization for the arts. In the 1935–36 essay "The Origin of the Work of Art," he continues to speak of the world as a context for finding meaning, but now the earth is said to enclose what remains unintelligible and stands as a limit for hermeneutics. The inclusion of earth makes his hermeneutical framework more complex, but it also serves to challenge what is ordinarily meant by the origin of a work of art. For Heidegger this origin has very little to do with either artistic intentions or experiences of an existential sort. This is because he sees the artist as caught up in an opposition between the world as we know it and an earth that both grounds and resists this world.

So far, hermeneutic orientation has been discussed primarily with reference to the world as the overall sphere of theoretical, practical, and reflective concerns. But the relation between world and earth was not overlooked by Kant. We saw Kant contrast earth and world in relative terms, whereby earthly content provides empirical limits that can, in principle, be transformed into intelligible worldly bounds. Although all orientational hermeneutic contexts are worldly, territory and habitat clearly retain some earthly traces. A human habitat still reminds us of our earthly roots, and a territory as a shared context assumes that the earth is capable of being cultivated. We saw Kant speak of the earth as a territorial sphere that is possessed in common in the state of nature. Only on the basis of a communal civic state can individual possession of any part of this territory be lawfully justified in worldly terms. But this kind of gradual transition from earth to world is rejected by Heidegger, who posits instead an inherent opposition between world and earth that will never be fully overcome.

In "The Origin of the Work of Art," Heidegger points to the Greek temple as "setting up (*auf-stellen*) a world" as well as "setting forth (*her-stellen*) the earth."³⁶ The temple opens up a world of meaning, but at the same time it "sets this world back again on earth, which itself only thus emerges as native ground."³⁷ According to Heidegger, the world that is "unconcealed" by the temple "strives to surmount" the earth, for "as self-opening it cannot endure anything closed. The earth, however, as sheltering and concealing, tends always to draw the world into itself and keep it there."³⁸ Any truth "unconcealed" or disclosed by the worldly character of the work of art is thus temporary and threatened by the power of the earth to draw it back into itself. The earth is not just a material medium such as clay or marble, but stands for a primitive sphere of concealment that closes us off from the truth. What artists can contribute through their work is to establish a temporary clearing between earth and world to produce insight into the nature of being.

Heidegger's essay on the origin of the work of art was first published in a collection of essays entitled *Holzwege*: Wood-paths. The opening lines of this volume read: "Wood is an old name for forest. A wood has paths that usually become overgrown and suddenly end where no one has passed before."³⁹ Such wood-paths are like temporary clearings that lead away from the world and point to uncharted terrain. These clearings must be maintained if they are not to be overgrown and reclaimed by native plant life. The thoughts inspired by forest clearings do not mark out a direct path toward the world of scientific and cultural communication. But even if winding wood-paths lead us nowhere, insofar as we are then required to circle back from this earthly cul-de-sac, the experience could still have hermeneutic value and add indirectly to our understanding of the world.

Viewed from a Lyotardian perspective, Heidegger's position may be said to hold that the earth is not "presentable" in worldly terms. But does this mean that the earth is inherently "unpresentable" or that it can be apprehended in Lyotard's words as "the unpresentable in presentation itself?"⁴⁰ The unpresentable can be imagined purely formally and negatively in the way that Kant conceived the sublime, namely, as surpassing all human measure.

36. Heidegger, "The Origin of the Work of Art," in *Poetry, Language, Thought*, trans. Albert Hofstadter (New York: Harper and Row, 1971), 46.
37. "Origin of the Work of Art," 42.
38. "Origin of the Work of Art," 49.
39. Heidegger, *Holzwege* (Frankfurt am Main: Vittorio Klostermann, 1963), 3.
40. Jean-Francois Lyotard, "Answering the Question: What is Postmodernism?," in *The Postmodern Condition: A Report on Knowledge* (Minneapolis: University of Minnesota Press, 1984), 81.

But for Lyotard, the postmodern is that moment in the modern that allows disruptive contents to be presented "without concern for the unity of the whole."[41] Whereas Kant's modern sublime projected what is unpresentable into the field of the supersensible, the postmodern sublime suggests that the unpresentable may be subliminal and submerged in the mysterious recesses of the earth. This way of correlating Lyotardian language with Heideggerian thinking shows that the earth need not stand solely for what is concealed and unpresentable as such, but for an unpresentable moment in what is presentable in the world.

Even in Heidegger's description, the work of art does not keep its earthly origins self-enclosed or concealed. As much as worldly meaning content tends to rise above earthly material, earth will eventually "jut through the world."[42] The earth finds a way of presenting or manifesting itself, even though it may be indirectly in terms of mere symptoms. The earth cannot express itself, but the plant life it can sustain gives us some indication of its underlying character.

Just as the earth is not completely closed off from us, so the world is not fully open and transparent. The world of hermeneutics consists of multiple contexts whose distinctive functions can be made more or less intelligible through the procedures of higher understanding. But this world also includes more deeply rooted institutional networks that are more difficult to discern. This exposes a tension between social, economic, and cultural systems that are formed to deal with the changing needs of the times and more entrenched institutions that continue to exert their power from behind the scene. The point is to recognize that the various contexts that are relevant to interpretation may either reinforce or counteract each other. Different contexts can disclose themselves at the various levels of understanding, from elementary to higher to critical, which underscores the need for judgmental discretion in determining the most appropriate contexts for interpretation.

Whether or not a work of art is to be conceived as rooted in the earth, it clearly can assert its own measure against the world at large. It may indirectly express or present what was initially inexpressible or unpresentable, thus marking a limit point for what we have been able to understand. The hermeneutical challenge for the arts as part of the development of human culture is to find the proper context that makes it possible for content to become expressible and communicable. This could require a newly configured context or a new way of relating already available worldly contexts.

---

41. "Answering the Question: What is Postmodernism?," 80.
42. "Origin of the Work of Art," 49.

However, the way Heidegger approaches their interpretation, the arts seem to fall outside of any cultural historical context and stand on more primordial ground. Each work is expected to throw us back to the origin of things. As Heidegger writes, "whenever art happens . . . history either begins or starts over again." This and his claim that art "founds history"[43] have been seen as providing a basis for social experience.[44] But if art has a social dimension for Heidegger, it is not one of public engagement. There is little evidence that he is interested either in the communal consensus-building functions that the arts have often been credited with or in the way that Dilthey and Gadamer see artists as responding to their predecessors and contemporaries. These more human interactive modes of artistic experience seem to be of little interest to Heidegger. What Heidegger's philosophy of art points to instead is the way the arts tap into what he calls a "people's endowment."[45] "Endowment" is a translation of "*ein Mitgegebenes*"—that which is given with. Heidegger uses the idea of endowment to claim that poets bring out what the ethos of their nation implicitly brings with it as their destiny. But we can use the idea of artistic endowment in a less problematic way. The relevant background that is "given with" and orients the artist in being creative is neither originating in Heidegger's nationalistic sense nor reducible to the "inborn predisposition (*ingenium*)"[46] that Kant ascribes to an individual state of mind. To delimit the endowment and initial orientation of the creative artist, we must take a closer look at how artists work with their medium.

THE MEDIAL CONTEXTS OF WORKS OF ART

What sets the arts apart from the other subject matters discussed so far is that they establish their own contexts to focus and frame the world in distinctive ways. Thus the general, reflective contexts used to interpret the historical world need to be supplemented with interpretive concepts adapted to the conditions of artistic creativity. Hermeneutics should be able to recognize these inherent contexts through an examination of artistic content.

43. "Origin of the Work of Art," 77.
44. See Kai Hammermeister, *The German Aesthetic Tradition* (Cambridge: Cambridge University Press, 2002), 184.
45. "Origin of the Work of Art," 77. Bernasconi notes that in later versions of the essay, Heidegger "omitted all reference to the *Volk*, to decision, and to 'great art' as such," in Robert Bernasconi, *Heidegger in Question* (Atlantic Highlands, NJ: Humanities Press International, 1993), 116.
46. *Critique of the Power of Judgment*, 186; Ak 5: 307.

Traditionally, artistic content has been conceived primarily in terms of meaning content (*Gehalt*), but works of art are also notable for the ways they present material content (*Inhalt*). The latter is generally identified as the "medium" or material base for representing meaning. It is widely assumed that the meaning content gives the initial shape to the material content. However, the confluence of meaning content and material content in works of art is better understood as present from the start in what I will call a "medial context" that orients artists to their work.

The idea of a "medial" context employs the dual meaning of "medium" as a material substance and also an agency or means. That is, the artistic medium is conceived to be not only a material substrate or base, but also a means of transmission for what is expressed or communicated in works of art. Whether the medium is inert physical material, as in the case of marble, clay, and paint, or the living language of words and musical tones, the function of the medium is already culturally conditioned and has the potential to communicate meaning. Medial contexts can provide the frame of reference for the convergence of material and meaning content in any art form. This convergence can also be thought of in terms of the overall stylistic qualities that give works of art their distinctive medial presence.

The relation between artists and their work is not merely one of transferring mental content to a material medium. The artist is immersed in an imaginary medial context that not only includes what has been assimilated over time, but also takes account of contemporary conditions and developments. In some ways a medial context may seem comparable to the "endowment" that Heidegger claimed to be "given with" the artist, but it is not a national ethos that befalls artists as their destiny. Medial contexts can be accepted, modified, or rejected. Even when painters approach their blank canvas aware of current conventions, stylistic tendencies, and other visual expectations, they are free to refine or even defy them.

Medial contexts possess some of the commonality assigned to the medium of objective spirit,[47] but they lack the stability of the customs embedded in this tradition-based medium. An artistic medial context rarely has an institutional basis in a community nor does it attain the disciplinary status that often attaches to the general sociocultural systems specified by the human sciences. Like the medium of inherited commonality, an artistic medial context is orientational. But it is a more informal context focused on aesthetic sensitivity and artistic innovation. A medial context orients the artist techni-

---

47. For an explication of objective spirit, see chapters 1 and 7 above.

cally, and for hermeneutics it provides the background frame of reference for discerning stylistic innovations.[48] This attendant stylistic use of the medial context for the interpretation of artworks by spectators and art critics need not, however, bring about anything as organized as the "status-conferring" social systems being discussed in contemporary aesthetics.[49] Artistic medial contexts have a self-delimiting intermediary scope and are informal in nature, which makes them all the more relevant for our times, in which new media are being explored.

We saw intimations of an artistic medial context in Dilthey's suggestion that musical genius is measured by the capacity to become absorbed "in the tonal sphere as if it alone existed."[50] What was described earlier as the contextual coherence of a musical composition can now be said to reflect the composer's immersion in a developing medial context. The composer does not merely find external sounds to express inner feelings, but works with a tonal medium that involves conventions about harmony and dissonance that are at least in part inherited and transmitted over time.

The feelings expressed by composers are musical from the start and are generated in a tonal medium. What they offer us is more than representation or expression: they offer a new medium-focused way of responding to the world. Whatever content is being expressed is already informed by a whole web of associations, and through the artist's creativity it can receive a new shape. What is expressed in a major composition constitutes a further articulation of that web and gives it a distinctive stylistic form. This link between expression and articulation can be used to show how a medial context both affects and is affected by artistic productivity.

The medial context of works of art could be called their sphere of material transmissibility and meaning communicability. Their integral unity exists

---

48. See also Makkreel, *Dilthey, Philosopher of the Human Studies*, 399–413, where the style of a work of art was characterized as a determinate-indeterminate quality that serves to articulate the objective spirit of a time and place. The idea of a medial context is less tied to the overarching scope of objective spirit, but can take into account relevant background conventions.

49. See George Dickie, *Introduction to Aesthetics: An Analytic Approach* (New York: Oxford University Press, 1997), 84–86. The institutional analysis of art by George Dickie defines the art world as a "bundle" of social systems and more informal subsystems that can confer the status of a work of art on an artifact by treating it as a potential *"candidate for appreciation."* Dickie's institutional framework provides no endorsement of artworks as actually being worthy of aesthetic appreciation. This sets it apart from medial contexts, which are mainly about aesthetic conventions and expectations.

50. "The Understanding of Other Persons," *SW* 3, 242.

most prominently in poetic and musical language. With the growing influence of modern technology and the digital revolution, the relation between meaning content and material content in the visual arts has also become more intimate. Whereas dabs of paint on a canvas are inert, the pixels of digital images are transmissible. Digitization produces a material transmissibility that parallels meaningful communication. This is just one example of the ever-increasing confluence of material content and meaning content in today's visual arts, which will be further discussed below. To make sense of this fluid art scene in which new combinations of media are being explored, it is all the more relevant to orient our understanding of them in terms of medial contexts. As the arts become less and less concerned with representing the world at large, the medial presentation of meaning comes to stand out as central for artistic communication.[51]

Current medial communication can be contrasted with the problem of communicability as it has been considered so far. In chapter 5, we approached the arts in relation to the Enlightenment concern with universal standards of taste and also looked for ways in which aesthetic spectators can be moved beyond their narrow feelings within their local habitat. With Kant's cosmopolitan field as the background, our discussions pointed to the more general contexts of a territory of human interchange and cultural systems. His concern was to account for the possibility of sharing feelings when the natural language we have inherited fails us. Pure aesthetic feeling was meant to be expansive by leading us outward into the world at large. And as distinctive as artistic expression may be, Kant's assumption was that it refers back to common sources, albeit to emulate rather than to imitate them.

What is transmissible and communicable within our more historically bounded artistic medial contexts opens up a much greater degree of complexity. The historicism of the nineteenth century led to an increasing awareness of multiple traditions and a loss of faith in common sources. What we inherit and assimilate may have various, even incompatible, sources. Today's world is global due to the increased transmissibility of the media being used, but this has only exacerbated the problem of recognizing commonality. Broader access to information allows the medial contexts of modern artists to be more eclectic and subject to shifting currents. In this atmosphere, the point of artistic productivity is less to imitate or emulate than to high-

---

51. Medial presentation as activity has long been central to such traditional arts as the ballet, where the dancer's body in motion is made the medium for performing a composition. Today we also have visual performance artists who use their own body as a medium of composing.

light what is novel or to present another stylistic perspective on what is familiar.

No art form has experimented more with stylistic innovation than twentieth-century painting, starting with Cubism and moving in rapid succession through Constructionism, Geometric Abstraction, Abstract Expressionism, Surrealism, to more nascent movements. Painting had always been either decorative or representational, but the use of collage to focus our attention back to the canvas did not become common until the early twentieth century. Media such as paper, sand, and wood were glued onto the painted canvas to interrupt its ordinary representational function. But we can trace this more medium-focused approach to painting back to the great landscapes of Paul Cézanne. What is distinctive about his landscapes and makes them pioneering is their power to bring a whole scene into relief by drawing everything forward onto what can be called a medial plane of visibility. His canvases bring what is perceivable to the fore as a structural but fragmented whole that exhibits the interplay of the angular and the curved, the static and the dynamic. Here the available medial context for meaningful presentation is articulated within the material presence of the medium.

We spoke above of reflexive awareness as the self-referential aspect of experience that can relate one's reflective context back to oneself. Similarly, the medial context of a work of art can be said to give its meaning content a reflexive or indexical with-itselfness that constitutes its presence. This reflexivity is especially evident in poetry, where we attend not only to the meaning of words but to how they sound. When these two aspects of poetic language reinforce each other, we linger and allow reflective meaning to be felt reflexively. Although the literary prose of a novel may not attain this reflexive intensity of poetic medial presence, it can evoke a more extensive imaginative presence. There are few modes of artistic presence that are as absorbing as a dramatic performance on the stage. And now that novels and dramas can be accessed in filmed versions as well as in print, they attain a life of their own in which the individual imagination merges with a more public mode of presentation. The optical and technical reproducibility of the medium of the film gives its virtual sphere an unprecedented scope.

But of all the arts, architecture most concretely illustrates the idea of a medial contextual presence that draws the world into itself and frames it in ways that can anchor us. Technological advances in the use of building materials and in making computer projections and calculations have allowed architects to draw our attention from afar with the monumental scale of their skyscrapers. But they have also been able to become more innovative in finding subtle, creative ways to accommodate buildings to their surroundings. Architects such as Le Corbusier have been able to give a flowing movement to their structures and remake architecture as an expanded sculptural medium that envelops us. Frank Lloyd Wright has used this adaptability to introduce a visual tension in the Guggenheim museum between the configurations of the exhibition space and the art that is placed there. Frank Gehry's unorthodox use of building materials allows for an exhilarating interplay between curvilinear shapes and surface sheen. More generally, contemporary architecture has allowed us to inhabit the world in new ways, while also integrating its products with their earthly base.

Not surprisingly, some architects have been intrigued by Heidegger's essay "Building Dwelling Thinking," for one of its central themes is that building is a form of dwelling that binds us to the earth.[52] However, the medial presence of architectural works refers to both earth and world. The Greek temple that Heidegger invokes already marks more than a temporary clearing between earth and world; it also establishes a medial space that holds them together. More generally, the medial context of an architectural work exhibits both material and meaning content in a creative tension.

THE MEDIAL PRESENTATION OF THE COMMONPLACE IN CONTEMPORARY ART

Over the course of this chapter, the traditional conception of artistic expression as essentially an individuating form of self-expression has been placed in a broader context as part of a process of public or worldly articulation. In so doing, we have increasingly moved from the expressive and representational functions of art to consider those of manifestation and medial presentation.

Rudolf Arnheim, as one who sought to preserve the centrality of expression in the arts, did so by pointing beyond personal feeling to the universal import of expressiveness. He writes that the "perception of expression fulfills its spiritual mission only if we experience in it more than the resonance of our own feelings. It permits us to realize that the forces stirring in ourselves are only individual examples of the same forces acting throughout the universe."[53] According to Arnheim, the expressiveness of natural oppositions like rising

---

52. See Pavlos Lefas, *Dwelling and Architecture: From Heidegger to Koolhaas* (Berlin: Jovis Verlag, 2006).

53. Rudolf Arnheim, "The Expressiveness of Visual Forms," in *Art and Visual Expression* (Berkeley and Los Angeles: University of California Press, 1966), 434.

and falling, dominance and submission, harmony and discord is directly presented in perception. The isomorphism between physical downward forces and mental depressive tendencies posited by Arnheim's Gestaltist psychology represents in effect a psycho-physical generalization of the resonance between material and meaning content ascribed above to artistic medial contexts. The result of this isomorphism is to expand the medial context of artistic creativity to give equal weight to natural and human forms of expressiveness.

For Arnheim the function of the arts is to reappropriate the universal expressiveness of life that has been lost sight of in our scientific age. However, the more prominent tendency in the contemporary arts has been to turn away from the universal patterns that orient us to the world at large and focus on commonplace patterns that pervade the mundane aspects of our everyday life. Ordinary human products and artifacts that we take for granted and use almost absent-mindedly are presented for our notice. The medium of photography has especially encouraged this tendency by exhibiting workaday scenes as well as close-ups that highlight the details of manufactured products such as can openers, Coke bottles, etc.

Jacques Rancière, for one, has referred to this as the egalitarian aesthetics of photography. This turn to everyday phenomena, as well as the presentation of ready-mades and found objects, can be seen as part of what Rancière has spoken of as "the appropriation of the commonplace."[54] In his own way, Arthur Danto has also thematized the commonplace through what he calls the "transfiguration of the commonplace" in contemporary art. Works of art may be physically "indiscernible" from ordinary things, yet they can be endowed with the "'is' of artistic identification."[55] This act of designating a common object as art shifts aesthetic appreciation from the level of mere perception to that of interpretation.

Nevertheless, the embrace of the commonplace has different implications for these two critics. Rancière endorses the commonplace politically as a democratization of the arts. To this extent he can be related to Walter Benjamin, who was one of the first to take note of the way technical reproducibility has removed artworks from the restrictive contexts that were prized for their uniqueness. The "original use value" of the arts derived from their relation to ancient cults and rituals. This traditional function gave the arts a distinc-

---

54. Jacques Rancière, *The Politics of Aesthetics*, trans. Gabriel Rockhill (London/New York: Continuum, 2006), 33.

55. Arthur Danto, "The Artworld," in *Philosophy Looks at the Arts*, ed. Joseph Margolis (Philadelphia: Temple University Press, 1978), 138–39.

tive "aura" that set them apart from the everyday.[56] Even as these religious functions were gradually relaxed, the arts continued to maintain their special aura through the "cult of beauty" that Benjamin characterized as a "secularized ritual."[57] This tradition is finally broken by the postindustrial technology that makes things readily reproducible and has spawned new art forms like photography and film that are capable of bringing everything close to us. "For the first time in world history, technical reproducibility emancipates the work of art from its parasitical dependence on ritual," he writes, "and begins to be based on another practice—politics."[58] This new relation of the arts to the broader political sphere is welcomed by Benjamin, but he also recognizes potential risks. Although new media such as film can give artists a political opening and the means to explore change, they can just as easily lead to the aesthetic glorification of dictators and the status quo.

Instead of looking to the broader public of the mass media, Arthur Danto focuses on the cognoscenti of the art world and their response to the Pop art of the 1960s. Warhol's *Brillo Box* can be appreciated as a work of art, Danto writes, only if one has "mastered a good deal of artistic theory as well as a considerable amount of the history of [mid-twentieth-century] New York painting."[59] In short, it requires a familiarity with that New York gallery scene as an institutional context, which fosters the requisite sophistication to identify Rauschenberg's installation entitled *Bed* as a work of art and not view it as simply a commonplace bed that is covered with streaks of paint. The appreciation of it as a work of art depends on our capacity to recontextualize ordinary life. This new attitude can involve entering the kind of institutional "artworld"[60] that Danto speaks of, but it can also proceed more informally in relation to what we have called artistic medial contexts.

Contemporary artists increasingly confront us with phenomena that have been taken out of their normal life-context and require a medial reorientation. This is most evident in the ready-mades introduced by Marcel Duchamp,

56. See Walter Benjamin, *Das Kunstwerk im Zeitalter seiner technischen Reproduzierbarkeit* (Frankfurt am Main: Suhrkamp Verlag, 1970), 20.

57. *Das Kunstwerk*, 20.

58. *Das Kunstwerk*, 21.

59. "The Artworld," 142.

60. Danto and Dickie are both interested in the institutional contexts of art, but in contrast to Dickie, Danto regards artworks as more than candidates for potential appreciation. Dickie thinks that there is no difference in kind "between the appreciation of art and the appreciation of nonart" (*Introduction to Aesthetics*, 440), whereas Danto thinks there is.

who isolated a urinal from the normal context of its use to exhibit its pristine porcelain surface. To create his *Bicycle Wheel*, Duchamp disassembled a wheel from a bicycle and attached it to a stool. Balancing a bicycle wheel on a stool removes it from its usual functional context and allows it to be relocated within a medial context in which the black elegance of the wheel contrasts with the white sturdiness of the stool. Warhol's *Brillo Box* is not a ready-made, but a decontextualized, presentation of the commodity widely available on store shelves. His painted Brillo box gives us an artifactual presentation that defines its own medial context.

But medial reorientation is not limited to the presentation of the commonplace. We can find precedent for it in the aesthetic reorientation introduced by great Cubists like Georges Braque and Pablo Picasso, who deconstructed objects in order to reassemble them in a way that provides multiple viewpoints on them. The face that is representationally meaningful as an integral part of a living body is simultaneously viewed as a separable and geometrically divisible object. Letting go of the representational function of painting altogether, the abstract expressionist Franz Kline could import fragments of calligraphy into his works, not for their meaning function as written language, but for their figural qualities. Similarly, the numbers in a Jasper Johns painting are removed from their mathematical context and held captive at the level of material embodiment.

By allowing one context to playfully comment on another, contemporary artists often introduce hybrid medial contexts in which personal technique and impersonal technology are allowed to converge for artistic effect. Again Warhol stands out for effectively exploiting the potentials of the advertising medium by highlighting the way in which the serial reproducibility of an iconic image like Marilyn Monroe can be exhibited with its own reiterations. Here the traditional distinction between a prized original and less valuable copies seems to fade just as it does in photography and film for Benjamin.[61] Warhol's silkscreens were intended to have an assembly-line effect, giving each of the repeated images roughly the same informational value. More recent paintings by Wade Guyton submit the canvas itself to digital technology and invite the spectator to consider "how machines, humans and images interact haltingly today."[62] The Chinese artist Ai Weiwei in turn exploits information technology to "stage" the way he presents his materials. With the use

---

61. See Benjamin's comments on film, *Das Kunstwerk*, 23–32.
62. From a caption at the Whitney Museum of American Art, October 2012.

of videos and blogs, he aims to bring out "the semantic cultural references that adhere" to these materials.[63]

Throughout this commentary on the contemporary scene, we have seen some of the ways in which artistic productivity has been transformed through technological innovations that have made the material content of art more readily transmissible. This sets up a tension in the aesthetic medial context between the transmissibility of material content, which operates primarily at the level of what is assimilated as elementary understanding, and the communicability of meaning content that aims at higher understanding.[64] The role of artistic creativity in this context is to provide an informal heuristic understanding that moves beyond the assumptions of elementary understanding without committing to the disciplinary conclusions of higher understanding. This heuristic cultivation of meaning in the arts offers a technique-based mode of challenging conventions and experimenting with new options.

TRANSITIONAL MODES OF UNDERSTANDING

The essential aim of this work has been to demonstrate the fundamental significance of orientational contexts for interpretation. The common-sense frames of reference that are characteristic of elementary understanding are not as well defined as the disciplinary contexts of the sciences or the reflective framework of philosophy, and are always in need of revision. The efforts of hermeneutics to relate these contexts become especially urgent in transitional periods when traditional assumptions and accepted conventions are being challenged. In this chapter we have traced a movement from earlier perspectives that assign the arts a representational or expressive function to those that also bring out their articulative and presentational functions.

Reflective judgment was shown to be important for opening up new meaning contexts whenever we need to augment the available conceptual tools of understanding. This expansive mode of judgment also has the capacity to differentiate among orientational contexts and to consider the most appropriate ways of relating them. We started with the four interpretive contexts of field,

---

63. See Lotte Philipsen, "De Pont: Ai Weiwei" (Tilburg, the Netherlands: De Pont Museum), www.scribd.com/doc/106791564/ePDF-aiweiwei-V3-ny. See also Hans Ulrich Obrist, *AI WEIWEI SPEAKS with Hans Ulrich Obrist* (London: Penguin Books, 2011).

64. For the distinction between what is commonly assimilated as elementary understanding and what is acquired through disciplinary means as higher understanding, see chapters 1 and 7.

territory, domain, and habitat that Kant introduced at the beginning of the *Critique of Judgment* with reference to our cognitive access to nature. Some of these contexts were also applied to aesthetic appreciation. Whereas ordinary perception relates the territory of what is experienced to the theoretical domain of necessary laws, we have shown that aesthetic appreciation relates this same territory to the habitat of what is contingently pleasurable. Each of these four contexts serves to bring out a distinctive modal perspective on the world, and reflective assessment is needed to adjudicate which context takes precedence in interpreting historical life and human productivity. It was also shown that the immanent purposiveness that Kant goes on to assign to organisms enables us to interpret them as domain-like systems that are functionally self-regulating. The sociocultural systems subsequently articulated by the human sciences with the aim of deepening historical understanding were then specified as organizational contexts that are both cognitive and normative.

Finally, the artistic medial contexts introduced here have provided less formal, technique-based ways of making sense of things. These weblike contexts can also be used to illustrate some creative ways of dealing with the fluidity of our present world of technological innovation. Medial contexts can thus be said to provide a kind of transitional understanding.

The contemporary art world has been exhibited as a sphere in transition, where very little is simply what it is or seems to be. Here the reflective coordination of contexts required for narrative understanding is often replaced by their seemingly random juxtaposition. Whether the "liberation" of the arts from traditional contexts is taken to be political or merely exploratory in the way that Danto speaks of the "atmosphere of artistic theory,"[65] the effect has been to produce a kind of response in which aesthetic fascination often proves to be more important than reflective and critical appreciation. This new medial art world makes artistic appreciation dependent on acknowledging certain declarative and performative gestures to which the audience is invited to consent.

In chapters 4 and 5 we spoke about prejudices as involving parochial prejudgmental consent that can gradually be transformed through broader experience and higher understanding into legitimate critical assent. The customs and beliefs that were at first implicitly consented to can either gain our judgmental assent or be replaced with other explicit convictions. Today's audience of the art scene is invited to give a different kind of consent, one that simply sets aside conventional prejudices without the further aim of encouraging

---

65. "The Artworld," 140.

reflective judgmental assent. This expectation of an open-minded provisional consent is meant to provoke thought—not so much to produce an exemplary consensus, but to suspend what has been taken for granted.

The extent to which individual assent and public consent can merge in aesthetics was analyzed in terms of several levels of consensus and used to question Kant's Enlightenment idea that the cultivation of good taste eventually produces univocal approbation. Instead, the continuing value of his aesthetic theory was located in its power to relate the harmonious interplay of the cognitive faculties to the communicability of states of mind. This makes possible a reflective attunement that does not need an omnilateral justification but can approach the kind of multilateral legitimacy that we have advocated.[66] Our capacity to have expansive feelings that transport us beyond ourselves can also be applied to the artistic medial spheres that invite our provisional consent.

However, hermeneutics must go beyond aesthetic attunement to consider what kind of consensus is feasible in responsibly pursuing the interpretation of human life for its challenges as well as its achievements. The idea of worldly orientation has served throughout this work to consider the extent to which local commonalities can lead to more widely shared universals. Yet there are limits to that kind of integrative process, and in recognition of this, hermeneutics must explore the various orientational contexts that are relevant to the interpretation of human life and culture and consider to what extent these contexts may overlap. The peculiar contribution of the arts is to provide medial contexts that can bring into focus those moments in which different perspectives intersect and hold them in suspense. Ultimately, the task of hermeneutics is not to fuse divergent perspectives, but to consider to what extent various disciplinary approaches can coexist and contribute to understanding. If two disciplinary approaches produce conflicting results, each of them must be reexamined. Perhaps both results will need to be qualified. The optimal outcome will be to have various approaches reinforce each other to provide a sense of differentiated relatedness.

Although hermeneutics is a cooperative project that is worked out in a multidisciplinary manner, interpreters have an individual responsibility to vouch for the legitimacy of their interpretation. This is a normative task, and aesthetics has been shown to play an intermediary role in this project as we advance from experiential assimilation and cognitive acquisition to reflective appropriation. In the chapter on narrative history, we spoke of assimila-

---

66. See chapter 6.

tion, acquisition, and appropriation as three stages of historical transmission. However, it has become evident that we have grown increasingly dependent on the contemporaneous transmissibility made possible by information technology. The preponderance of what we accumulate as life-knowledge today comes not from our cultural heritage, but from information that is accessible through all the media of communication that constantly surround us. The Internet gives us access to a virtual world that can readily overwhelm us with digitally generated information that has not been cognitively vetted. What can be downloaded from search engines such as Google provides an aggregate of diverse sources whose impact is to make proper assimilation more difficult and cognitive acquisition less likely.

The project of a hermeneutical critique is complicated by the fact that the disciplinary contexts of the human sciences must now contend with more impersonal and technological media-driven contexts. Because much of what is transmitted through the mass media is information that is unsorted and unreliable, the disciplinary results of higher understanding have become more difficult to attain. In an age where instantaneous responsiveness is prized, there is rarely time for a responsible consideration of the appropriate judgmental contexts. Nevertheless, we have seen that the imaginative capacity to focus on intermediary medial contexts can play a heuristic role in facilitating the transition from elementary to higher understanding. A further task of interpretation is to circle back from higher understanding to determine whether it has done justice to elementary understanding and to what extent the common sense embodied there needs to be altered. But the final task is to expand the hermeneutic circle into the sphere of critical understanding and bring reflective judgment back into the picture.

The current art scene has played a kind of transitional role between elementary and higher understanding by generating imaginative medial spheres that explore techniques of reorienting ourselves to the world around us. The arts allow us to see the world in new ways and augment elementary understanding with the possibility of an elemental re-understanding that we have called heuristic. Moreover, there has always been an intermediary role for the arts in stimulating us to move from the higher understanding made possible by cognitive inquiry to a third, more reflective, level of critical understanding. For this the literary arts have been especially important in helping to shape our overall worldview. To move toward this more comprehensive understanding or knowledge, all the contemporary advances that have been made in the area of medial presentation will have to be matched by another aspect of artistic creativity, namely, a subtlety of discernment. Here the way Kant's aesthetics has been explicated in terms of reflective schematization and symbolic presentation remains as relevant as ever. The greatest contribution that the arts can make is to widen our horizon by suggesting how intuitable relations within contexts that are familiar to us can be adapted to illuminate relations within other less familiar contexts. The reflective analogies that result from this use of the creative imagination have more than an aesthetic value: an orientational hermeneutics has the capacity and responsibility to explore their more general import.

BIBLIOGRAPHY

Allison, Henry. *Kant's Transcendental Idealism: An Interpretation and Defense*. New Haven, CT: Yale University Press, 2004.
———. *Kant's Theory of Taste*. Cambridge: Cambridge University Press, 2001.
Ameriks, Karl. *Interpreting Kant's Critiques*. Oxford: Clarendon Press, 2003.
Arendt, Hannah. *Lectures on Kant's Political Philosophy*. Edited by Ronald Beiner. Chicago: University of Chicago Press, 1992.
———. *Responsibility and Judgment*. Edited by Jerome Kohn. New York: Schocken Books, 2003.
Aristotle. *Poetics*. Princeton, NJ: Princeton University Press, 1985.
Arnheim, Rudolf. *Art and Visual Expression*. Berkeley and Los Angeles: University of California Press, 1966.
Baumgarten, Alexander Gottlieb. *Aesthetica*. Hildesheim: Georg Olms, 1961.
———. *Reflections on Poetry*. Translated by Karl Aschenbrenner and William B. Holther. Berkeley: University of California Press, 1954.
Benjamin, Walter. *Das Kunstwerk im Zeitalter seiner technischen Reproduzierbarkeit*. Frankfurt am Main: Suhrkamp Verlag, 1970.
Bernasconi, Robert. *Heidegger in Question*. Atlantic Highlands, NJ: Humanities Press International, 1993.
Bleicher, Josef. *Contemporary Hermeneutics: Hermeneutics as Method, Philosophy and Critique*. London: Routledge and Kegan Paul, 1980.
Bourdieu, Pierre. *An Invitation to Reflexive Sociology*. Chicago: University of Chicago Press, 1992.
Brandom, Robert. *Making It Explicit: Reasoning, Representing and Discursive Commitment*. Cambridge, MA: Harvard University Press, 1994.
Carr, David. *Time, Narrative, and History*. Bloomington, IN: Indiana University Press, 1986.

Chignell, Andrew. "Belief in Kant." *Philosophical Review* 116, no. 3 (2007): 323–60.
Cohen, Alix. *Kant and the Human Sciences: Biology, Anthropology and History.* New York: Palgrave Macmillan, 2009.
Crowell, Steven. *Husserl, Heidegger, and the Space of Meaning: Paths toward Transcendental Phenomenology.* Evanston, IL: Northwestern University Press, 2002.
Damasio, Antonio. *Looking for Spinoza: Joy, Sorrow and the Feeling Brain.* San Diego: Harcourt Inc., 2003.
Danto, Arthur. *The Analytic Philosophy of History.* Cambridge: Cambridge University Press, 1968.
———. "The Artworld." In *Philosophy Looks at the Arts,* edited by Joseph Margolis 132–44. Philadelphia: Temple University Press, 1978.
Davidson, Donald. *Inquiries into Truth and Interpretation.* Oxford: Oxford University Press, 1984.
Derrida, Jacques. *Specters of Marx.* New York: Routledge, 1994.
Dickie, George. *Introduction to Aesthetics: An Analytic Approach.* New York: Oxford University Press, 1997.
Dilthey, Wilhelm. *Das Erlebnis und die Dichtung.* Göttingen: Vandenhoeck & Ruprecht, 1970.
———. *Die Jugendgeschichte Hegels.* Vol. 4 of *Gesammelte Schriften.* 26 vols., 1904–2006. Göttingen: Vandenhoeck & Ruprecht, 1963.
———. *The Formation of the Historical World in the Human Sciences.* Selected Works (*SW*) 3. Edited by Rudolf A. Makkreel and Frithjof Rodi. Princeton, NJ: Princeton University Press, 2002.
———. *Hermeneutics and the Study of History. SW* 4. Edited by Rudolf A. Makkreel and Frithjof Rodi. Princeton, NJ: Princeton University Press, 1996.
———. *Introduction to the Human Sciences. SW* 1. Edited by Rudolf A. Makkreel and Frithjof Rodi. Princeton, NJ: Princeton University Press, 1989.
———. *Poetry and Experience. SW* 5. Edited by Rudolf A. Makkreel and Frithjof Rodi. Princeton, NJ: Princeton University Press, 1985.
———. *Understanding the Human World. SW* 2. Edited by Rudolf A. Makkreel and Frithjof Rodi. Princeton, NJ: Princeton University Press, 2010.
Dray, William. "'Explaining What' in History." In *Theories of History,* edited by Patrick Gardiner, 403–08. New York: The Free Press, 1959.
Ferrara, Alessandro. *Reflective Authenticity: Rethinking the Project of Modernity.* London: Routledge, 1998.
Flynn, Thomas. *Sartre, Foucault, and Historical Reason.* Chicago: The University of Chicago Press, 1997.
Forster, Michael. *Kant and Skepticism.* Princeton, N.J.: Princeton University Press, 2010.
Foucault, Michel. *Discipline and Punish: The Birth of the Prison.* New York: Vintage Books, 1979.

Frank, Manfred. *Das individuelle Allgemeine, Textstrukturierung und Textinterpretation nach Schleiermacher.* Frankfurt am Main: Suhrkamp Verlag, 1985.
Gadamer, Hans-Georg. *Hegel's Dialectic: Five Hermeneutical Studies.* Translated by D.C. Smith. New Haven, CT: Yale University Press, 1976.
———. *The Relevance of the Beautiful and Other Essays.* Translated by Nicholas Walker. Edited by Robert Bernasconi. Cambridge: Cambridge University Press, 1986.
———. *Truth and Method.* 2nd revised ed. Translation revised by Joel Weinsheimer and Donald Marshall. New York: Crossroad, 1992.
———. *Wahrheit und Methode.* 2nd ed. Tübingen: J.C.B. Mohr, 1965.
Gallagher, Shaun. "Hegel, Foucault, and Critical Hermeneutics." In *Hegel, History and Interpretation,* edited by Shaun Gallagher, 145–66. Albany: SUNY Press, 1997.
Gasché, Rodolphe. *The Idea of Form: Rethinking Kant's Aesthetics.* Stanford, CA: Stanford University Press, 2003.
Ginsborg, Hannah. "Thinking the Particular as Contained under the Universal." In *Aesthetics and Cognition in Kant's Critical Philosophy,* edited by Rebecca Kukla, 35–60. Cambridge: Cambridge University Press, 2006.
Gjesdal, Kristin. "Between Enlightenment and Romanticism." *Journal of the History of Philosophy* 46, no. 2 (April 2008): 285–305.
Grondin, Jean. *Einführung in die philosophische Hermeneutik.* Darmstadt: Wissenschaftliche Buchgesellschaft, 1991.
———. "The Neo-Kantian Heritage in Gadamer." In *Neo-Kantianism in Contemporary Philosophy,* edited by Rudolf Makkreel and Sebastian Luft, 92–110. Bloomington, IN: Indiana University Press, 2010.
Guyer, Paul. *Kant and the Claims of Taste.* Cambridge, MA: Harvard University Press, 1979.
———. *Kant and the Experience of Freedom.* Cambridge: Cambridge University Press, 1996.
Habermas, Jürgen. *Between Facts and Norms: Contributions to a Discourse Theory of Law and Democracy.* Cambridge, MA: MIT Press, 1996.
———. *Knowledge and Human Interests.* Translated by Jeremy J. Shapiro. Boston: Beacon Press, 1972.
———. *The Theory of Communicative Action.* Vol. 2. Translated by Thomas McCarthy. Boston: Beacon Press, 1987.
Hammermeister, Kai. *The German Aesthetic Tradition.* Cambridge: Cambridge University Press, 2002.
Hance, Allen. "The Hermeneutic Significance of the *Sensus Communis*." *International Philosophical Quarterly* XXXVII, no. 2 (June 1997): 133–48.
Hegel, Georg Wilhelm Friedrich. *Enzyklopädie der philosophischen Wissenschaften im Grundrisse* (1827). Vol. 19, *Gesammelte Werke.* Hamburg: Felix Meiner Verlag, 1989.

———. *Phenomenology of Spirit*. Translated by A.V. Miller. Oxford and New York: Oxford University Press, 1979.

———. *Science of Logic*. Translated by W.H. Johnston and L.G. Struthers. London: Allen and Unwin, 1961.

———. *Vorlesungen über die Philosophie der Religion. Werke*. Vols. 16 and 17. Frankfurt am Rhein: Suhrkamp Verlag, 1978.

———. *Wissenschaft der Logik. Werke*. Vols. 5 and 6. Frankfurt am Rhein: Suhrkamp Verlag, 1976.

Heidegger, Martin. *Being and Time*. Translated by J. Macquarrie and E. Robinson. New York: Harper & Row, 1962.

———. *Holzwege*. Frankfurt am Main: Vittorio Klostermann, 1963.

———. "The Origin of the Work of Art." In *Poetry, Language, Thought*. Translated by Albert Hofstadter, 17–87. New York: Harper and Row, 1971.

———. "Phänomenologische Interpretationen zur Aristoteles (Anzeige der hermeneutischen Situation)." Edited by Hans-Ulrich Lessing. *Dilthey-Jahrbuch* 6 (1989).

———. *Sein und Zeit*. Tübingen: Max Niemeyer Verlag, 1979.

———. *Supplements*. Edited by John van Buren. Albany: SUNY Press, 2002.

———*Unterwegs zur Sprache*. Pfullingen: Verlag Günther Neske, 1959.

———. "Wilhelm Diltheys Forschungsarbeit und der gegenwärtige Kampf um eine historische Weltanschauung." Edited by Frithjof Rodi. *Dilthey-Jahrbuch* 8 (1993).

Hirsch, E.D. *Validity in Interpretation*. New Haven, CT: Yale University Press, 1967.

Kant, Immanuel. "An Answer to the Question: 'What is Enlightenment?'" Translated by H.B. Nisbet. In *Kant: Political Writings*, edited by Hans Reiss, 54–60. Cambridge: Cambridge University Press, 1991.

———. *Anthropology from a Pragmatic Point of View*. Translated by Robert B. Louden. Cambridge: Cambridge University Press, 2006.

———. *Bemerkungen in den "Beobachtungen über das Gefühl des Schönen und Erhabenen."* Herausgegeben und kommentiert von Marie Rischmüller. Hamburg: Felix Meiner Verlag, 1991.

———. *Critique of Pure Reason*. Translated and edited by Paul Guyer and Allen W. Wood. Cambridge: Cambridge University Press, 1998.

———. *Critique of the Power of Judgment*. Translated and edited by Paul Guyer and Eric Matthews. Cambridge: Cambridge University Press, 2000.

———. "Idea for a Universal History with a Cosmopolitan Purpose." In *Kant: Political Writings*, 41–53.

———. *Kant's gesammelte Schriften, herausgegeben von der Preussischen Akademie der Wissenschaften zu Berlin*. 29 Vols. Berlin: Walter de Gruyter, 1902–97.

———. *Lectures on Logic*. Edited by J. Michael Young. Cambridge: Cambridge University Press, 1992.

———. *The Metaphysics of Morals*. Translated by Mary Gregor. Cambridge: Cambridge University Press, 1996.

———. "On the Miscarriage of All Philosophical Trials in Theodicy." In *Religion within the Boundaries of Mere Reason and Other Writings*, translated and edited by Allen Wood and George Di Giovanni, 15–30. Cambridge: Cambridge University Press, 1998.

———. *Prolegomena to Any Future Metaphysics*. Translated by Paul Carus. Edited by Beryl Logan. London and New York: Routledge, 1996.

———. *Reflexionen zur Logik*. In *Kant's gesammelte Schriften*. Vol. 16. Berlin: Walter de Gruyter, 1902–97.

———. "What Does It Mean to Orient Oneself in Thinking?" In *Religion within the Boundaries of Mere Reason and Other Writings*, translated and edited by Allen Wood and George Di Giovanni, 1–14. Cambridge: Cambridge University Press, 1998.

———. "What Is Orientation in Thinking?" Translated by H.B. Nisbet. In *Kant: Political Writings*, edited by Hans Reiss, 237–49. Cambridge: Cambridge University Press, 1991.

Kisiel, Theodore. "Hegel and Hermeneutics." In *Beyond Epistemology*, edited by Frederick Weiss, 197–220. The Hague: Martinus Nijhoff, 1974.

Kneller, Jane. *Kant and the Power of Imagination*. Cambridge: Cambridge University Press, 2007.

Korsgaard, Christine. "Reflective Endorsement." In *The Sources of Normativity*, edited by Onora O'Neill, 49–89. New York: Cambridge University Press, 1996.

Kukla, Rebecca, ed. *Aesthetics and Cognition in Kant's Critical Philosophy*. Cambridge: Cambridge University Press, 2006.

Le Goff, Jacques. *History and Memory*. New York: Columbia University Press, 1992.

Lefas, Pavlos. *Dwelling and Architecture: From Heidegger to Koolhaas*. Berlin: Jovis Verlag, 2006.

Lessing, Hans-Ulrich, Rudolf Makkreel, and Riccardo Pozzo, eds. *Recent Contributions to Dilthey's Philosophy of the Human Sciences*. Stuttgart-Bad Cannstatt: Problemata, frommann-holzboog, 2011.

Longuenesse, Beatrice. *Kant and the Capacity to Judge: Sensibility and Discursivity in the Critique of Pure Reason*. Princeton, NJ: Princeton University Press, 2001.

Lyotard, Jean-Francois. "Answering the Question: What is Postmodernism?" In *The Postmodern Condition: A Report on Knowledge*, 71–82. Minneapolis: University of Minnesota Press, 1984.

———. *The Differend: Phrases in Dispute*. Translated by Georges Van Den Abbeele. Vol. 46, *Theory and History of Literature*. Minneapolis: University of Minnesota Press, 1988.

Makkreel, Rudolf A. "The Cognition-Knowledge Distinction in Kant and Dilthey and the Implications for Psychology and Self-Understanding." *Studies in History and Philosophy of Science* 34 (2003): 149–64.

———. "The Confluence of Aesthetics and Hermeneutics in Baumgarten, Meier, and Kant." *The Journal of Aesthetics and Art Criticism* 54, no. 1 (1996): 64–75.

———. *Dilthey, Philosopher of the Human Studies*. Princeton, NJ: Princeton University Press, 1975. Revised with a new afterword, 1992.

———. "From Authentic Interpretation to Authentic Disclosure: Bridging the Gap between Kant and Heidegger." In *Heidegger, German Idealism, & Neo-Kantianism*, edited by Tom Rockmore, 63–83. New York: Humanity Books, 2000.

———. *Imagination and Interpretation in Kant: The Hermeneutical Import of the "Critique of Judgment."* Chicago: University of Chicago Press, 1990. Revised 1994.

———. "Kant, Dilthey, and the Idea of a Critique of Historical Judgment." *Dilthey-Jahrbuch für Philosophie und Geschichte der Geisteswissenschaften* X (1996): 61–79.

———. "Life-Knowledge, Conceptual Cognition and the Understanding of History." In *Dilthey und die hermeneutische Wende in der Philosophie*, edited by Gudrun Kühne-Bertram and Frithjof Rodi, 97–107. Göttingen: Vandenhoeck & Ruprecht, 2008.

———. "Reflection, Reflective Judgment and Aesthetic Exemplarity." In *Aesthetics and Cognition in Kant's Critical Philosophy*, edited by Rebecca Kukla, 223–44. Cambridge: Cambridge University Press, 2006.

———. "The Role of Judgment and Orientation in Hermeneutics." *Philosophy & Social Criticism* 34, no. 1–2 (2008): 29–50.

Marx, Karl. *Theses on Feuerbach*. In *The Marx-Engels Reader*, edited by Robert Tucker, 107–109. New York: W.W. Norton & Co., 1972.

Meier, Georg Friedrich. *Anfangsgründe aller schönen Wissenschaften*. Vol. 1. Halle, 1755 Hildesheim: Georg Olms, 1976.

———. *Versuch einer allgemeinen Auslegungskunst*. Düsseldorf: Stern-Verlag Jannsen & Co., 1965.

Mink, Louis. "History and Fiction as Modes of Comprehension." In *Historical Understanding*, edited by Brian Fay, Eugene O. Golob, and Richard T. Vann, 42–60. Ithaca, NY: Cornell University Press, 1987.

———. "Philosophical Analysis and Historical Understanding." In *Historical Understanding*, 118–146.

Mensch, Jennifer. *Kant's Organicism*. Chicago: University of Chicago Press, 2013.

Munzel, G. Felicitas. *Kant's Conception of Moral Character: The Critical Link of Morality, Anthropology, and Reflective Judgment*. Chicago: University of Chicago Press, 1999.

Nagel, Thomas. *The View from Nowhere*. Oxford: Oxford University Press, 1986.

Nancy, Jean-Luc. "Sharing Voices." In *Transforming the Hermeneutic Context: From Nietzsche to Nancy*, eds. Gayle Ormiston and Alan Schrift. Albany: SUNY Press, 1990.

Nietzsche, Friedrich Wilhelm. *Beyond Good and Evil*. Translated by Walter Kaufman. New York: Vintage Books, 1989.
———. *On the Genealogy of Morals*. Translated by Walter Kaufman and R.J. Hollingdale. New York: Vintage Books, 1989.
———. *Untimely Meditations*. Translated by R.J. Hollingdale. Cambridge: Cambridge University Press, 1986.
———. *Zur Genealogie der Moral*. In *Kritische Studienausgabe*. Band 5. Herausgegeben von Giorgio Colli und Mazzino Montinari. Berlin/New York/Munich: DTV/Walter de Gruyter, 1988.
Nuzzo, Angelica. *Ideal Embodiment: Kant's Theory of Sensibility*. Bloomington, IN: Indiana University Press, 2008.
Obrist, Hans Ulrich. *AI WEIWEI SPEAKS with Hans Ulrich Obrist*. London: Penguin Books, 2011.
O'Neill, Onora. "Experts, Practitioners and Practical Judgement." *Journal of Moral Philosophy* 4, no. 2: 154–66.
Palmer, Richard E. *Hermeneutics: Interpretation Theory in Schleiermacher, Dilthey, Heidegger and Gadamer*. Evanston, IL: Northwestern University Press, 1969.
Pasternack, Lawrence. "The Development and Scope of Kantian Belief." *Kant-Studien* 102 (2011): 290–315.
———. "Kant's Doctrinal Belief in God." In *Rethinking Kant*. Edited by Oliver Thorndike. Newcastle upon Tyne: Cambridge Scholars Publishing, 2011.
Philipsen, Lotte. "De Pont: Ai Weiwei." Tilburg, the Netherlands: De Pont Museum. www.scribd.com/doc/106791564/ePDF-aiweiwei-V3-nyePDF_aiweiwei_V3_ny.
Pippin, Robert. *Hegel's Idealism: The Satisfactions of Self-Consciousness*. Cambridge: Cambridge University Press, 1989.
Quine, Willard Van Orman. *Word and Object*. Cambridge, MA: MIT Press, 1960.
Rancière, Jacques. *The Politics of Aesthetics*. Translated by Gabriel Rockhill. London/New York: Continuum, 2006.
Redding, Paul. *Hegel's Hermeneutics*. Ithaca, NY: Cornell University Press, 1996.
Ricoeur, Paul. *Freud and Philosophy*. Translated by Dennis Savage. New Haven, CT: Yale University Press, 1970.
———. *From Text to Action, Essays in Hermeneutics*, II. Translated by Kathleen Blamey and John B. Thompson. Evanston, IL: Northwestern University Press, 1991.
———. *Time and Narrative*. 3 Vols. Chicago: University of Chicago Press, 1984.
Risjord, Mark. *Woodcutters and Witchcraft: Rationality and Interpretive Change in the Social Sciences*. Albany: SUNY Press, 2000.
Rodi, Frithjof. *Das strukturierte Ganze: Studien zum Werk von Wilhelm Dilthey*. Weilerwist: Velbrück Wissenschaft, 2003.
Royce, Josiah. "The Doctrine of Signs." In *The Problem of Christianity*, 343–62. Chicago: University of Chicago Press, 1968.

———. "Perception, Conception, and Interpretation," In *The Problem of Christianity*, 273–96.
———. "The Will to Interpret." In *The Problem of Christianity*, 297–320.
Sartre, Jean-Paul. *Critique of Dialectical Reason*. Vol. 1. Translated by Alan Sheridan Smith. Vol. 1. London: Verso, 1991.
———. *Nausea*. Translated by Lloyd Alexander. New York: New Directions, 1969.
———. *The Philosophy of Jean-Paul Sartre*. Edited, with an introduction by Robert D. Cumming. New York: Random House, 1965.
Schleiermacher, Friedrich. *Die christliche Sitte nach den Grundsäzen der evangelischen Kirche im Zusammenhange dargestellt*. Berlin: G. Reimer, 1843.
———. *Hermeneutics: The Handwritten Manuscripts*. Edited by Heinz Kimmerle. Translated by James Duke and Jack Forstman. Missoula, MT: Scholars Press, 1977.
———. *Hermeneutik und Kritik*. Edited by Manfred Frank. Suhrkamp: Frankfurt, 1977.
Serres, Michel. *Hermes: Literature, Science, Philosophy*. Baltimore: Johns Hopkins University Press, 1982.
Sgarbi, Marco. *Kant on Spontaneity*. London: Continuum International Publishing Group, 2012.
Shell, Susan Meld. *The Embodiment of Reason: Kant on Spirit, Generation and Community*. Chicago: The University of Chicago Press, 1996.
Vico, Giambattista. *The New Science of Giambattista Vico*. Edited by Thomas Goddard Bergin and Max Harold Fisch. Ithaca, NY: Cornell University Press, 1948.
Waldenfels, Bernhard. *Antwortregister*. Frankfurt am Main: Suhrkamp, 1994.
White, Hayden. *Metahistory: The Historical Imagination in Nineteenth-Century Europe*. Baltimore: Johns Hopkins University Press, 1973
Wright, Georg Henrik von. *Explanation and Understanding*. Ithaca, NY: Cornell University Press, 1971.
Zammito, John. *The Genesis of Kant's "Critique of Judgment."* Chicago: The University of Chicago Press, 1992.
Zuckert, Rachel. *Kant on Beauty and Biology: An Interpretation of the "Critique of Judgment."* Cambridge: Cambridge University Press, 2007.

INDEX

acquisition, 83, 131, 148, 188, 194–97, 222–23; vs. appropriation, 9, 83, 194, 197; vs. assimilation, 9, 83, 194–95; of conceptually mediated cognition, 9; and higher understanding, 144–45, 171; and historical narratives and, 177; reflective, 166, 167, 171; and scientific cognition, 114
adjudication, 7, 123; and hermeneutics, 5, 123–27
advents and events, 186, 187, 194
aesthetic consensus: Kant and, 102; levels of, 102–7, 109; and reflective consensus, 102
aesthetic differentiation, 38, 40
aesthetic ideas, 42, 111, 203–4, 207
Alexandrians, 17–18, 26
allegorical interpretation, 18
Amadeus (Shaffer), 180
amphiboly: of concepts of reflection, 62, 75; Kant and, 62, 75–77, 144; of moral reflection, 75–77, 143, 144; of reflective orientation, 74–78, 170, 172; of "sensitivizing" concepts and "intellectualizing" appearances, 62
appropriation, 2, 9, 80, 83, 132, 133, 168; vs. acquisition, 9, 83, 194, 197; vs. assimilation, 9, 83, 194, 197; of cognition as knowledge, 90–91; of the commonplace, 217; critical,

126, 166, 177, 188; and critical understanding, 144–45, 166, 197; Dilthey and, 9, 24–25; Heidegger and, 24–25; and historical narratives, 177; of historical situations and events, 177, 190, 196, 197; moment of, 131–32; of prejudices, 103–4; reflective, 83, 133–34, 144, 145, 154, 197, 222; of reflective judgments, 162; and reflective knowledge, 9, 83, 114, 145, 172, 195; reflective-reflexive, 166, 167, 171; and transmission, 194, 196
archetypes, 111, 112
Arendt, Hannah, 109n30
Aristotle, 18, 25–26, 207
Arnheim, Rudolf, 216–17
art: medial contexts of works of, 211–16; medial presentation of the commonplace in contemporary, 216–20
articulation, 78, 208; from conceptual classification to judgmental, 81–84; and expression, 37, 199, 207, 213; and interpretation, 32; reflective, 140
arts: contemporary, 217–19, 221; "The Origin of the Work of Art" (Heidegger), 207–11
artworld, 217–18, 221
ascriptive and attributive modes of imputation, 7, 53, 127–30, 138, 140, 145
ascriptive imputation, 142, 186

assent, 104; aesthetic, 100; and consent, 5, 100, 109, 118–19, 164, 221–22; of conviction, 90–91; defined, 87; judgmental, 5, 84, 87, 89, 94, 97, 101, 109, 164–65, 171, 221–22; and reflective judgment, 100, 221–22; subjective modes of, 91–92; universal, 102

assimilation, 2, 9, 83, 194, 196, 222–23; vs. acquisition, 9, 83, 194–95; vs. appropriation, 9, 83, 194, 197; defined, 196; and elementary understanding, 188, 220; less and more active modes of, 188; and life-knowledge, 83, 188; and reflective knowledge, 83; reflexive (mode of), 166, 167, 170

assimilative understanding, 9

Ast, Friedrich, 15

attributive characterizations, 191, 192

attributive evaluations, 186

attributive imputation, 7, 53, 127–30, 133, 138, 140–43, 145, 171, 186, 192

attributive judgments, 129–30, 192

Auslegung, 42, 45–47, 63, 134. *See also* interpretation

authentic interpretation, 143, 144, 171, 201–3; and intersubjective legitimacy, 133–37

authentic self-understanding, 126, 136

authentic theodicy, 135, 136, 142. *See also* theodicy

authentic understanding, 25–27, 32, 93; defined, 25

Being and Time (Heidegger), 24–25, 27–30, 208

Benjamin, Walter, 217, 218

Bernasconi, Robert, 211n45

Bible and biblical interpretation, 14, 15, 44, 46, 160. *See also* God

boundaries (*Grenzen*): vs. limits (*Schranken*), 62–63, 67–69, 72–74

bounds (*Grenzen*), 62–63; vs. limits (*Schranken*), 5, 67–68, 72–74, 77, 80, 121, 127, 130–31, 146, 151 (*see also under* limits (*Schranken*)); philosophy and the reflective specification of, 69–74; as positive, 62–63, 67, 144; and reflective judgments, 5, 67, 68

Brandom, Robert, 110n32

Braque, Georges, 219

Carr, David, 178–80

categorial cognitive validity claims, universal, 97

categorial concepts, 65

categorial conditions, 146, 147

categorial critique, 147. *See also* critique: as constitutive and categorial

categorial rules, 146

categorial schemata, 112

categorial structures, 148

categories, 15, 31–32, 84–86, 92; Dilthey's, 31–32, 147, 149–51; of human sciences, 31, 147, 149, 151; Kant's, 15, 61, 84–86, 92, 147, 150–51; of life, 32, 149–51; of natural sciences, 149

causal and non-causal explanation, 8, 154, 157, 175–76, 183–89

causal imputation, 185–86

causality, 134; and conceptual cognition, 182; Dilthey on science and, 148–49; and fate, 181, 182; historical, 181, 185, 187; Kant on, 85, 148; Kant on purpose and, 161; Nietzsche on, 184; schema of, 70, 86

causes and influences, 186–88

certainty: apodictic, 91, 93, 98; Dilthey on, 154; empirical vs. rational, 93–94; Kant on, 43, 44, 87–94, 97, 98, 132, 142, 171; vs. reliability, 22, 83, 88, 89; subjective, 22, 83

Cézanne, Paul, 215

character: empirical and intelligible, 141–42; Kant on, 139–41; physical and moral, 139–40

character formation, 140

characterization: attributive, 191, 192; vs. description, 139; Kant on, 64, 139–44, 151; pragmatic, 137–43, 171

charity in interpretation, 201

Chignell, Andrew, 89

Chladenius, Johann Martin, 14

cognition, 56; Baumgarten and sensible, 200–201; Dilthey on, 18–19, 21–22, 24, 25, 42, 117, 119, 149, 183; Heidegger and ontical, 25; and hermeneutics, 3, 5, 25, 80, 117, 169, 172, 200; historical, 19, 28; is not possible without inquisitive interest, 120; Kant on, 4, 42, 64, 71, 84–98, 101, 104, 107, 112, 134, 147; prejudices as productive of, 50; and reflection, 58; science, higher understanding, and, 3; scientific, 80, 84, 112, 114; symbolic, 42. *See also* conceptual cognition

cognition (*Erkenntnis*) and knowledge (*Wissen*), distinction between, 3, 28, 82–98; cognition appropriated and legitimated as reflective knowledge, 145; in Dilthey, 13, 20–22, 82, 116; in Kant, 84, 87, 91–92, 116–17, 147

cognitive exchange and communal conspectus, Josiah Royce on, 55–59

commonality vs. universality, 28, 29, 32, 74

commonplace: appropriation of the, 217; prejudice as, 93. *See also under* medial presentation

communal consent, 5, 91, 171

communal conspectus and cognitive exchange, Josiah Royce on, 55–59

communal sense as orientational principle for reflective judgment, 102

communal truths, 35, 41

communicability, 90, 104, 213–14; aesthetic, 102, 107, 109, 114–16, 182, 199, 204, 222; Kant and, 90, 102, 106, 107, 108n27, 115, 199, 203, 204, 207, 222; and meaning, 199, 212–14, 220; and persuasion, 89; of representations, 44; and Royce, 108n27; of states of mind, 107, 222; universal, 89

communication: dialogical, 51–52, 55, 171; symbolic, 204–5; and transmission, 9, 74, 97, 199, 212–14

communicative action, Habermas on, 16

completeness: and comprehensiveness in critique, 170; in critical hermeneutics, 169–72

conceptual cognition, 9, 20–23, 27–29, 42, 58, 83, 166, 196; epistemology as the analysis of, 22; and life-knowledge, 22, 27, 83, 98, 123, 172, 182; and objective spirit, 28; reflective consciousness as a necessary condition for, 122; sensible cognition, 200

concrete universal, 164

conscience, defined, 143

conscientiousness and truthful interpretation, 141–43

consensus: four levels of, 222. *See also* aesthetic consensus

consent, 97, 116, 164; and assent, 5, 100, 109, 118–19, 164, 221–22; communal, 5, 91, 171; external, 131; formal, 133; hermeneutic, 133; implied, 104; judgmental, 101, 145; normative, 104, 110; prejudgmental, 109; provisional, 222; public, 164–65, 222; univocal, 184

constraint vs. restraint, 7, 121. *See also* limits (*Schranken*): vs. bounds (*Grenzen*)

contemporaneity vs. simultaneity, 40

content: material, 8, 212, 214, 220; meaning, 9, 85, 96, 198, 199, 210, 212–18, 220

contexts: interpretive, 72, 112, 113, 150, 161, 163, 164, 186, 205–7, 220–21, 224. *See also* meaning contexts; medial contexts of works of art; orientational contexts; referential contexts/spheres of reference

contextual reconfiguration, 107, 114; and reflective schematization, 105–8

contextual reorientation, 158

contextual type, 112

contextualization, 71, 73, 83, 167, 191, 199, 208

continuity vs. discontinuity, 82. *See also under* narrative histories; narrative theory

conviction, 87

Corbusier, Le, 216

countertypes, 112–13

critical appropriation, 126, 166, 177, 188

critical hermeneutics, 14, 33, 52, 147, 162, 163, 167, 168, 175, 193; completeness in, 169–72

critical interpretation, 40, 123, 198

critical reflection, 155

critical sciences, 154, 155

critical understanding, 18, 123, 144–45, 166–67, 197, 223

critique: as constitutive and categorial, 146–51; of historical judgment, xi, 7, 161; of historical reason, 18, 117, 147, 161; as reflective and judgment-centered, 4, 7, 33, 161–64, 169–72, 177; as regulative and emancipatory, 7, 151–61, 169. See also *specific topics*

Danto, Arthur, 213n49, 217, 218, 218n60, 221
Davidson, Donald, 201
demystifying hermeneutics, 159
depth hermeneutics, 152, 154–56
depth interpretation, 159
Derrida, Jacques, 28n43
description vs. characterization, 139
descriptive vs. intentionalist theoretical understanding, 189
determinant judgments, 109, 133, 141; defined, 6; Kant and, 2, 5–7, 27, 59, 61, 66, 84, 94, 112, 129, 137, 138, 163–65; and reflective judgments, 2, 5, 6, 59, 60, 66, 78, 84, 94, 98–99, 104, 106, 112, 115, 127, 129n25, 129n35, 130, 137, 138, 145, 163–65
determinant schematization, 110–12
dialectical reconciliation, 47, 55, 171. *See also* dialectics
dialectics, 17, 55; Gadamer and, 48–50; Hegel and, 34, 45–50; tension between hermeneutics and, 45
dialogical approach to human understanding, 55
dialogical communication, 51–52, 55, 171
dialogue, Gadamer and, 34, 48–49, 51–52, 115, 156
Dickie, George, 218n60
differend, 52
digital technology, xi, 9, 214, 219
dijudication, 7, 128, 129, 142, 144, 163
Dilthey, Wilhelm, 3, 6–8; on cognition, 18–19, 21–22, 24, 25, 42, 117, 119, 149, 183; on cognition-knowledge distinction, 13, 20–22, 82, 116; on human sciences, 1, 17, 19–22, 25, 49, 50, 147–51, 157, 183, 192; on knowledge, 13, 21, 23; on manifestations of life and their interpretive contexts, 205–7; on understanding (*Verstehen*), 27, 59, 150–51. See also *specific topics*

disciplinary approaches, 58–59, 69, 80, 222
disciplinary cognition, 171
disciplinary consciousness, 29
disciplinary contexts, 9, 98, 145, 168, 172, 181, 196–97, 223
disciplinary differentiation and coordination, 81
disciplinary discourse, 29, 125–26
disciplinary explanations, 191
disciplinary frames of reference, 162
disciplinary standards and norms, 133
disciplinary topology of hermeneutic judgment, expansive, 193
discipline, culture of, 138
Discipline and Punish: The Birth of the Prison (Foucault), 192
disciplining techniques of normalizing judgment, 193
distanciation, technique of, 156
doctrinal determinacy, 136
doctrinal vs. authentic modes of interpretation, 134–35, 201
dogmatic determination, 136
domain(s), 4, 65–67, 75, 83, 106, 170; defined as a context, 4, 5, 64–66, 220–21; and Dilthey's thought formations, 205; Kant on, 64–66, 73–75, 132, 151, 170, 206, 221; and law, 4, 5, 8, 65–67, 73–75, 79, 106, 114, 124, 132, 133, 162, 170, 184, 187, 204–6, 221; and other referential contexts/spheres of reference, 4, 64–66, 75, 170, 220–21
Dray, William, 178, 190, 191
Droysen, Gustav, 186–87
Duchamp, Marcel, 218–19

earth and world, 130–31; Heidegger on, 199, 208–11, 216; Kant on, 199, 208. *See also* worldly orientation
earthly limits: Kant on, 5, 62–63, 68, 130–31. *See also* worldly bounds

elementary understanding: and assimilation, 188, 220; and objective spirit, 29, 98, 122
empirical vs. rational certainty, 93–94
emulation, 169; and exemplarity, 108–11, 115
endowment, 211–12
Epicurus, 20
epistéme (determinate observational understanding), 26, 27, 32
epistemology (*Erkenntnistheorie*), 22, 153–54; vs. theory of knowledge (*Theorie des Wissens*), 22; transcendental, 98
Erlebnis (lived experience), 35, 38–41; vs. *Erfahrung* (experience), 38
events and advents, 186, 187, 194
explanation: causal and non-causal, 8, 154, 157, 175–76, 183–89; causal vs. structural, 157; conceptual, 191; as framed by understanding, 8, 186; in human sciences, 6, 154, 157–59, 183–84, 186, 188–89; intentionalist, 188–91; teleological, 161, 176, 188–91; vs. understanding, 6, 157–58. *See also* imputation: causal
Explanation and Understanding (Wright), 188–89
expression, 199, 203–7, 216; and articulation, 37, 199, 207, 213; and manifestation, 1, 14, 37, 141, 199, 205, 206

feelings, self-absorbed vs. world-oriented, 35
Fichte, Johann Gottlieb, 16, 56, 196
field(s), 64–65, 72; defined as a context, 4, 64–66, 220–21; Kant and, 4, 64, 75, 210, 214; logical, 65, 205; of logical possibility, 66, 67, 75, 79, 133, 203–5; and other referential contexts/spheres of reference, 4, 64–66, 75, 170, 220–21; of the supersensible, 210
Flacius, Matthias, 14
Foucault, Michel, 80, 192–94

Gadamer, Hans-Georg, 1, 34, 39, 40, 51–52, 93, 116, 159, 160, 199; and aesthetic differentiation, 38; Dilthey and, 38–40, 42, 48, 50; Habermas and, 124, 168, 168n63;

Hegel and, 35, 41, 43, 44, 48–49; Heidegger and, 1, 5, 13, 26–27, 34, 49, 50, 93, 116; on interpretation and dialogue, 34, 48–52, 115, 156; Kant and, 35, 42, 43, 49, 51, 95; Paul Ricoeur and, 156, 159; on prejudice, 48–50, 93, 95, 116; Schiller and, 51; *Truth and Method*, 34, 42, 51
Gehry, Frank, 216
generation, 195–97
generative (continuity) narrativists, 178. *See also under* narrative histories
genius: creative, 16; defined, 203; Dilthey on, 213; Kant on, 203, 204, 207; musical, 207, 213
Ginsborg, Hannah, 109n29
God, 43–47, 71, 75–77, 134–36, 141, 182
Grondin, Jean, 200n3
Guyton, Wade, 219

Habermas, Jürgen, 6, 53, 123; on communicative action, 16; on emancipatory critique, 152, 154, 156, 160; Gadamer and, 124, 168, 168n63; and hermeneutics, 124, 126, 152–56; *Knowledge and Human Interests*, 152–56; Paul Ricoeur and, 7, 147, 152, 156, 160; and regulative critique, 7, 147, 156, 160; on self-formative process, 153; and self-reflection, 153–56; social critique, 168; and universality, 156
habitat(s), 68, 73–74, 78–80, 95, 98, 168; and contingency, 5, 65, 66, 73–74, 78, 79, 95, 124, 130, 162–62, 170; defined as a context, 4–5, 65–67, 208, 220–21; and familiarity, 4, 66n32, 83, 95, 108, 206; and other referential contexts/spheres of reference, 4–5, 64–66, 75, 78, 79, 95, 107, 108, 115, 130, 162–63, 170, 206, 208, 221
Hegel, Georg Wilhelm Friedrich, 198; on concrete universals, 164; and dialectic, 34, 45–50; Dilthey and, 28; Gadamer and, 35, 41, 43, 44, 48–49; on interpretation, 44–47; Kant and, 35; on language, 43, 44; and objective spirit, 28, 95, 102; Royce and, 56, 57

238 Index

Heidegger, Martin: *Being and Time*, 24–25, 27–30, 208; "The Origin of the Work of Art," 207–11
Hempel, Carl, 190
hermeneutical circle, 25, 123, 158, 223
hermeneutics: critical, 14, 33, 52, 147, 162, 163, 167–72, 175, 193; methodological vs. phenomenological, 1; reflective, 8, 13, 53, 63, 124–26, 159, 161n49, 162, 177, 196; a responsive hermeneutics and a transformative critique, 166–69; restorative vs. demystifying, 159. See also *specific topics*
higher understanding, 9, 29, 32, 98, 123, 144, 155, 166, 167, 171, 181, 194, 196, 210, 220–23; and acquisition, 144–45, 171; science, cognition, and, 3
Hirsch, E. D., 198
historical cognition, 28; reliability, 19
historical interpretation: delimiting the appeal to causes in, 184–86; Nietzsche's challenge to the objectivity of, 176–77
history, narrative approaches to, 178–80
human sciences: Dilthey on, 1, 17, 19–22, 25, 49, 50, 147–51, 157, 183, 192; explanation in, 6, 154, 157–59, 183–84, 186, 188–89; understanding (*Verstehen*) and, 17, 19
Hume, David, 20, 62
Husserl, Edmund, 28n43, 120
hypotypes and hypotyposis, 112

ideal and real types, 112
imagination, transcendental synthesis of the, 85–86
imaginative symbols, 112
imitation, 94–96, 103; vs. emulation, 110, 214 (*see also* emulation)
immanent purposiveness, 59, 72, 137, 148, 151, 161n49, 221; vs. external purposiveness, 60
imputation: ascriptive, 7, 53, 127–30, 133, 138, 140–43, 145, 171, 186, 192; attributive, 7, 53, 127–30, 133, 138, 140, 141, 143, 145, 171, 192; causal, 185–86

incommensurable contexts and the possibility of universalist history, 181–84
information, 58–59, 132, 214, 219, 223; digitally generated, 198, 223; transmission of, 9, 74, 97, 199
intention and reflective understanding, 13, 34, 134, 136, 158, 189–91, 198, 200–203
intentional context, Georg Friedrich Meier on representational signs and their, 200–202
intentional explanation and hermeneutical contextualization, 188–91
intentionalist fallacy, 202
intentionalist vs. descriptive theoretical understanding, 189
interpretation(s): allegorical, 18; and articulation, 32; charity in, 201; conscientiousness and truthful, 141–41; critical, 40, 123, 198; defined, 45–46; depth, 159; doctrinal vs. authentic modes of, 134–35, 201; Gadamer on dialogue and, 48–51; Hegel on, 44–47; interpreting as cognizing meaning and knowing truth, 84–88; legitimacy of, 130–34; as a mode of reflective judgment, 98–99; religious, 44 (*see also* Bible and biblical interpretation); and understanding, 154, 157–58, 161, 164, 167–68, 177, 208, 223. See also *Auslegung*; authentic interpretation; historical interpretation; will to interpret; *specific topics*
interpretive contexts, 72, 112, 113, 150, 161, 163, 164, 186, 205–7, 220–21, 224. See also orientational contexts
intersubjective legitimacy, 90–91, 143, 162
intersubjectivity, 5, 7, 42, 57, 101, 106, 108, 113, 115, 124–25, 128, 133, 136, 143, 147, 171, 203–4; and universality, 36, 90–91, 107

Johns, Jasper, 219
judgmental articulation, from conceptual classification to, 81–84
judgment(s): and evaluation, 100, 101, 105–7, 113, 123, 128–29, 163, 166, 193; kinds of (*see*

Index   239

determinant judgments; preliminary judgments; reflective judgments); normative vs. normalizing, 192–93; and prejudgments, 50, 84, 93–98, 101, 103–4, 108, 109; and prejudice, 2, 49, 53; provisional, 93–99, 104, 130; and theoretical assent, 100, 221–22. See also *specific topics*
judication: vs. adjudication, 7 (*see also* adjudication); vs. dijudication, 7 (*see also* dijudication)

Kant, Immanuel: on aesthetic consensus, 102; amphiboly and, 62, 75–77, 144; on cognition, 4, 42, 64, 71, 84–98, 101, 104, 107, 112, 134, 147; *Critique of Judgment*, 4, 35, 42, 44, 59, 63, 66, 70–72, 102, 106, 110, 127, 136–38, 148, 203, 221; *Critique of Pure Reason*, 44, 59–64, 67, 69, 70, 72, 84–90, 106, 138, 141, 147; and determinant judgments, 2, 5–7, 27, 59, 61, 66, 84, 94, 112, 129, 137, 138, 163–65; and expressing what was inexpressible, 202–5; interpretive contexts of (*see* orientational contexts); *The Jäsche Logic*, 79, 80, 88, 93–94, 96, 108, 163; on knowledge and knowing, 5–6, 84–98; levels of aesthetic consensus, 101–5; *Metaphysics of Morals*, 75–76, 127–28, 130, 141–42; on opining, believing, and knowing, 88–92 (*see also under* cognition (*Erkenntnis*) and knowledge (*Wissen*)); on prejudices, 2, 5, 49, 53, 84, 93–98, 103, 104, 121, 169, 188; on purposiveness, 60, 66, 67, 72–74, 104–6, 134–37, 148, 151, 161, 221; *Religion within the Boundaries of Mere Reason*, 14; and transcendental topic, 61–64; on the understanding (*Verstand*/ explanation), 27, 59, 150
Kline, Franz, 219
knowing, Kant on, 5–6, 84–98
knowledge: appropriation of cognition as, 90–91; Dilthey on, 13, 21, 23; Kant on, 5–6, 84–98; and legitimacy, 116–23; theory of knowledge (*Theorie des Wissens*), 22. See *also* cognition (*Erkenntnis*) and knowledge (*Wissen*); life-knowledge; reflective knowledge
Knowledge and Human Interests (Habermas), 152–56
Korsgaard, Christine, 110n33

lawfulness, 66, 73, 204
legitimacy: intersubjective, 90–91, 143, 162; and knowledge, 116–23; unilateral, bilateral, omnilateral and multilateral modes of, 131–33; vs. validity, 3, 92
"Life and Cognition" (Dilthey), 149–50
life-categories, 149–51
life-context, 37, 118, 196, 206, 218
life-knowledge: and assimilation, 83, 188; and conceptual cognition, 22, 27, 83, 98, 123, 172, 182; and objective spirit, 28, 32; vs. reflective knowledge, 22–23
life-manifestations: classes of, 205–6; in Dilthey, 28, 37, 205–6; vs. expressions, 37, 206
limits (*Schranken*): vs. boundaries (*Grenzen*), 62–63, 67–69, 72–74; vs. bounds (*Grenzen*), 5, 67–68, 72–74, 77, 80, 121, 127, 130–31, 146, 151; negative, 62, 67, 144, 169
Lyotard, Jean-Francois, 52, 209–10

manifestation(s): and expression, 1, 14, 37, 141, 199, 205, 206; of life and their interpretive contexts, 205–7. See *also* life-manifestations
Marx, Karl, 4, 47, 152, 155, 159
mass media, 218, 223
mathematics, 69–72, 82, 112
meaning: category of, 31, 150; and communicability, 199, 212–14, 220; explication of, 46, 108, 123; presentation of, 111–12, 214–15; and schemata, 86, 92, 97, 106, 108
meaning content, 9, 85, 96, 198, 199, 210, 212, 214–17, 220; and material content, 9, 212–18, 220
meaning contexts, 53, 64, 74, 77–78, 80, 100, 110, 116, 118, 125, 162, 177, 195, 206, 220

240 *Index*

meaning/significance/import, 89
meaning-truth relation, 53, 62, 75, 84–87, 91–92
medial contexts of works of art, 58, 211–16
medial presentation of the commonplace in contemporary art, 216–20
medium, 58, 212; of inherited commonality, 28, 73–74, 79, 95, 122, 151–52, 212 (*see also* objective spirit); meanings of, 212
Meier, Georg Friedrich, 205, 207; on representational signs and their intentional context, 200–202
Melanchthon, Philipp, 14
Metaphysics of Morals (Kant), 75–76, 127–28, 130, 141–42
Mink, Louis, 178–79, 181, 183, 186–88
moral and physical character, 139–40
moral reflection, amphiboly of, 75–77, 143, 144
morality: symbolization and, 15, 111, 112. See also *Metaphysics of Morals*
Munzel, G. Felicitas, 140n67

Nagel, Thomas, 80
narrative histories: continuity vs. discontinuity, 177–79; generative vs. genealogical, 175–78, 196
narrative theory, 175, 178, 194; continuity vs. discontinuity conceptions of, 181; types of, 181
nature and purposiveness, 60, 66, 67, 136
Nietzsche, Friedrich Wilhelm: challenge to the objectivity of historical interpretation, 176–77; and judgment as verdict, 177; and monumental, antiquarian, and critical history, 176
noumenal possession, 132
nous, 25–27

objective spirit, 30, 98, 122, 151–52, 212; definitions and meanings of, 28, 28n43, 29; Dilthey and, 25, 28, 29, 36, 45, 95, 102, 122, 151, 152, 213n48; and elementary understanding, 29, 98, 122; Hegel and, 28, 95, 102; inherited commonality of, 28, 32, 73–74, 95, 98; Kant and, 98, 102; and life-knowledge, 28, 32; and medial contexts, 212

O'Neill, Onora, 129n25
ontico-temporal analysis of world-time, 30
orientation, xi, 81, 114; contextual, 177, 205 (*see also* orientational contexts); hermeneutic, 122, 208; and reflective judgment, 59–60; spatial, 78, 105, 119, 122; worldly, 78–80. *See also* reflective orientation; *specific topics*
orientational capacity to take a stance, 167
orientational contexts, 67, 70, 74, 106, 170, 205, 222; and expansive mode of judgment, 224; for interpretation, 224; kinds of (*see* domain(s); field(s); habitat(s); medial contexts of works of art; medial presentation; objective spirit; systems; territory(ies)). *See also* orientation: contextual
orientational hermeneutical contexts, 208
orientational hermeneutics, 80, 132, 167, 175, 193, 198, 199, 224
orientational principle for reflective judgment, 102
orientational reflection, 61. *See also* reflective orientation
orientational task of hermeneutics, 75

Pasternack, Lawrence, 90
"Perception, Conception, and Interpretation" (Royce), 55–56
performance, 214n51
Pergamene school of philology, 18
persuasion, 87–89, 91–98; vs. conviction, 88–94
phenomenology, 158–59
phronesis, 26–27, 32
Picasso, Pablo, 219
pragmatic, different senses of, 138
pragmatic predisposition, 138
prejudgments, 50, 84, 93–98, 101, 103–4, 108, 109

prejudice(s): appropriation of, 103–4; Gadamer on, 48–50, 93, 95, 116; Kant on, 2, 5, 49, 53, 84, 93–98, 103, 104, 121, 169, 188; and superstition, 49, 95
preliminary judgments, 2, 5, 53, 104, 116, 133, 189, 190; and the provisionality of reflective judgments, 93–99
presentation (*Darstellung*): of meaning, 111–14; and representation (*Vorstellung*), 45, 111; symbolic, 70–71, 111, 113
prototypes, 112, 135
psychology, 67–69, 84, 157, 191, 217
purposive arrangement among particulars, 60
purposive order, 151, 161
purposive systems: organized, 73–74; vs. productive systems, 125
purposive unity of things, 72
purposive world order, 135
purposiveness: aesthetic, 111, 127; and counterpurposiveness, 134, 135; Dilthey on, 125, 148–49; efficacy of, 149; indeterminate sense of, 149–50; Kant on, 60, 66, 67, 72–74, 104–6, 134–37, 148, 151, 161, 221; and nature, 60, 66, 67, 136; reflective, 59, 111, 138, 161, 162; regulative, 148, 161; teleological, 59, 60. *See also* immanent purposiveness

Quine, Willard Van Orman, 201

Rancière, Jacques, 217
Ranke, Leopold von, 19
Raphael, 108
rational vs. empirical certainty, 93–94
Rauschenberg, Robert, 218
reason, practical and theoretical, 15
referential contexts/spheres of reference, 4, 64–66, 75, 170, 220–21
reflection, 155, 160–63, 165–67; and reflexivity, 132–33, 165–67, 197; transcendental, 62, 117–18, 122, 140. *See also* self-reflection
reflective acquisition, 166, 167, 171
reflective and aesthetic consensus, 102
reflective critique, 4, 7, 33, 161–64, 169–72, 177

reflective hermeneutics, 8, 13, 53, 63, 124–26, 159, 161n49, 162, 177, 196
reflective judgment(s), 60, 66–68, 75.105, 108, 126, 145, 162, 204, 220–23; about God, 134, 136; aesthetic model of, 7, 127; appropriation of, 162; and assent, 100, 221–22; and bounds, 5, 67, 68; communal sense as orientational principle for, 102; contextualizing function, 112–13; and decisional judgment, 127; defined, 6; and determinant judgments, 2, 5, 6, 59, 60, 66, 78, 84, 94, 98–99, 104, 106, 112, 115, 127, 129n25, 129n35, 130, 137, 138, 145, 163–65; diagnostic use of, 129, 171, 186, 197.9; and habitat, 66; interpretation as a mode of, 98–99; as interpretive, 113, 114; Kant and, 6, 52, 59–61, 66, 67, 70–73, 75, 100, 135, 138, 140, 163, 165, 166; orientation and, 59–60; preliminary judgments and the provisionality of, 93–99; and reflexivity, 164, 166; and Ricoeur's singular causal imputation, 186; task of, 5, 106, 165, 206; of taste, 113; and universality, 72–73, 163
reflective judication, 7
reflective knowledge, 9; and appropriation, 9, 83, 114, 145, 172, 195; and assimilation, 83; vs. life-knowledge, 22–23
reflective orientation, 59, 76, 79; an amphiboly of, 74–78, 170, 172; modes of, 68, 78. *See also* orientational reflection; *specific topics*
reflective orientational hermeneutics, 93
reflective purposiveness, 59, 111, 138, 161, 162
reflective schematization and contextual reconfiguration, 105–8
reflective topology, 63–65, 168; and judgmental contexts, 63–69
reflective vs. regulative, 7, 161–62, 172
reflective-reflexive appropriation, 166, 167, 171
reflexive assimilation, 166, 167, 170
reflexive awareness, 119–22, 143, 166, 167, 194, 215

reflexivity, 24; first- and second-order, 166, 167; and reflection, 132–33, 165–67, 197; vs. reflection, 32–33; from reflection to, 164–66; and reflectiveness, 119, 121, 122, 133, 143, 164–67, 171, 191, 215; vs. reflectiveness, 166; as self-referring/self-referential, 32–33, 143, 167, 215

regulative critique, 7, 147, 151–61

regulative purposiveness, 148, 161

religious interpretation, function of, 44

representation (*Vorstellung*), 43–44, 166, 199–202 205, 213; vs. presentation (*Darstellung*), 45, 111, 214–16, 220

responsiveness, reflective vs. instantaneous, 223

restorative hermeneutics, 159

Rickert, Heinrich, 119

Ricoeur, Paul, 7, 44, 147, 152, 156–60, 185–86

Royce, Josiah, 55–59

Roycean conspectus, 59, 77, 115, 132

Sartre, Jean-Paul, 152, 179

Schelling, Friedrich Wilhelm Joseph, 15, 20, 195

schema of causality, 70, 86

schemata: categorial, 112; and meaning, 86, 92, 97, 106, 108; and symbols, 15, 70, 112

schematism of analogy, 15

schematization: determinant, 108–12; mathematical, 70, 112 (*see also* mathematics); reflective/contextual, 53, 65, 105–8, 111–14, 162–63, 223–24; symbolic, 15, 70, 111–13, 224

schematizing: with concepts, 105, 106, 108; without concepts, 105, 106, 114 (*see also* schematization: reflective/contextual)

Schiller, Friedrich, 51, 187

Schlegel, Friedrich, 187, 195–96

Schleiermacher, Friedrich, 1, 13–17, 34, 40, 43, 81–82, 195–96, 202

science(s), 3; causality and, 148–49; critical, 154, 155. *See also under* cognition

self-cognition, 68

self-formative processes, 153, 155

self-reflection, 22, 32, 83, 153–56; in Dilthey, 22, 32, 153–54; in Habermas, 153–56

self-understanding, 9, 84, 126, 136, 167, 182

Semler, J. S., 15

sense-certainty, 43, 44

sophia, 26–27, 32. *See also* authentic understanding

spiritual-cultural facts, 119

Stoics, 18, 20

structural regularities, 114, 117

structural relations, 20, 117

structuralism, 156–59

style, 115, 178, 206

superstition, 49, 95

symbolic cognition, 42; of God, 75

symbolic communication, 204–5

symbolic presentation, 70–71, 111, 113

symbolic schematization, 15, 70, 111–13, 224

symbolism, 111; Dilthey on moral, 15; Kant and, 16, 42, 43, 69–71, 111–13, 204–5. *See also* symbolization

symbolization, 113, 204–5; aesthetic, 42, 43; and contextual types, 112; and countertypes, 112–13; *Gegenbildung* as, 113; and morality, 111, 112. *See also* symbolism

symbols: imaginative, 112; and schemata, 15, 70, 112

systems: organized purposive, 73–74; purposive vs. productive, 125

technique, 50, 154, 192–93

technology, 153, 215, 218–21, 223; digital, xi, 9, 214, 219

teleological explanation, 161, 176, 188–91

teleological purposiveness, 59, 60

temporality, 24–26, 29–32, 81

territory(ies): defined as a context, 4–5, 64–65, 208, 220–21; of human experience, 71, 72, 74, 83, 108, 162; and other referential contexts/spheres of reference, 4–5, 64–66, 75, 78, 79, 95, 107, 108, 115, 130, 162–63, 170, 206, 208, 220–21

theodicy, 134–37, 142
theoretical cognition (*Erkennen*), 3, 119
thirdness and third idea, 56–57
time, 24, 31–32; as advancing, 31. *See also* temporality
tonal medium, 213
topology, 3, 73, 193; reflective, 63–65, 168
tradition, 34, 93, 96, 160, 168, 194
transcendental analysis, 117
"Transcendental Analytic" (Kant), 84, 92
transcendental concepts, 69, 85, 117
transcendental conditions of experience, 118
"Transcendental Doctrine of Method, The" (Kant), 84
"Transcendental Doctrine of Power of Judgment, The" (Kant), 92
transcendental ego, 44
transcendental epistemology, 98
transcendental function, 153
transcendental illusions, 67, 95
transcendental logic, 85, 86
transcendental possibilities, 64
transcendental principles, 60, 140
transcendental reflection, 62, 117–18, 122, 140
transcendental rules, 204
transcendental structure, 153
transcendental synthesis of the imagination, 85–86
transcendental theory of cognition and rational knowing, 93
transcendental topic, Kant's, 61–64
transcendental truth, 86
transitional understanding, 9, 220–24
transmissibility, material, 213, 214
transmission: and communication, 9, 74, 97, 199, 212–14; hermeneutics and historical, 194–97, 223
transposition, 158, 182
Truth and Method (Gadamer), 34, 42, 51. *See also* Gadamer, Hans-Georg
truth claims, 86, 87, 91, 92, 97, 143
truth conditions, 85, 86

truth standards of reason, 92
truth-assessment, 85, 91, 98–99
truthful in itself, 37, 40, 43, 207
truthfulness, 141–45, 164; as normative, 164
truth(s), 34, 35, 37, 41–43, 48–50, 96–97; communal, 35, 41; empirical, 86; search for, 92; transcendental, 86; vs. truthful, 37
types: and archetypes, 111–12; and countertypes, 112–13; ideal and real, 112; and prototypes, 112, 135
typification and the intuitive presentation of meaning, 111–14

ultimate vs. final purpose, 138
understanding: authentic, 25–27, 32, 93; better, 17, 39; critical, 18, 123, 144–45, 166–67, 197, 223; descriptive vs. intentionalist, 189; and historical understanding, 17, 19; and intention, 13, 34, 134, 136, 158, 189–91, 198, 200–203; transitional modes of, 9, 220–24. *See also* elementary understanding; higher understanding
understanding (*Verstand*), 17; as discursive intellect, 150; faculty of, 59
understanding (*Verstehen*), 17, 39, 202; and explanation, 6, 154, 157–59, 183–84, 186, 188–91; and human sciences, 17, 19; and reexperiencing, 158. *See also* critical understanding; elementary understanding; higher understanding; self-understanding
"Understanding of Other Persons and Their Manifestations of Life, The" (Dilthey), 28, 37. *See also* Dilthey, Wilhelm
universalist history, 184, 197; incommensurable contexts and the possibility of, 181–84; vs. universal history, 184
universalistic demands of disciplinary consciousness., 29
universality, 19, 28, 42–44; abstract, 44, 163; and aesthetics, 36, 42, 107, 115, 127; vs. commonality, 28, 29, 32, 74; Habermas and, 156; and intersubjectivity, 36, 90–91, 107; of language, 16; and reflective judg-

universality (*continued*)
  ments, 72–73, 163; and understanding, 39–40

validity: general vs. universal, 101–4; and legitimacy (*see* legitimacy); objectivity and universal, 19, 89
Vermeer, Johannes, 108
Vico, Giambattista, 18
von Wright, Georg Henrik, 188–91

Warhol, Andy, 218, 219
Weiwei, Ai, 219–20
White, Hayden, 178

will to interpret, 57, 185
"Will to Interpret" (Royce), 56–57
Windelband, Wilhelm, 19
world/earth. *See* earth and world
worldly bounds, 62–63, 131. *See also* earthly limits
worldly orientation, 78–80
world-oriented vs. self-absorbed feelings, 35
world-time, ontico-temporal analysis of, 30
worldviews, 18, 20, 23, 24, 32, 83, 223; types of, 20, 23, 32
Wright, Frank Lloyd, 216
Wright, Georg Henrik von. *See* von Wright, Georg Henrik

www.ingramcontent.com/pod-product-compliance
Lightning Source LLC
Chambersburg PA
CBHW021941290426

44108CB00012B/917